Barth and God's Story

DAVID F. FORD

BARTH AND GOD'S STORY

BIBLICAL NARRATIVE AND THE THEOLOGICAL METHOD OF KARL BARTH IN THE **CHURCH DOGMATICS**

WIPF & STOCK · Eugene, Oregon

Wipf and Stock Publishers
199 W 8th Ave, Suite 3
Eugene, OR 97401

Barth and God's Story
A Biblical Narrative and the Theological Method
of Karl Barth in the Church Dogmatics
By Ford, David F.
Copyright©1985 by Ford, David F.
ISBN 13: 978-1-60608-056-6
Publication date 7/3/2008
Previously published by Peter Lang, 1985

CONTENTS

Karl Barth as a narrative theologian

We live in a time when one can win elections on the ticket of being "born again", when a non-Christian producer can make a fortune with a musical on "Jesus Christ Superstar", when a British actor can fill a theatre night after night just by reciting the Gospel of Mark, when each new Bible translation becomes a bestseller (and that irrespective of its quality), when two well-known Marxists, namely Roger Garaudy and Milan Machoveč, in spite (or perhaps because) of their knowledge of critical exegesis confess their admiration for the biblical stories <u>in their present narrative and mythical form</u>. We live also in a time when we, the pastors and theologians, find it more and more difficult to present the biblical stories in such a way that people want to listen to us.

There must be something <u>in the form</u> of biblical stories (and not merely in their theological content) that they exercise such an attraction on the educated and uneducated, on Christian and non-Christian. It is therefore only logical that my colleague, David Ford, presents one of the most widely read theologians of our time as a "story teller", or to be precise, as one who is re-telling the biblical stories: "To me, Barth is claiming that God chooses to bring people to faith through certain stories; that this does not depend on us being able to verify the stories historically or affirm them as inerrant; but that it does depend on us following the stories carefully and trusting that their subject, who is still alive to confirm them, is rendered adequately for God's purpose." (p. 22) "Die Offenbarung steht, nein sie geschieht in der Schrift, nicht hinter ihr."[1] "When the Bible speaks of revelation it does so in the form of narrating a story or a series of stories"[2], and this form of revelation is inseparable from its content.[3] Dogmatics is therefore "much less a system than the narrative of an event"[4]. This event effects "an absolute alteration of the world"[5] and thus the Bible effects a takeover of our world of meaning.

David Ford examines the legitimacy of Barth's narrative interpretation and points to its sources; they are to be found in the Alemannic songs for children by Barth's pastor, Abel Burckhardt. Barth says of them: They were "the text-book in which, at the beginning of the last decade of the last century, I received my first theological instruction in a form appropriate to my then immaturity. And what made an indelible impression on me was the homely naturalness with which these very modest compositions spoke of the events of Christmas, Palm Sunday, Good Friday, Easter, the Ascension and Pentecost as things which might take place any day in Basel or its environs like any other important happenings. History? Doctrine? Dogma? Myth? No - but things actually taking place.... The yawning chasm of Lessing did not exist. The contemporaneity of Kierkegaard was not a problem. The Saviour Himself was obviously the same yesterday and today. All very naive, and not worth mentioning at all in academic circles? Yes, it was very naive, but perhaps in the very naivety there lay the deepest wisdom and the greatest power, so that once grasped it was calculated to carry one relatively unscathed - although not, of course, untempted or unassailed through all the serried ranks of historicism and anti-historicism, mysticism and rationalism, orthodoxy, liberalism and existentialism, and to bring one back some day to the matter itself. As far as it was still possible in the 19th century, and not without an obvious influence of Pietism, good Abel Burckhardt stood firmly on the older christology, presumably of a moderate Reformed type. But, obviously, in all simplicity he had in fact overcome its deadness, and he gave us an impulse to overcome it again. For that reason - academic circles or nor - he deserves to be mentioned in this connexion."(7)

Barth a narrative theologian! Is that an attempt to up-date good old Barth? In reading Ford's work together with Barth's Dogmatics, one will notice that in fact on many pages Barth tells stories, most of them biblical stories. He tells them in the mood of a post-critical naivety, as one who believes that Jesus is risen and alive (p. 52), as one who is aware that neither exact historiography nor literature can provide categories for adequately representing the event of Christ's advent (p. 68). Barth's chief way of presenting his theology is "through the dominance of one story over all others" (namely the biblical story). This "story is like a finger which, for all its shaking and its warts, points to Christ; and it is the only witness we have, so that it must be...the criterion against which world-views are measured" (p. 182). This biblical story is both: Something which is foreign to us (an "extra nos") and something in which we find ourselves (tua res agitur). Barth's statement that at the university he only continued what he had begun in the confirmation classes in Safenwil thus becomes clearer, also the importance he lays on humour and phantasy: "Imagination, too, belongs no less legitimately to the human possibility of knowing. A man without an imagination is more of an invalid than one who lacks a leg."(8)

It is not surprising that the literary quality of Barth's works had been fully recognised, amongst other things by conferring on him a literary prize. Humorously he writes on this to a friend: At Darmstadt "not Ebeling, nor Fuchs, nor any one of the new school of hermeneutics or cybernetics with their emphasis on that which happens in language (Sprachgeschehen) but I shall receive a 'Sigmund-Freud-Prize' (of all things!) in praise of my scientific prose."(9)

The qualification of Barth as a theological story-teller is an original discovery (10), the critical analysis of Barth's stories even more so. Ford does not deny Barth the right to do academic theology as a narrative interpreter. He only asks - and rightly so - Is the story, which Barth tells us, a truthful and realistic re-telling? It is here that Ford discovers that the hero of Barth's story, Jesus Christ, sometimes eclipses the context. He mentions the example of Judas in relation to the doctrine of election (p. 93) or the human nature of Christ in Barth's treatment of the doctrine of the two natures (p. 131). In other passages Barth tells the story in such a way that important elements of the original story are lost or new elements, not contained in the original story, are introduced.

I suppose that Barth would answer this criticism with the same argument he used in order to conclude a long scholarly debate with Bultmann: "In heaven (in the highest storey of the mythological world) we shall visit the apostle Paul together - I however only after a long chat with W.A. Mozart - and he may explain to us what he really meant."(11)

Whether we like it or not, Barth is now part of the history of Christ-

ianity, to be precise - although contrary to Barth's own understanding - of
a Christianity which is exactly defined and definable. It makes sense therefore to publish this work in the "Studies in the Intercultural History of
Christianity". An Anglican from Ireland, who teaches at an English University may be well placed to help us better to understand this culturally
conditioned Christianity. In particular the author may show us in Karl
Barth's narration an intercultural bridge over the troubled waters between
Africa and Europe. I suppose that the way David Ford reads Karl Barth will
hardly make more disciples for Karl Barth but perhaps it will help to make
him understood in unexpected places.

Dr W.J. Hollenweger,
Professor of Mission,
University of Birmingham

NOTES

(1) K. Barth, Prolegomena zur christlichen Dogmatik, 344; Ford, p. 23.

(2) CD I/1, 362.

(3) CD I/1, 285, 367.

(4) CD I/1, 321.

(5) CD I/1, 161.

(6) CD I/1, 177; cp. on the whole passage Ford,

(7) CD IV/2, 112f; Ford, pp. 16 f.

(8) CD III/1, 91; Ford, pp. 108 f.

(9) Letter of 30.10.1968 to Pastor R. Karwehl, in: Karl Barth, Briefe
1961-1968 (Gesamtausgabe, Zürich 1975), 513; cp. also 481, 520.

(10) cp. on this too H. Anselm, "Gott als Dichter. Aspekte zum Selbstver-
ständnis narrativer Religionspädagogik", Theologia practica 1981 (in
preparation; special mention of Barth as a narrative theologian is
made in this article).

(11) Karl Barth/Rudolf Bultmann, Briefwechsel 1922-1966 (Gesamtausgabe,
Zürich 1971), 203; Ford, pp. 56-46, Note 63.

8

PREFACE

Narrative has been one of the richest themes in recent Christian theology. Its importance in all religions and cultures is obvious, and one of the most powerful factors in the way the Bible crosses barriers of time and place is its inclusion of so many good stories. But what happens when these stories are rigorously examined and reflected upon in theology? What is the relationship of theological to literary interpretation? How can stories be central to a theology while keeping their integrity as vivid, universal literature?

There is no general answer to such questions. I have taken one modern theologian of international significance, Karl Barth. By concentrating on that part of his method which has to do with narrative, I have attempted both to offer a new assessment of his achievement and also to open a door into his works that will help to make them accessible to those of many backgrounds and cultures with a keen interest in narrative and literature.

The preparation of this work has itself been a fascinating experience of how issues in theology and literature are understood in various cultures. In each university in which work has proceeded I have been deeply grateful to those who have taught and given so much time in discussion.

In U.S.A. the inspiration for this approach to Karl Barth came through the writings, teaching and friendship of Professor Hans Frei of Yale University. There too the assistance of Professor David Kelsey and Professor Lindbeck was most valuable, and to Dr. Robert Kruger I owe the decisive encouragement to embark on the project. I am grateful too to the Charles and Julia Henry Trustees for the fellowship which took me to Yale for a year.

In England, I am most deeply indebted to Professor Sykes and Professor Donald Mackinnon. The years in Cambridge University were extremely rich, and their contribution immense. My gratitude too goes to Dr. George Newlands, Professor Nicholas Lash, Dr. Richard Roberts, Father Herbert Slade, S.S.J.E., and, as a major influence on my literary criticism (through his works and conversations), Professor Peter Stern. Since coming to Birmingham there has been yet another delightful round of exchanges, and Rev. Daniel Hardy and Professor Walter Hollenweger have been of particular help in this project.

On the Continent there were yet more debts incurred at a crucial time in this book's genesis. Professor Eberhard Jüngel of Tübingen University not only discussed the work in progress but also gave me four months of extremely generous hospitality in his own house. Dr. and Frau Hinrich Stoevesandt likewise showed great kindness and hospitality during my time at the Barth-Archiv in Basel. My deep gratitude goes to Dr. Ingolf Dalferth, Dr. Hans-Anton Drewes, Father Philip Rosato S.J., Professor Jürgen Moltmann and Professor and Frau Dietrich Ritschl.

Then there is the ever-present Irish contribution. First of all, beyond any adequate expression, there is my mother, to whom this book is dedicated: she has given endless support, spiritual and practical. Also my very special thanks go to Mrs. Smith for all her typing.

In the most recent typing for publication in its present form my warm thanks go to Mrs. I. Browne.

A previous form of this book, little altered, was accepted for the degree of Doctor of Philosophy by the University of Cambridge, and is deposited in the library there under the title Biblical Narrative and the Theological Method of Karl Barth in the Church Dogmatics.

A note on references: I have usually quoted German works in translation if they exist (E.T. = English Translation). I quote German page numbers with S. (= Seite), English with p. (= page).

CHAPTER 1. INTRODUCTION

"A student had prepared a paper on a christological
issue he felt is evoked by a section of the Church Dogmatics.
The first question was addressed to him by a peer. As
frequently happens, it was in reality not a question but a
charge, that he had seriously misconstrued the issue because
he had misunderstood Barth's method.

"The debate that ensued was as convoluted as spirited.
It moved from one complex methodological issue to two others;
and from each of these to two others. It continued in white
heat for a polarizing hour. Throughout the hour, Barth peered
over his spectacles (and his glasses), stroked and smoked his
outsized pipe, sipped his Rhenish wine, and spoke not one word.

"As the debate was beginning to move into a second hour,
it suddenly occurred to one of the students that there was,
as we say, a 'resource person' present, who might possibly
be able to throw light on the issues and adjudicate the dispute. He turned and ricocheted the previous question to Barth.

"After a full minute of heavy silence, Barth raised his
head and above the welter of complex formal issues that had been
strewn on the table:

"'If I understand what I am trying to do in the Church
Dogmatics, it is to listen to what Scripture is saying and tell
you what I hear.'

"What can be made of this simplistic, obviously heuristic
ploy? I wish to suggest that it be taken seriously."(1)

I wish to take up that suggestion by trying to show Barth's characteristic way of being true to his maxim of sola scriptura in the Church Dogmatics.(2)

(i)

There are many other ways of treating the C.D. as a unity. The most
straightforward is to follow Barth's own progress from prolegomena through
the doctrines of God, creation and reconciliation.(3) Yet the C.D. invites
other ways too. Its volumes are not parts of the whole like separate stages
on a journey or links in an argument. They are rather like a spiral round
and round the same subject matter, repeatedly taking it in hand (4) and insisting that each major doctrine includes all the others.

Proposals about how best to understand this subject matter abound. The
maxim of solus Christus is a popular standpoint (5). Sola gratia has also
been taken as the pervasive theme (6), as have the doctrine of the Trinity(17),
the doctrine of justification (8), the doctrine of eternity and time (9), the
doctrine of the Holy Spirit (10), and apologetics (11), with F.-W. Marquardt

11

even taking Barth's political biography as the key to the unity of his theology and his theological method (12). Marquardt is trying to meet what he calls "das Gebot sorgsamer immanenter Interpretation" (13) of Barth's theology, which he sees adequately attempted only in the studies of von Balthasar and Berkouwer (14). This book is making another such attempt.

(ii)

My standpoint is Barth's interpretation of biblical narratives, and it can be supported as worthwhile on several grounds.

Primarily there is the evidence, which I present in later chapters, that certain narratives are of central importance to Barth's doctrines of God, creation and reconciliation, and that his use of these narratives helps to understand both the unity and the method of his theology.

Secondly, there is the neglect of this subject in the major works on Barth. Of those mentioned above only Marquardt discusses Barth's exegetical method at any length (15), and, while much of what he says is borne out by this dissertation (16), his treatment is on a general level and does not explore the role of narrative in Barth's dogmatic proposals. There are, of course, in the works of theologians and biblical scholars innumerable discussions of pieces of Barth's biblical interpretation but, as the coming chapters will show, Barth insulates his dogmatic conclusions against refutation in this way, the main insulator being his understanding of the relation of Jesus Christ to biblical narrative which ensures that his conclusions are not based on "proof-texts".(17) Between the generalization of Marquardt and the examination of particular cruces of interpretation there is a wide field of study in the exegesis of the C.D. One might, for example, examine how (from the O.T.) the patriarchs, the Exodus, the law, the prophets and the wisdom and apocalyptic literature, and (from the N.T.) the individual evangelists, the Acts of the Apostles, Paul, Hebrews, Peter and the Apocalypse are each interpreted and contribute to the C.D. None of these, however, has the pervasive role of the theme I have chosen. The only possible exception is Paul. After Der Römerbrief (18), however, Barth laid increasing emphasis on both O.T. and N.T. narratives (19), and his doctrine of election puts Paul's thought firmly in this context (20).

Thirdly and finally, my approach is suited to elucidating the places in Barth's method where major verdicts for or against it need to be given. Barth was very suspicious of "methodology" and the claim of theology to be "systematic", since he detected in them attempts to secure by human means what can only be given freely by God. What I mean by "method" is, however, something which can be discerned in any theology which tries to justify its position by argument. Barth uses a wide variety of arguments in the C.D., appealing to the Bible and to other sources as varied as historical studies, marriage manuals and the music of Mozart. My concern is with that family of arguments which employs biblical narratives. I have selected some of these narratives - the Gospels, Genesis 1 and 2, and those stories which Barth interprets in support of his doctrine of election - and have examined their role in his arguments for some major doctrinal conclusions. I show where Barth is traditional, where he innovates, where he invites decisions about the relation between theology and history, philosophy or science, and above all where the main "scandal" of his theology lies for most post-Enlightenment world-views: in his claim that history is a predicate of revelation and that a subject-centred must give way to christocentric anthropology. This helps to clarify possible agreements and disagreements with him in a way that does justice to his arguments.

Many of the debates about Barth's thought, especially on the Continent, are about whether Barth can be described under the heading of one or more "-isms". Proposals include Platonism, Hegelianism, Kantianism, intellectualism, rationalism, irrationalism, monism, dualism, biblicism, revelation positivism, christomonism, docetism, panactualism, monoactualism, universalism, occasionalism, over-optimism, pessimism, modernism. Such debates have been helpful in preparing this study and if pressed to invent such a label I would choose "monism of the Gospel story", noting that the differentiations within the story (not least between God and men) give this monism a distinctive meaning. This perspective on Barth clarifies what is at issue in the other "-isms" and above all recognizes that since Barth draws his main conclusions from stories the crucial test of his theology is whether his interpretation and assessment of those stories is convincing.

The above justification of my project will, I hope, be confirmed in the following nine chapters. Chapter 2 treats the development of Barth's exegesis of narratives up to the prolegomena to the C.D. Chapter 3 draws from C.D.IV.1 some of the basic issues of narrative interpretation, in preparation for Chapter 4. There, parallels are drawn between what literary critics say about realistic novels and what Barth says about certain biblical narratives, and I also set his hermeneutics in a historical context. Chapter 5 does a detailed analysis of the use of narratives in Barth's doctrine of election in C.D.II.2 (with an appendix on his doctrine of evil) and Chapter 6 does the same for Barth's doctrine of creation in C.D.III.1. Chapter 7 suggests that his argument for the two natures of Jesus Christ is both circular within the Gospel story and also requires the support of his understanding of time and eternity, as described in Chapter 8. Chapter 9 sums up and criticizes the C.D. as a spirituality of knowledge dependent on reading the Bible in a certain way, and Chapter 10 draws some further conclusions. The aim throughout is neither to cover the whole range of Barth's thought nor to do justice to the many influences upon it, but to relate it at key points to the only documentary authority that he regarded as a primary source for theology.

NOTES to Chapter 1

(1)   Robert C. Johnson, "The Legacy of Karl Barth", in Reflection Vol. 66, No. 4, May 1969 (New Haven, Conn.), p. 4.

(2)   Hereafter referred to as C.D., the German original as K.D.

(3)   Otto Weber's Karl Barth's Church Dogmatics. An Introductory Report on Vols. I.1 to III.4 (London 1953), by faithfully summarizing and commenting on the C.D. illuminates its coherence in this way.

(4)   Johnson, op. cit., suggests this, comparing the C.D. to Augustine's retractationes.

(5)   For a thorough exposition of it see Hans Urs von Balthasar, Karl Barth, Darstellung und Deutung seiner Theologie (Köln 1962). (The Theology of Karl Barth (New York 1972) is an abridged translation of the 1962 German edition). Von Balthasar supports his christocentric interpretation by an analysis of Barth's method under the heading of analogy.

(6)   G.C. Berkouwer, The Triumph of Grace in the Theology of Karl Barth (London 1956).

(7)   E. Jüngel, Gottes Sein ist im Werden (Tübingen 1966).

(8)   Hans Küng, Justification. The Doctrine of Karl Barth and a Catholic Reflection. With a letter by Karl Barth (London 1964). Henri Bouillard, Karl Barth. Vol. I Genèse et Évolution de la Théologie Dialectique; Vol. II, Parts 1 and 2 Parole de Dieu et Existence Humaine (Aubier 1957), makes the theme of simul justus et peccator dominant, but his is less an exposition from one viewpoint than the others mentioned here.

(9)   Richard Roberts, Eternity and Time in the Theology of Karl Barth. An Essay in dogmatic and philosophical theology. Unpublished Ph.D. thesis (Edinburgh University 1975).

(10)   P.J. Rosato, Karl Barth's Theology of the Holy Spirit. God's noetic realization of the ontological relationship between Jesus Christ and all men. Unpublished doctoral dissertation (Tübingen University 1975).

(11)   H.-G. Fritzsche, Das Christentum und die Weltanschauungen. Zugleich eine Einführung in die Kirchliche Dogmatik Karl Barths unter vorwiegend "apologetischem" Gesichtspunkt (Hamburg-Bergstedt 1962).

(12)   Theologie und Sozialismus. Das Beispiel Karl Barths (München 1972, zweite Auflage), especially S.333 ff. on the unity of Barth's work and the methodological importance of politics.

(13)   Op. cit. S. 339.

(14)   See notes 5 and 6 above.

14

(15) Op. cit. S. 94 ff.; cf. "Exegese und Dogmatik in Karl Barths Theologie" in Die Kirchliche Dogmatik von Karl Barth. Registerband, herausgegeben von Helmut Krause (Zürich 1970). Bouillard, op. cit., does have much criticism of parts of Barth's exegesis, but does not offer an overall interpretation as Marquardt does.

(16) His main points are about Barth's focus on the "Konkretheit" of the Bible, his faithfulness to the text, and the all-encompassing "Bewegung der Gottesgeschichte".

(17) See below Chapters 3, 5, 6, 7, 8, 9, 9. Cf. Richard Roberts' illuminating discussion of the conflict between Barth and O. Cullmann over the interpretation of the "biblical view of time" and of James Barr's criticism of both sides of the debate. Roberts concludes that Barth cannot be refuted at the level at which Cullmann and Barr are arguing (op. cit. pp. 211 ff.).

(18) München 1922. (Zweite, völlig veränderte Auflage). E.T. of 6th Edition The Epistle to the Romans (Oxford 1933).

(19) See below, Chapter 2.

(20) See below, Chapter 5. The symbol of this could be seen in the way Judas and Paul are related in C.D.II.2. Another sign of it is the theological estrangement of Barth and Bultmann. The division between these men has dominated Protestant theology in Germany (and often elsewhere) since the 1940's. Bultmann and his school have offered a comprehensive alternative to Barth's understanding of the Bible, and Barth wrote the C.D. fully aware of the challenge. At various points in this dissertation I will compare the two in order to show how their differences are illuminated by their contrasting interpretations of narratives; and my first chapter of commentary on the C.D., Chapter 3 below, will deal with C.D.IV.1, of which Barth himself said in the preface that it was written with Bultmann in mind. Their main difference could be summed up as being over the interpretation of Paul: whether to use Bultmann's existential hermeneutic, or, with Barth, to insist on Paul's reference to historical events (especially the crucifixion and resurrection) which have "objectively" changed the situation. Where Bultmann's understanding of Paul is consistent with giving minimal treatment to the synoptic Gospels in his Theology of the New Testament Vol. I (New York 1951), Barth was led to make even his doctrine of the immanent Trinity reflect the relations between events in the Gospels (see below Chapter 8).

One problem in understanding the development of Barth's exegesis of biblical narratives is that he did no extensive interpretation of them until the
C.D. In the C.D., however, Barth gives a rare piece of spiritual autobio-
graphy which is important enough to be quoted at length. The context is the
"actualisation" of christology, and in an excursus he says that the festivals
of the church year invite us to "participate with supreme realism" in the
history of Jesus Christ, and continues:

> "I must interpose at this point a small but sincerely
> grateful tribute. It is to a theologian who cannot be called
> great, but to whom I am greatly indebted. I refer to Abel
> Burckhardt, who a hundred years ago - a contemporary of the
> more famous Jacob Burckhardt - was the second pastor at the
> minster here in Basel. He composed and edited a collection of
> songs for children in the local district. This was the text-
> book in which, at the beginning of the last decade of the last
> century, I received my first theological instruction in a form
> appropriate to my then immaturity. And what made an indelible
> impression on me was the homely naturalness with which these
> very modest compositions spoke of the events of Christmas,
> Palm Sunday, Good Friday, Easter, the Ascension and Pentecost
> as things which might take place any day in Basel or its en-
> virons like any other important happenings. History? Doctrine?
> Myth? No - but things actually taking place, os that we could
> see and hear and lay up in our hearts. For as these songs were
> sung in the everyday language we were then beginning to hear
> and speak, and as we joined in singing, we took our mother's
> hand, as it were, and went to the stall at Bethlehem, and to
> the streets of Jerusalem where, greeted by children of a
> similar age, the Saviour made His entry, and to the dark hill
> of Golgotha, and as the sun rose to the garden of Joseph.
> Was this representation, like the unbloody repetition of the
> sacrifice of Christ in the Roman doctrine of the Mass? Was
> it the kind of faith which in that rather convulsive doctrine
> is supposed to consist in a re-enactment of the crucifixion
> of Christ in our own existence? Again, no. It was all present
> without needing to be made present. The yawning chasm of
> Lessing did not exist. The contemporaneity of Kierkegaard was
> not a problem. The Saviour himself was obviously the same
> yesterday and today. All very naive, and not worth mentioning
> at all in academic circles? Yes, it was very naive, but per-
> haps in the very naivety there lay the deepest wisdom and the
> greatest power, so that once grasped it was calculated to carry
> one relatively unscathed - although not, of course, untempted
> or unassailed - through all the serried ranks of historicism
> and anti-historicism, mysticism and rationalism, orthodoxy,
> liberalism and existentialism, and to bring one back some day
> to the matter itself. As far as was still possible in the 19th
> century, and not without an obvious influence of Pietism, good

Abel Burckhardt stood firmly on the older christology,
presumably of a moderate Reformed type. But, obviously,
in all simplicity he had in fact overcome its deadness,
and he gave us an impulse to overcome it again. For that
reason - academic circles or not - he deserves to be
mentioned in this connextion."(1)

This suggests a thread through the period up to the C.D. for which it is
worthwhile searching. Although the subject of this study is the C.D., Barth
was over forty-five years old when C.D.I.1 was published, and there is much
in his earlier years which helps to illuminate my theme. I will not, however, attempt to give a full account of the genesis of his thought. There
are already some excellent works dealing with this (2) and with their help
I will merely draw out evidence which will confirm Barth's retrospective
verdict of C.D.IV.2. I will first give a summary of Barth's position in
relation to some of his teachers and contemporaries and will then go through
his works in chronological order.

(i)

I begin with someone who did not teach Barth and whose conclusions were
almost invariably rejected by him: Ernst Troeltsch (3). Troeltsch's historical relativism represents an extreme in opposition to the idea that the
Gospel events could have happened in nineteenth century Basel, and Barth,
even in his most "liberal" period before 1911, always stopped short of
Troeltsch's position on the role of history in theology (4). Bultmann, on
the other hand, was much influenced by Troeltsch (5) in deciding virtually
to exclude the Gospel narratives from his data for theological reflection,
and in this divergence (6) one can see a major element in their lifelong
differences.

The questions posed by Troeltsch's work and later asked by Bultmann and
his school, as well as by most liberal theologians, represent what is perhaps
the most common viewpoint from which to criticise Barth's hermeneutics (7).
Barth never wrote the intended chapter on Troeltsch in his treatment of Protestant theology in the nineteenth century (8), nor did he give any single
thorough exposition of his reply to criticisms from this direction (9). There
are numerous passages in his works which do offer replies, and in the course
of this dissertation I hope to show how Barth's determination to preserve
"the deepest wisdom and the greatest power" found in Jacob Burckhardt's hymns
is supported by a distinctive understanding and use of biblical narratives
(10). Yet Troeltsch always remains with his critical attack on the foundation
of Barth's hermeneutics, and Barth's rejection of him from the outset signifies a recognition of the mortal threat that he was to Barth's whole theology.

Barth's own introduction to historical criticism of the Bible was at
Berne University in 1906. His father, Fritz Barth, taught him, but his con-
servatism did not impress his son so much as did the approach of Rudolf Steck,
Hermann Lüdemann (both former students of F.C. Baur) and Karl Marti (a student
of Wellhausen) (11).

Adolf von Harnack, less of a philosopher than Troeltsch and also less radical in the conclusions he drew about the "hermeneutical gap", continued Barth's education in the historical problems of theology. Barth was his enthusiastic (12) student in Berlin from 1906 to 1908, but soon afterwards he began to move away from Harnack's views (13). The eventual result was a head-on collision in 1923 when Harnack had an exchange with Barth which, as it focuses some enduring issues between Barth and liberal historical scholarship (and a fortiori, Troeltsch), I will discuss below in its chronological order.

The teacher who influenced Barth most after 1908 was Wilhelm Herrmann. Barth wrote of him in 1928:

> "Herrmann is the one from whom I have learned something
> most basic, something which, once I followed it out to its
> consequences, caused me to see everything else in a wholly
> different way, even to interpret this most basic matter
> quite differently from him."(14)

Rumscheidt (15) speculates plausibly that the basic matter was Herrmann's doctrine of the autopistia of faith, which stressed God's transcendence, and ruled out any proof of his existence, thus freeing faith from the need to legitimate itself by appeal to rational or historical evidence. Barth's new interpretation of this was to reject Herrmann's basis for it, the inner life of Jesus, and substitute his own concept of revelation. This concept was always linked with his exegesis of Scripture, and so one way of understanding its changing content is to trace the development of his exegesis, as I do below. My main conclusion there can be anticipated: Barth "objectivized" Herrmann's autopistia by concentrating on the biblical narratives understood not as evidence for Jesus' consciousness but as representing a world of meaning in events which cannot be transcended. Again there is a contrast with Bultmann. He had also been Herrmann's student, and also rejected his concept of "the inner life of Jesus", but his measure of agreement with such critics as Troeltsch made it impossible for him to follow Barth. He did not, however, follow Troeltsch in the search for "real history", but instead, like Herrmann, stressed the "non-objectifiable" element of Christianity, and, unlike Herrmann, located it in the eschatological event of salvation which can be known only in the subject's act of decision(16).

(ii)

I will now tell how Barth arrived at an exegesis which was both independent of historical criticism and yet not "subjectivist".

In his parish of Safenwil after 1911 Barth was driven to reconsider his liberal theology by finding it inadequate to the demands of preaching, and the attitude of many of his liberal teachers to the First World War confirmed his suspicion of their theology. There were many influences on Barth's thought in these years, but two which had enduring results were Herrmann Kutter's stimulus to him to rethink his notion of God (17), and his grappling with the Bible in sermon preparation, which led to his decision that biblical

exegesis was the basis on which to build his own theology. The two come together in his 1916 lecture "Die Neue Welt der Bibel" (18) where he says
bluntly: "The contents of the Bible are 'God'."(19)

The lecture begins with a series of scenes from O.T. and N.T. stories to
indicate the strange new world of the Bible, next dismisses any reduction of
its contents to history, morality or religion, and then, after a little summary of the biblical story from Abraham to Paul, asks: "Is that all of God
and His new world, of the meaning of the Bible, of the content of the contents?" (20)   Barth answers in the affirmative: we find God in the new world
of the biblical events.(21) There is as yet no concern as to how the events
can yield a full doctrine of God but already there is Barth's version of Herrmann's autopistia: and not only is God found through the biblical events but
Barth insists that the Bible interprets itself.(22) This concept of "Selbst-
auslegung" is one which, as Lindemann says, remained for Barth "zeitlebens
bestimmend".(23) One of my tasks in this dissertation is to show how this
concept, whatever its other drawbacks, helps in the interpretation of realistic narratives in a way which general hermeneutical principles such as
those of Bultmann do not.

As he began his commentary on Romans, Barth's dissatisfaction with the
theological context of liberal exegesis led him back to authors favoured by
his father, such as J.T. Beck (24). Lindemann (25) analyses three of the
conservative exegetes mentioned by Barth as his mentors at this time: Beck,
J. Chr. K. von Hofmann and A. Schlatter. Each of the three has a hermeneutical circle which excludes historical criticism (26), and to these should be
added Martin Kähler who attacked the quest for the historical Jesus, saw the
biblical facts as above history ("übergeschichtlich") and proposed a hermeneutical circle between the biblical text and the faith-experience of the
individual (27). Barth's circle in his Römerbrief was to be different, but
recognizably from the same stable.

In the first edition of Barth's Römerbrief (1919) there is a confidence
that "die Sache" intended by Paul is still accessible through the text, and
there is a great stress on its objectivity, for "Im Objektiven liegt die Wahr-
heit" (28). "Historie" is seen to offer only a "Chaos sinnloser Beziehungen
und Begebenheiten" (29), and the history of O.T. and N.T. is taken as the
world of meaning, with the resurrection as the starting point for christology.
There are many of the themes of the second edition, but several crucial and
explosive elements had yet to be added, in particular the thought of Overbeck,
Kierkegaard and Dostoyevsky (30). The second edition is rightly taken as much
the more important work. There the attack on liberal exegesis sharpens, as
does the disjunction, the "infinite qualitative distinction" (31), between
God and man, eternity and time. I wish to make three points about this work.
Firstly, in it Barth's own hermeneutical circle emerges as one which is within the Gospel story and focuses on the relation of crucifixion to resurrection. As Lindemann says:

"Es ist der schon bekannte hermeneutische Zirkel:
Christus als der wahre Ursprung lässt uns im Kreuz die
vorher unbewusste Frage nach dem Ursprung radikal stellen
und gibt uns in der Auferstehung die "wirkliche" Antwort.(32)

The dialectical thought-form has the relation between these two events as its main exegetical basis (33). The stress is on the negation embodied in the crucifixion, which is so radical a judgment on everything human that time itself cannot contain the Yes of the resurrection (34).

Barth later criticised himself for his handling of time and eternity in this edition, chiefly for not doing justice to the temporality of salvation history (35), and his continual preoccupation with this theme of time will in Chapter 8 below be interpreted by me as his search for a suitable metaphysics for the Gospel story. The Römerbrief shows an early stage in that search. The interpretation of the relation of cross to resurrection as paradoxical is destined to disappear when in Barth's later work Jesus' person is seen as an identity rendered by them, but the basic principle of solving theological problems in a world of meaning defined by this story is constant. Besides, while Jesus' life is seen by Barth as summed up in his death (36), the time of revelation is taken as all of the years A.D.1-30 (37) and there are hints of his later use of the structure of the Gospel narratives to support theological conclusions (38). The whole style of the Römerbrief is expressionist and does not easily accommodate the "Nachdenken" of narratives which is fundamental to the C.D.; but in its own vivid way, with much distinctly non-mimetic mathematical imagery (39), it states the "scandal of particularity" which is essential to all Barth's story-based theology.

Secondly, while Barth took much from Kierkegaard (such as the concepts of the infinite qualitative distinction, the moment, the divine incognito, eternal contemporaneity, paradox, and the category of decision) he did not take over his account of the paradox in the individual's interiority, with its tendency to absorb the "what" of belief into the "how". In this Barth is true to the "objectivity" of the first edition, and it signifies his refusal of the existentialist way which Bultmann was to follow. How, then, without such an approach, is faith to be seen as something a man can have? Barth is so concerned to deny all "religious" ways of understanding faith, hope and love which confuse them with human natural capacities that he gave no adequate answer to this, but there are the beginnings of what will later emerge as his solution. Barth makes no attempt to say how one may come to faith, but the crucial test of Christian life is that a great reversal has happened and one's own life is now somehow included in the story of Jesus:

"Those who love God were preordained to bear witness
to the death of Jesus and consequently to His resurrection;
and, whatever precise form their lives may take, these
must be lived under the final tribulation of men who fully
recognise that there exists no third intermediate thing
between the unknown God and the altogether too well known
world. They proclaim and show forth the tribulation of
Jesus in Gethsemane, a tribulation which begins with the
Baptism in Jordan and ends with the Crucifixion in Golgotha.
To accompany Him along His road and become messengers on
His behalf - that is to say, to allow the word of reconciliation to be spoken over them as a genuine condemnation
against which they have no defence (1 Cor V. 19-20) - this
it is to love God."(40)

Thirdly, the sustained attack on "religion" in the second edition has as a principal effect that the very use of the word "God" is problematical. "God" is no longer someone Christians can assume they have in common with other religious people, even (or especially) within the Church. Since the crucifixion is seen to have an epistemological role in rebutting all claims to knowing God except paradoxically through itself and the resurrection, there is no longer any connection between the Gospel and religion or natural theology. This means that God is to be described only through that story (41) and we shall see the consequences of this in the C.D.

The reaction of writers such as Jülicher, Schlatter, Althaus and Bultmann to the second edition was a mixture of agreement with Barth on the need for theological exegesis and disagreement on the way he related it to historical critical method (42). This objection had extensive implications, for it involved the issue of how the text and revelation are related, and also the status of theology vis-a-vis preaching. It was Barth's exchange with Harnack in 1923 which clarified how deep the differences went. The correspondence is not very long, but Rumscheidt has shown, by setting it in its context in Barth's and Harnack's thinking and in the theological situation of the time, what an important confrontation this was.

As Rumscheidt says:

"The issue in the correspondence between Harnack and Barth is the way man speaks about God."(43)

Harnack could not see that there was any third way between basing one's faith on knowledge gained from investigation which aimed to discover the historical Jesus, and having a subjectivist faith which has no safeguard against an imaginary picture of Jesus (44). Harnack's own method (45) led him to distinguish a "simple Gospel" preached by Jesus (about the Kingdom of God, the Fatherhood of God and the infinite value of the human soul) which is the essence of Christianity, ideal and timeless, and a second Gospel about Jesus (including for example the incarnation, death and resurrection, and theories of redemption) which was of secondary importance (46): exactly the reverse of the emphasis Barth had developed.

In the correspondence Barth denies any direct knowledge of God, even of his fatherhood, from history (47). The great obstacle to such directness is the crucifixion, and this is a "scandal" which is not contained in the "simple gospel" and shatters its world-view. Here Barth asserts the priority of Harnack's second Gospel and its absolute claim as the Christian world of meaning. Yet this extreme stress on the historical particularity of revelation goes with denying the events any revelational value in themselves. This is an enduring tension in Barth's theology. At this stage in his career it is commonly seen as the problem of the Word in the words of Scripture, and the relation is such that he can say:

"Faith is the acceptance of this unbelievable testimony of the Scriptures."(48)

It is only as Barth comes to see the issue rather as the discerning of Jesus Christ's identity in the events of O.T. and N.T., and develops his major

doctrines within a new understanding of the relation of time to eternity that
the testimony emerges as "believable", not in the sense of systematically
producing belief in its hearers, but by being a providential account of a
providential history with discernible patterns and continuities. One indic-
ation of Barth's development is that whereas at this time a favourite word
of his for the Gospel story is "parable" (49), as he thought out his own
concept of analogy there was more stress on "correspondence" between the
story and its divine subject.

What, then, was Barth's third way that Harnack would not see? It was
a rejection of Harnack's historical method and an avoidance of "subjectivity"
by stressing the referential, ostensive, testimonial nature of Scripture.
There is no possibility, he says, of "going from testimony to 'direct statement'" (50), but yet the Bible gives the only way to its object, in parabolic
form. Faith, he claims, happens in relation to this testimony and not in
relation to a reconstructed historical Jesus or simple Gospel. To Harnack
this appeared as "an invisible ridge between absolute religious scepticism
and naive biblicism" (51). To Rumscheidt Barth's dialectical approach to
God through a story that hides its "yes" in a "no" seems to do for theology
what the complementarity principle does for physics (52). To me, Barth is
claiming that God chooses to bring people to faith through certain stories;
that this does not depend on us being able to verify the stories historically
or affirm them as inerrant; but that it does depend on us following the stories carefully and trusting that their subject, who is still alive to confirm
them (53), is rendered adequately for God's purpose.

(iv)

In the years that followed, up to the publication of C.D.I.1 in 1932,
Barth systematically worked out a doctrine of the Word of God. It had many
surprises for his contemporaries, not least the mere fact that he thought
the task possible and worthwhile. His chief colleagues of the "dialectical
theology" group parted company with him during those years (54). Each break
can be symbolised by an emotion-laden concept - "Vorverständnis" (Bultmann)
(55), "Schöpfungsordnungen" (Gogarten) (56) and "Anknüpfungspunkt" (Brunner)
(57), and the issue in each case can be subsumed under the heading of natural
theology, which Barth's developing doctrine was increasingly rigorous in
excluding (58). It was a period of polemics against several traditional theological positions too, such as Roman Catholicism, pietism, liberalism, verbal
inspiration and biblicism (59), and here also the touchstone was his new
doctrine of the Word of God. I will briefly sketch the stages in its growth.

In 1924 Barth published Die Auferstehung der Toten (60), a work whose
exegesis of 1 Cors. 15 was similar in style to that of the second edition of
his Römerbrief, but which laid more stress on the principle of "Nachdenken"
(61), and in which the concern for ontology, for a basis for the relation of
God to man other than antithesis, can be discerned (62). By the time of his
exegesis of Philippians (63) his style is much more sober and the concern
for the incarnation, the positive role of the Word in history (64), echoes
what he wrote in his Prolegomena zur christlichen Dogmatik which appeared
the same year. That work centres on reconciliation in Jesus Christ rather
than on the dialectical relationship between man and a wholly other God -

God is now rather the Lord, his otherness is expressed in his lordship and freedom rather than his antithesis to man, and this positive doctrine of God is elaborated in a doctrine of the Trinity which has the main elements of that in C.D.I.1 (65). The doctrine of the Word in which the Trinity is discovered is of the Word as Dei loquentis persona, as actus purus, communicating itself (66); and the "Urgeschichte" in which this happens is definitely a "geschichtliches Ereignis" (67), though history is the predicate of revelation, not vice versa. Along with this emphasis on the historical form of revelation went a balanced, dogmatic recommendation of reflection (Nachdenken) (68) on the whole narrated world of the Bible, as also did the accompanying assurance that "Die Offenbarung steht, nein sie geschieht in der Schrift, nicht hinter ihr" (69) and a strong assertion of the unity of O.T. and N.T. (70). The major innovation in this work is the doctrine of the Trinity in such close dependence on the doctrine of revelation, and I discuss the implication of this for my theme in Chapter 8 below.

After the Prolegomena zur christlichen Dogmatik Barth was intent on purifying his theology from any remaining suggestion of it depending on philosophy, and to do this he needed a comprehensive theological basis. His search for this culminated in his book on Anselm (71). Colin Gunton, in his dissertation on Barth's and Hartshorne's doctrines of God (72) makes an illuminating comparison between the way the two interpret Anselm's proof of God's existence (73). He supports at length his opinion that Hartshorne's proof of God depends on "the mutual logical implication of a limited number of key concepts" (74), and that this a priori philosophical system corresponds to the role of the creed and church authority in Anselm. In contrast, Barth's interpretation of Anselm results in an a posteriori proof of God from his revelation; and Barth distinguishes his position from Anselm's by having "a more biblical centre". Gunton suggests that:

> "Barth's conception of revelation in his equivalent of
> the proof of God from God as he finds it in Anselm...
> Barth's phrase 'God reveals Himself as the Lord' performs
> for him the same function that 'that than which no greater
> can be conceived' performed for Anselm: it provides him
> with reasons for using the word 'God' in rational discourse."(75)

I would add to this that the posterius from which Barth takes his notion of God is mainly biblical narratives interpreted as rendering God's identity, and that this feature (which includes his "christocentricity") is what fundamentally distinguishes him from Anselm. What Anselm gave him was a systematic grounding for his exegesis which denied any vantage point outside the hermeneutical circle (76), and achieved an unprecedented integration of Deus revelatus and Deus in se(77).

(v)

The relevant aspects of Barth's approach to exegesis up to C.D.I.1 have now been described. Except for those sections on the Trinity and on time which are discussed in Chapter 8 below, I am not going to discuss C.D.I.1, 2 in detail, for several reasons.

Firstly, there is the lack of novelty as regards my theme.

Secondly, these volumes engage at great length in conceptual clarificat-
ion and related polemics, especially about the concept of revelation, with a
strong emphasis on the divinity of the Word; whereas my concern is with how
Barth handles narratives in practice, and therefore the later volumes are
more relevant. Besides, I.1 and 2 seem to me to be surprisingly inessential
to understanding the later volumes (with the above-mentioned exceptions of
the Trinity and time). This is partly because Barth repeats himself, but is
also due to the nature of his method. His exhaustive account of what revelation is must still be followed by exegesis which proves all dogmas de novo
from Scripture.

Thirdly, there is the change in Barth's own concept of revelation. Biblical narratives are, as my analysis has shown, a factor of growing importance in the years before C.D., but both then and in C.D.I.1, 2 his main model
of revelation is of a strongly I-Thou, confronting and verbal nature, whereas
from II.2 onwards the mediation of the story becomes more pervasive, and the
doctrine of revelation takes on many characteristics of a doctrine of providence, with God ordering events and the accounts of them in significant patterns to be understood, Spiritu Sancto adiuvante, by the free act of reflection (78). There is no dichotomy; it is a matter of emphasis, and the change
might be ascribed to the subject matter of the later volumes; and it is possible to demonstrate retrospectively the continuity of his hermeneutics; but
for my purposes a lengthy analysis of I.1, 2 is superfluous. So I will merely
list some of the elements which show the continuity.

In I.1 perhaps the most important section for my thesis is on God's language as God's act (79) for there is set out Barth's understanding of the Word
of God being identical with God's act and so becoming history. This goes
with the previous identification of God's Word with his Son, whose essence
is in turn identical with his language, action and passion (80) as mediated
indirectly through Scripture. Barth is clear that the Bible is not to be
measured by human criteria as regards what it may say (81), and he insists
on the incomparability and particularity of its message (82), and on only
posing problems in theology that are raised by Scripture (83). Further,
"when the Bible speaks of revelation it does so in the form of narrating
a story or a series of stories" (84), and this form of revelation is inseparable from its content (85). Dogmatics is therefore "much less a system
than the narrative of an event" (86). This event effects "an absolute alteration of the world" (87) and thus the Bible effects a takeover of our world
of meaning (88).

Such themes are repeated in I.2, and there Barth is more explicit about
his method. The formal task of dogmatics is to listen to Jesus Christ as
attested in Scripture (89), and to adopt the biblical writer's outlook, approach and method (90), and then to teach the result. The method is one of
reporting an event (91), that of reconciliation (92). Of special relevance
to my thesis is the description of what an exegete ought to do (93). He
should find Jesus Christ to be the unifying content of Scripture, and engage
in the three-fold operation of observation (Beobachtung, explicatio), reflection (Nachdenken, meditatio) and appropriation (Aneignung, applicatio).

"Observation" concentrates on the text with "literary-historical" methods.
The literary tools include source-criticism, lexicography, grammar, syntax,
and appreciation of style (94). The history to be considered includes that
of before and after the text was written, as well as all sources for the
events in the text. But then Barth says that we must be open to the possibility that the picture given in the text will

> "determine and modify, shatter and remould my previous
> picture of that time, then of the whole historical process,
> and in the end perhaps even of historical reality generally."(95)

Thus the way is prepared for his own adoption of the narrated world of the
Bible, though he does not do this in a context of historical arguments.
Further, he claims that such openness includes and improves on general hermeneutics, and that biblical hermeneutics is not claiming any special priv-
ileges (96). Such statements could be taken as his blessing on my inquiry.

"Reflection" is crucial for my dissertation. My use of "literary" includes Barth's use of reflection as well as observation. (The narrow meaning
of "literary" for Barth is understandable in the context of his theological
background (97), but one result of it has been to inhibit the sort of comparison which I will make between Barth's handling of biblical stories and
what literary critics say about novels.) Barth's characteristic way of
thinking is dominated by the association of "reflection" with the notions
of correspondence, analogy and similar words. His epistemology is his own
version of the correspondence theory of truth, an attempt to reflect the
truth of Scripture. He recognises the inevitability of philosophical and
other presuppositions in reflection, and gives guidance on how to prevent
distortion of exegesis which may result (98).

His stress is on the experimental, hypothetical, pluralist nature of
reflection, and my task is to try to assess some of his hypotheses.

Thirdly, there is "appropriation", the culmination of true observation
and reflection, involving the orientation of one's whole existence by Scripture (99). This is the goal of Barth's ascesis of Bible reading and is the
subject of my ninth chapter.

My final comment on I.2 is to note the role of the Virgin Birth in
Barth's scheme. As will appear in subsequent chapters, the years A.D. 1-30
constitute Barth's overarching narrative world, and there is great emphasis
on the resurrection as its culmination. The Virgin Birth does for the beginning what the resurrection does for the end by defining the stretch of time
which is "eternalized" and so embraces all history (100). Jacob Burckhardt
has been given theological backing, for now the first Christmas really does
still happen in Basel.

This chapter has followed the thread of Barth's attention to biblical
narratives, especially the central Gospel events. It has shown how he uses
them to present a hermeneutical circle and a world of meaning which are central to his doctrine of revelation and do not appeal either to historical
reconstruction or to the author's or believer's subjectivity. In the next
chapter I will outline this position in its fully developed form.

(1) IV.2, pp. 112 f.

(2) Bouillard, op. cit. Vol. I; T.F. Torrance, Karl Barth: An Introduction to his early theology 1910-1931 (London 1962); Hans Urs von Balthasar, op. cit.; W. Lindemann, Karl Barth und Die Kritische Schriftauslegung (Hamburg-Bergstedt 1973); M. Rumscheidt, Revelation and Theology. An Analysis of the Barth-Harnack Correspondence of 1923 (Cambridge 1972).

For a thorough account of the period see E. Busch, Karl Barth, His Life From Letters and Autobiographical Texts (London 1976).

(3) On the relationship of Troeltsch to Barth and some contemporaries see Robert Morgan, "Ernst Troeltsch and the dialectical theology" in Ernst Troeltsch and the Future of Theology, ed. J.P. Clayton (Cambridge 1976).

(4) Cf. Bouillard, op. cit., pp. 83 f.

(5) For an assessment of how much see Morgan, op. cit., esp. pp. 56 ff.

(6) Bultmann notes acutely their differing attitudes on history in a letter to Barth on 31 December 1922 and attributes it to different "Bildungs-erlebnis" - Karl Barth - Rudolf Bultmann. Briefwechsel 1922-1966, herausg. B. Jaspert (Zürich 1971), S. 9.

(7) For the most thorough critique of the early Barth from this viewpoint see Lindemann, op. cit., S. 82 ff.

(8) Die Protestantische Theologie im 19. Jahrhundert (Zürich 1952. E.T. London 1972).

(9) The correspondence with Harnack, discussed below, is the clearest early example of the irreconcilability of the two positions. cf. Barth's prefaces to the second and third editions of his Epistle to the Romans.

(10) E.g. Chapter 3 below.

(11) Barth's final verdict in 1968 on this period was:

"Was ich jenen Berner Meistern trotz allem verdanke: ich habe damals das Gruseln verlernt, habe nämlich die "historisch-kritische" Schule in ihrer älteren Gestalt damals so gründlich durchlaufen, dass mir die Äusserungen ihrer späteren und heutigen Nachfolger nicht mehr unter die Haut oder gar zu Herzen, sondern, als nur zu bekannt nur noch auf die Nerven gehen konnten." - Schleiermacher-Auswahl, heraus. H. Bolli (München 1968), S. 291.

(12) "He was chained to Harnack...in a kind of stupor so that even the Berlin Philharmonic could not lure him from his studies" - Boniface A. Willems, Karl Barth, p. 16, quoted in Rumscheidt, op. cit., p. 4. Willems is quoting what Barth said to him.

(13) Rumscheidt, op. cit., pp. 4 ff. describes the process. Cf. Bouillard, op. cit., Vol. I, Ch. II.

(14) Theology and Church (New York 1962), p. 239.

(15) Op. cit., pp. 4-5.

(16) Cf. Morgan, op. cit., pp. 41 ff., where Barth and Bultmann are described in relation to the two opposing poles, Herrmann and Troeltsch.

(17) "Bei Kutter lernte ich schlicht, das grosse Wort "Gott" wieder ernst, verantwortlich und gewichtig in den Mund zu nehmen" - in Schleiermacher-Auswahl, op. cit., S. 293.

(18) E.T. in The Word of God and the Word of Man (New York 1957).

(19) Ib. p. 46.

(20) Ib. p. 47.

(21) Ib. pp. 48-50.

(22) Ib. p. 34.

(23) Op. cit., S. 82.

(24) Schleiermacher-Auswahl, op. cit., S. 294 f.

(25) Op. cit., S. 14 ff.

(26) Beck reacted against literal and verbal inspiration positions and developed a theory of the "Theopneustie der biblischen Zeugen" which treated the biblical history as an organic whole (Realorganismus) to which theology must correspond with an organic conceptual whole (Begriffsorganismus). Hofmann had a christocentric interpretation of the biblical history, with historical and critical exegesis strictly subservient to the biblical history as the history of God ("die Geschichte Gottes") when understood by faith.

(27) See M. Kähler: Der sogenannte historische Jesus und der geschichtliche, biblische Christus (1st ed. 1892, 4th ed. München 1969). Cf. Lindemann, op. cit., S. 15.

(28) Der Römerbrief (Bern 1919), S. 80.

(29) Op. cit., S. 100.

(30) For a summary of the relationship between the first and second editions and of the new influences see Bouillard, op. cit., Vol. I, pp. 91 ff.

(31) The Epistle to the Romans, op. cit., p. 10.

(32) Op. cit., S. 30.

(33) For three meanings of "dialectic" in Barth's thought at this period
see Bouillard, op. cit., Vol. I, pp. 73 f. Cf. the discussion of
Barth's exchange with Harnack below; also H.U. von Balthasar, op. cit.,
Part Two, Ch. 2.

(34) Op. cit., p. 116, 103 ff., cf. p. 195.

(35) C.D.II.1, p. 635, on his exegesis of Roms 13,11 f.: "I missed the
distinctive feature of the passage, the teleology which it ascribes
to time as it moves towards a real end." Cf. Bouillard, op. cit.,
p. 76 on the lack of penetration of history by revelation: Roberts,
op. cit., p. 33 on the dichotomy between time and eternity.

(36) E.g. p. 159.

(37) E.g. p. 29: "The years A.D. 1-30 are the era of revelation and disclosure; the era which, as is shown by the reference to David, sets
forth the new strange definition of all time." Barth goes on to
identify this as the Urgeschichte. On Urgeschichte see Bouillard,
op. cit., pp. 99 f.; E. Thurneysen in Revolutionary Theology in the
Making (London 1966), p. 21; Jüngel, op. cit., S. 88 f.

(38) E.g. p. 281:

"This condemnation of sin dwelling in the flesh, this exposure
of the true nature of the flesh, this parable of the Spirit, takes
place, as has been frequently pointed out (on VI,6-8, VI,8), in
the ever-increasing deprivation and diminution of the life of
Jesus, emphasised first in the Temptation, then in Gethsemane and
finally on Golgotha."

(39) But note too that Dostoyevsky is the author most referred to in the
book, and his realistic novels (in which the way of sinners leads
to the Kingdom, and religion is exposed as unchristian, and even the
Grand Inquisitor is kissed by Christ) form a counterpoint to the
Gospels which is constantly present.

(40) P. 323. Cf. pp. 202, 223, 378, 383, 462.

(41) Bouillard even says of Barth's thought at this time: "La resurrection
est une periphrase du mot 'Dieu'" - op. cit., Vol. I, p. 49.

(42) See Lindemann, op. cit., S. 35 ff. Cf. Bultmann's complaint (Briefwechsel, op. cit., S. 9) in a letter to Barth about the third edn. that
there is no "Sachkritik" of Paul.

(43) Ib. p. 171.

(44) Ib. p. 116 ff.

(45) Summarised under six headings of Rumscheidt, ib. pp. 105-6.

(46) See Rumscheidt, op. cit., pp. 76 ff.

(47) See his reply to Harnack's fourth point, ib. pp. 32 f., and his attack on the "simple Gospel", pp. 44 f. and also especially pp. 48 f.

(48) Ib. p. 46.

(49) E.g. Rumscheidt, op. cit., pp. 48 f.

(50) Ib. p. 48.

(51) Ib. p. 53. On naivety see on Smend below, Chapter 4, pp. 50 f. On biblicism, a few years later Barth in Die christliche Dogmatik im Entwurf, I Lehre vom Worte Gottes. Prolegomena zur christlichen Dogmatik (München 1927), S. 435-440, goes to some trouble to refute the charge, his main point being that his object is not to repeat the words or even the theology of the Bible but to discern the Word in the words.

(52) Ib. p. 177 f.

(53) Barth's first reply to Harnack's first point is perhaps his most important of the debate:

> "'Historical knowledge' can be accomplished according to the assertion of the Gospel, only through an act of this 'content' itself. But 'critical reflection' would lead to the conclusion that this assertion is founded in the essence of the matter (the relation of God and man) and is therefore to be seriously respected. The 'scientific character' of theology would then be its adherence to the recollection that its object was once subject and must become that again and again..." ib. pp. 31 f.

(54) Though the final open break with Brunner only came in 1934.

(55) E.g. C.D. I.1, p. 39.

(56) See "Der heilige Geist und das christliche Leben" in Zur Lehre vom heiligen Geist (München 1930), S. 49-50. Cf. C.D.I.1, pp. 141 ff.

(57) See "Nein! Antwort an Emil Brunner", Theologische Existenz Heute, Heft 16, München 1934. Cf. C.D.I.1, p. 29 ff.

(58) Barth's own slogan could be summed up as a rejection of "Offenbarung und..." (religious consciousness or reason or civilisation or history of religion or creation or human existence). He expressed this most concisely at this period in "Das erste Gebot als theologisches Axiom" in Zwischen den Zeiten, 1933, S. 298-314.

(59) See Bouillard, op. cit., Vol. I, pp. 148 ff.; Lindemann, op. cit., S. 51 ff.

(60) München. E.T. London 1933.

(61) From the Foreword, S.IV: "Taube Ohren habe ich nur für das Verbot einer prinzipiell nachdenkenden - und selbst denkenden Exegese 'überhaupt'."

(62) See Roberts, op. cit., p. 40.

(63) Erklärung des Philipperbriefes (München 1927; E.T. London 1962).

(64) Cf. his conclusion:

> "So the letter ends with the same objectivity and superiority
> with which it began, and in which it is at once both one of
> the most remarkable evidences of how human a Christian can be
> and a testimony to an event that can only be designated as the
> very limit of what is understood as human history." (op. cit.,
> E.T., p. 128)

(65) Discussed below, Chapter 8. See Prolegomena zur christlichen Dogmatik,
S. 37 ff., 63 ff., 131 ff., 171 ff.

(66) Ib. S. 63, 81 f., 112.

(67) Ib. S. 230 ff.

(68) "Denken heisst Nachdenken" - ib. S. 102. (This idea was always central
to his notion of thinking, cf. his article, in answer to an atheist in
Zürcher Woche, 15. Jg., Nr. 24, 14.6.1963, S. 5 "Denken heisst: Nachdenken".)

(69) Ib. S. 344.

(70) E.g. ib. S. 240.

(71) Fides Quaerens Intellectum. Anselms Beweis der Existenz Gottes (München
1931. E.T. London 1960). In the preface to the second edition he wrote:
"In this book on Anselm I am working with a vital key, if not the key,
an understanding of the whole process of thought that has impressed me
more and more in my Church Dogmatics as the only one proper to theology."
(E.T. p. 11). Hans Urs von Balthasar, op. cit., Pt. II, Ch. III, gives
a good account of the place of the book in Barth's development of his
doctrine of analogy.

(72) London Univ. 1975.

(73) Op. cit., Ch. IV, V.

(74) Ib. Ch. V, p. 3.

(75) Ib. Ch. V, p. 10.

(76) Ib. Ch. V, p. 10.

(77) Lindemann, op. cit., S. 65 ff. is perceptive on this point.

(78) See below Chapter 8.

(78) John McIntyre in The Shape of Christology (London 1966), pp. 159 ff.
suggests that there was a change in Barth's main model of revelation

between C.D.I.1 and IV.2. In my terms, his point is that Barth places increasing emphasis on the story of Jesus Christ as the expression of the divine essence.

(79) I.1, pp. 162-184.

(80) Ib. p. 156. Cf. the criticism of Bultmann for concentrating on the verbal element and not doing justice to "the fact that N.T. tradition has set forth the revealing activity of Jesus as an intertexture, impossible to dissolve, of word and deed, and indeed of word and miracle". Ib. p. 458 f.

(81) E.g. ib. p. 120, 16 ff.

(82) E.g. ib. p. 29 f., 42, 60, 127, 131, 155, 164 ff., 170, 181, 222. Cf. p. 351 on O.T. and N.T. pointing to a "self-contained novum".

(83) Ib. p. 339.

(84) Ib. p. 362.

(85) E.g. p. 285, cf. p. 367: God "can and will and really does assume temporal form".

(86) Ib. p. 321.

(87) Ib. p. 164.

(88) Ib. p. 177: "Thus the world literally ceases to exist apart in a neutral attitude, over against revelation, the Bible, and proclamation."

(89) E.g. p. 802.

(90) Ib. p. 816.

(91) Ib. p. 862 ff.

(92) Ib. p. 719 ff.

(93) Ib. p. 719 ff.

(94) Ib. p. 723.

(95) Ib. p. 724.

(96) Ib. pp. 725-727.

(97) Lindemann, op. cit., S. 9 ff. gives an account of the usage of the term in German theology during Barth's formative years. The "literary" approach, as described e.g. by P. Wernle, differentiated between literary "Kritik" and literary "Verständnis". The former was about the prehistory of the document and problems of language, grammar, and sources. The latter deals with the hermeneutical circle formed by the place of the work in its tradition and context, the intention of its author, its

whole arrangement and style, and the text itself. Such a general hermeneutic omits just that approach of Nachdenken which is so suited to
realistic narrative and is, as Barth understood, in no systematic relation to the operation proposed by Wernle. Cf. below Chapter 4.

(98) I.2, pp. 728 ff. Cf. the constant efforts of literary critics to do
the same, and the dilemma of "the mirror and the lamp".

(99) Ib. pp. 736 ff.

(100) E.g. ib. p. 182:

"Now it is no accident that for us the Virgin Birth is parallelled
by the miracle of the empty tomb. These two miracles belong together. They constitute, as it were, a single sign, the special
function of which is to describe and mark out the existence of
Jesus Christ, amid the many other existences in human history, as
that human historical existence in which God is Himself, God is
alone, God is directly the Subject, the temporal reality of which
is not only called forth, created, conditioned and supported by
the eternal reality of God, but is identical with it."

CHAPTER 3.   THEOLOGY AND NARRATIVE: SOME ISSUES RAISED BY
             C.D.IV. §59

I now penetrate deep into the C.D. for my first chapter of analysis. I start with C.D.IV.1 in order, in preparation for my next theoretical chapter, to illustrate my theme with a sample of Barth's maturer thought, and also to begin the doctrine of reconciliation which is central to his whole dogmatic structure (1).

                              (i)

The problem in IV.1 which I treat in this chapter is whether there is any way to reconcile the various statements Barth makes about the story of Jesus Christ.

At the simplest level he takes it as any other story:

       "It came to pass, we have just said; as we do when we
       tell the story of something that happened in the world at
       a definite place and a definite point of time. To think
       the matter out further and to understand it in detail, all
       that remains actually for us to do is simply to recount it
       in the manner of a story which has come to pass (which it
       is), to bring it before ourselves as something that has
       objectively happened."(2)

As the last sentence implies, he makes a historical claim in addition:

       "It is a matter of history. Everything depends upon
       the fact that this turning as it comes from God fur us men
       is not simply imagined and presented as a true teaching
       of pious and thoughtful people, but that it happened in
       this way, in the space and time which are those of all
       men."(3)

Yet this history has peculiar features:

       "There is no question of appealing to His remembered
       form as it had necessarily appeared to His disciples before
       the verdict of the Holy Spirit was pronounced on His life
       and death, abstracted from the verdict of the Holy Spirit.
       In the editing and composition of the Evangelical narratives
       the interest and art and rules of the historian do not
       matter. What matters is His living existence in the com-
       munity and therefore in the world. What matters is His
       history as it has indeed happened but as it is present and
       not past."(4)

Within this story there is also a distinction:

> "The death of Jesus Christ can certainly be thought of as
> history in the modern sense, but not the resurrection."(5)

Barth, however, is not interested in assessing either event by historical
canons. He is content to reflect on both as they are given in the N.T., and
the differentiation of the resurrection narratives as sage (6) is based on the
"strong impression" got from reading the Gospels (7), not on the difficulty
of assessing their historicity. Besides, as the quotation from p. 320 above
implies, this history is not "dead" history.

> "He not only went the way from Jordan to Golgotha, but He
> still goes it, again and again."(8)

A concomitant of this is that it is an "inclusive" story (9), it is the
"sphere" in which we live, and

> "a report about ourselves is included in that report about
> God."(10)

Christ's death and resurrection are

> "the basis of the alteration of the situation of the men
> of all times."(11)

The question of a hermeneutical gap between the Gospels and today is a
technical or methodological issue (12) which is solved theologically by
Barth's answer to the question:

> "Supposing our contemporaneity with the Word of God made
> flesh, with the Judge judged in our place, is already an
> event?"(13)

Can Barth coherently say on the one hand that, for instance, the best explanation of the passion story is its "mere repetition" (14), and on the
other hand, that unlike other stories it does not need normal historical
verification, but is proved by Christ speaking through it now? (15)

If these two statements, and the previous ones, are consistent, the
obvious direction to look for their unity is in Barth's interpretation of
the Gospel story. The only reason he gives for flying in the face of general hermeneutical and historical procedure is that the nature of this story
demands it, for then he can be defended by saying the general rules are not
sufficiently inclusive. His simplest summary of what this story is about is:

> "It recounts this history and speaks of its inclusive power
> and significance in such a way that it declares a name,
> binding the history strictly and indissolubly to this name

34

and presenting it as the story of the bearer of this
name."(16)

The context of that sentence is an explanation of why his list of seven points
on the meaning of "God with us" needs to be restated with specific reference
to the story, where the meaning is given "concrete expression". He says
that

> "everything depends upon its concrete expression:
> the whole truth and reality of the report, and the whole
> secret of the communication of the matter".(17)

Special attention should therefore be paid to his treatment of the Gospel
story. §59, The Obedience of the Son of God, is the crucial section of IV.1
in this regard. §§57, 58 had continually stressed the importance of the
story for the doctrine of reconciliation, and the succeeding sections §§60-
63 look back to §59.

(ii)

Within §59 the first subsection is about the meaning of the incarnation
in the New Testament, introducing the theme of the whole section, The Obedience of the Son of God, by stressing the "decisive expressions" of Paul in
Phil. 2. The Gospels are appealed to in support of Paul's meaning, but there
is no detailed exegesis of them. The ancient creeds are supported

> "when under the concepts passus, crucifixus, mortuus,
> sepultus, they believed that they were saying everything
> that is decisive about the man Jesus".(18)

Barth also emphasises that the Word became Jewish flesh. The O.T. is
essential for knowledge of the incarnation, and it too focuses us on the
passion story:

> "In the Old Testament there is always the antithesis
> between the righteous God and the bitter things which man
> has to accept from Him without murmuring. In the passion
> story of the New Testament this is done away. It is God
> Himself who takes the place of the former sufferer and
> allows the bitterness of their sufferings to fall upon
> Himself.... What took place on the cross of Golgotha is
> the last word of an old history and the first word of a
> new."(19)

Barth discusses the mystery of God's presence in Christ's suffering
and looks to the story for a solution. (He says the identity of God and man
in Jesus Christ cannot be a postulate but must be derived from "what took
place in this man" (20).)In trying to understand this he rejects the notion
of a split in God Himself (21), and chooses rather to form his concept of

35

who God is from this story (22). The nature of God's glory is to be deduced from

> "its revelation in the divine nature of Jesus Christ.
> From this we learn that the forma Dei consists in the grace
> in which God Himself assumes and makes His own the forma
> servi".(23)

Modalism and subordinationism are criticised for trying to evade the cross of Jesus Christ (24) and the concepts of unity and obedience are re-interpreted in the light of the relationships within God (25). These relationships are seen in the Gospel story.

From all this it can be seen how the main function of §59.1 is to pre-pare for the following two subsections where the crucifixion and resurrection are treated. How the incarnation makes sense is to be decided only by refer-ence to their story. After explaining the meaning of judgment in the New Testament (26) he says that what took place in Jesus Christ was that he took our place in undergoing God's judgment (27). How are we to understand this? Barth says: by listening to the story (28). There follows an excursus which is a literary analysis of the story of Jesus from the beginning of his ministry to his resurrection (29), and which is of great importance to my argument. Parallel to it there is an excursus on the temptation and Geth-semane in §59.2, pp. 259 ff. In view of the many possible approaches to the Gospel narratives it is vital to a solution of the problem of their role in his theology that the nature of such analysis be noted.

His view on pp. 224 ff. (S. 246 ff.) is that the pattern of the synoptic Gospels represents the pattern of the atonement. In his ministry Jesus emerges as alone and superior to his disciples and other men, who are judged by his presence and their reaction to him. Then comes the contrast of the passion story in which the roles are reversed: now Jesus is the object of what happens, he suffers rather than acts, and instead of judgment falling on other men it falls on him. The Barabbas episode shows this best. Finally, the third part of the story, the Easter narrative, shows that the same per-son, the Judge who was judged, was acknowledged by God, was with his disciples again, and is still alive. Because his identity is known in his history, one must know that history in order to know him.

Barth repeats in various ways the distinction between this history and all interpretation or effects of it, and culminates with a statement of the irreversible relationship that is at the heart of his theology:

> "He Himself and His history as it took place then and
> there is identical with the Word of God, not with that
> which may result from the Word of God in the way of pro-
> clamation and faith and fulfilment in and through and
> from us men who hear it."(30)

What critical questions should be put to this excursus? The first is whether it is an answer to the question it asks: "What do we find in this history?"(31) How is Barth understanding "Historie"? Does what follows

36

give any basis for differentiating "Historie" from "Geschichte"? He claims that the "Historie" is factual (32), that there is almost no attempt by the evangelists to give an interpretation ("Deutung") and that they are content simply to say how the events happened (33). Yet apart from an admission that there may be <u>vaticinia ex eventu</u> (34) there is no attempt at historical criticism, and even that one instance is introduced not because of an interest in reconstructing what happened but because it is an exception to his theory and needs to be explained away. In short, he makes no distinction between the history-likeness of the Gospels and their correspondence to events that happened. This is clearest when he denies the Evangelists an interpretative role. At one level he is quite right: the story is for the most part an account of the interaction of men and events without explicit comments by the narrators; but he does not raise the question of how far the picture it conveys is the result of redaction by the authors or their sources, or how far even the pattern of exchange, which is so important to his theology, is a product of such redaction. The nearest he comes to granting the validity of the latter approach is in forestalling it by noting that the events of the passion narrative are substantially the same in all the Evangelists. I am not denying that Barth knows how the Gospels differ and can even make theology out of the differences. My point is that what count as historical facts for theological reflection are limited to the events as described in the Gospels, and that Barth does not admit verification by critical methods. In practice, therefore, "Historie" and "Geschichte" are synonymous, and he does not try to distinguish the story from a novel by historical methods.

The second critical question grows out of the answer to the first. Granted that the events of this story are not to be verified by referring them to whatever historical critics can reconstruct, does Barth offer an alternative referent? He does: the resurrected Christ. Until, on p. 227, we reach Barth's third part of the story, the resurrection, there is nothing to suggest that the Gospel is not a novel or a fictional short story. A novel too can render a character, and it might be impossible and unnecessary to be able to draw the line between fact and fiction in order to understand the character's identity. But in this story the referent is not just a historical character but one who is alive now as the same person. How does this affect the historical status of the story? Barth's answer that it makes the history "significant in and by itself" (35) does not answer the question of the reliability of the accounts. Yet when he sees the resurrection as summing up the Gospel and concentrating it on Jesus Christ, e.g.

> "He Himself was and is this event, the origin, the authority,
> the power, the object of the proclamation laid on the com-
> munity" (36),

and then goes on to claim that

> "He speaks for Himself whenever He is spoken of and His
> story is told and heard" (37),

he is implicitly ruling out the question of the reliability of the accounts as theologically irrelevant. If they are the means of knowing the person

37

they portray then they are significant in themselves without any other support. By making the identity of Jesus Christ the referent Barth creates a closed circle of the accounts and the presence of Christ. It is the history-likeness of the accounts and not their confirmation as "Historie" which is essential if they are to depict Jesus Christ. He is of course free to speak or not speak through the story (Barth is careful, for instance, when he suggests that the best service for Good Friday would be the repetition of the passion story, to add: "Spiritu Sancto adiuvante" (38)), and so there is no way of proving his presence disinterestedly by experiment. Yet this freedom from concern about the persuasiveness or apologetic value of the story (and even the question: Did it actually happen? can be seen as apologetic in intent) gives all the more freedom for purely literary analysis. The first thing to do is to try to hear what the story says, and Barth draws a sharp distinction between this and attempts not only to ascertain critically their historical reference but also to show the story's relevance to ourselves:

> "The relationship between the significant thing which He
> is in Himself and the significance which He may acquire
> for us is an irreversible relationship." (39)

There are several methodological implications of this position. The most obvious is the necessity for a literary analysis of the story such as Barth gives in this excursus. It is not meant to give the conceptual content of the story, but to make sure that one sees that it only "means" as it "tells", and to

> "find some way of making the accustomed unaccustomed
> again, the well-known unknown and the old new: that
> is, the outline of the evangelical history with which
> we are so familiar and the stimulating singularity of
> which we may so easily overlook, especially in the form
> in which it is presented in the synoptic Gospels."(40)

A corollary of this is the importance of the narrative framework of the rest of the Bible, which gives the context for the central story. This involves the question of the unity of the Bible and the role of typological exegesis. I will deal with this mainly on C.D.II.2 and III.1.

A further implication is the discrimination of genres in the Bible. If the stories are really myths then Barth's position is undermined. In the introduction to IV.1 he says that while writing the volume he had Bultmann's work constantly in mind. In the debate with Bultmann the decision about the nature of the narratives leads to the question of the "hermeneutical gap".

In addition there is the issue of How Barth argues from the narratives to his theological proposals, including the way he distinguishes and relates the life of Christ and the lives of Christians and the Church.

(iii)

The rest of §59.2 is a fourfold answer to the question of what Jesus Christ was and did for us. It can be seen as a commentary on the excursus in pp. 224 ff.

In the first part on Jesus as Judge, the supporting exegesis on p. 235 clearly harks back to pp. 224 ff. The excursus accompanying the second part, on Jesus as the judged, does the same, and includes the remarkable claim that the theological explanation Barth gives of what "the Gospel story says...factually" is the only one the story will bear, and agrees with that of "every Church which is worthy of the name of Christian" (41).

The third part of the answer, on the judgment (i.e. the passion and death), says that it is the identity of the one who was crucified rather than his human suffering which marks the uniqueness of the event, making it of universal importance. It is God who

> "gives Himself to be the humanly acting and suffering
> person in this occurrence" (42).

This does not mean (as the English translation at the end of the previous paragraph on p. 246 suggests) that we have to look for the meaning in God outside the story. Rather it leads on to a strong affirmation that the truth of Christian experience of God is discovered only through the story (43). The exegetical excursus of this third part is confined to quoting with brief comments N.T. passages which relate the death of Jesus Christ to sin.

The fourth part, on Jesus' obedience, concentrates in its exegesis (44) on Jesus in Gethsemane, expanding the brief reference on p. 226. Gethsemane is the turning-point from Christ's action to passion. Barth understands it in the light of the temptations, but sees the decisive difference between the two episodes in the form of the testing. Previously Satan spoke with words, now he speaks "in the hard language of facts" (45). God's answer to Jesus' prayer is given in the same language (46). Therefore "the answer of God was identical with the action of Satan" (47). Barth then expounds the prayer of Jesus as meaning the completion of his obedience to the Father. Earlier he had seen the "for us" of the Gospel represented best in Jesus' aloneness in Gethsemane (48). Thus, by seeing the crucifixion as the point of convergence of the intentions of Satan, God and the representative Jesus, Barth explains his doctrine of the atonement. It is a literary explanation, appealing to the interaction of characters and events in the narrative; and without it his theological conclusions are baseless (49).

§59.3, The Verdict of the Father, comments on the relationship between the crucifixion and resurrection in order to determine what the resurrection adds to the story. As the introduction on p. 283f. says, this is the basic transitional discussion which justifies Barth's inclusive christology. The following sections on sin, justifiction, community and faith are made to depend on this turn in the story. What sort of dependence that is, is a matter for the particular arguments in each section, but the presupposed fact of the relevance of the story to all men is to be proved from the resurrection.

Before his main discussion Barth argues against being too concerned
with the "hermeneutical gap", the distance between our time and that of
Christ's life on earth (50). He identifies this problem with others: that
of faith and history; and that of mysticism - the spatial counterpart of
the hermeneutical gap. Barth does not deny the gap in time but he claims
that it is a side-issue, to be resolved in the course of answering the main
question. The gap has

> "more the character of a technical difficulty in thinking
> than that of a spiritual or a genuine theological problem....
> It is a methodological question."(51)

The main question is the content of the story, where the problem becomes
the encounter of man with God acting and speaking in history. Barth suggests
that concern about the hermeneutical gap is an attempt to escape facing the
truth of this content (52). What this means for Barth's own method is a
choice of literary exegesis of the content rather than exploration of the
possibilities of the stories being meaningful today. There is a reversal
of the way the problem of the gap is posed. Instead of asking how the
story of Jesus Christ is comprehensible in some view of history, he starts
from Jesus Christ's contemporaneity with us, and asks:

> "How will it stand with us when we are alongside Jesus
> Christ and follow Him, when we are in His environment and
> time and space?" (53)

This means that the only standpoint which Barth will admit is one within the
story, and he makes the question more precise as follows: if Christ's death
has an inclusive, substitutionary character (which §59.2 concluded it had),
it means the death of all men, for whom the only question is then whether
there is anything for them beyond this death (54). The excursus on pp. 295-6
is a good example of the extent to which Barth insists on taking the story
as his criterion of reality, whatever common sense might object:

> "For then and there, in the person of Christ taking our
> place, we were present, being crucified and dying with Him.
> We died. This has to be understood quite concretely and
> literally.... (It is an) event which can be characterized
> only indicatively, in the form of a narrative, because is
> can be only as we look back to Golgotha."

Having thus concentrated the problem on the story he gives five conditions which a genuine sequel to the crucifixion must fulfil. Since, as he
says on p. 298, the conditions were arrived at on the basis of what the story
says the sequel actually was, the discussion of them filling the rest of the
section can best be seen as a reflection on the structure and content of the
story at its climax.

The first and fifth considerations show how the resurrection portrays
the identity of God:

> "It was the very model of a gracious act of God, the Son
> of God as such being active only as the recipient, God the
> Father alone being the One who acts, and God the Holy Spirit

alone the One who mediates His action and revelation."(55)

In the first consideration the stress is on the fact that it is the same
Father who willed the crucifixion and resurrection, in the fifth it is on
the Son's identity given through the same events.

The second consideration is that the resurrection is a new event which
continues the story by justifying what God did and Jesus suffered in the
crucifixion, and therefore (because of Jesus' substitutionary role) justifying
all men. Barth stresses that the resurrection is not "the noetic converse"
of the crucifixion (56), and the fourth consideration reinforces this by
maintaining that the resurrection is an historical event. He says that the
resurrection itself cannot be narrated, that the accounts of the forty days
have "obscurities and irreconcilable contradictions", that even 1 Cor. 15:
4-8 is not an attempt to prove the resurrection according to modern historical
criteria (57). He makes only one positive point in defence of the resurrection as an event in space and time: that this is the intention of the narratives (58). The whole burden of his case here (obviously with Bultmann in
mind) rests on his judgment about the nature of the narrative: that it is
realistic in the sense of saying what it intends without meaning to

> "speak of the non-spatial and timeless being of certain
> general truths, orders and relationships, clothing what
> it really wanted to say in the poetical form of a narrative".(59)

He is even willing to admit the labels "saga" and "legend" (60) as long as
the element of spatial and temporal particularity is retained. Not only do
the narratives themselves intend this, claims Barth, but any other interpretation cannot account for the relationship between the history of Jesus
Christ and that of the Church (61). He admits the possibility of faith
without the resurrection, but says that that is not the content of the narrative (62). So at this point his case against Bultmann is simply that the
text is to be understood as realistic narrative without the need for further
hermeneutical discussion (63). He says that the third consideration, on the
positive connection between the crucifixion and resurrection, is decisive for
understanding the relevance of the crucifixion to us (64). The resurrection
shows God's intention in the crucifixion to be our conversion to God (65),
so the two have the one purpose. The resurrection also makes this purpose
relevant to us now because it makes the Gospel story into our present reality:

> "But the fact that He is risen to die no more, to be
> taken from the dominion of death (Roms. 6:9), carries with
> it the fact that His then living and speaking and acting,
> His being on the way from Jordan to Golgotha, His being as
> the One who suffered and died, became and is as such His
> eternal being and therefore His present-day being every
> day of our time. That which took place on the third day
> after His death lifted up the whole of what took place
> before in all its particularity (not in spite of but
> because of its particularity) into something that took
> place once and for all." (66)

This is Barth's simplest justification for his theological method: that his
concentration on the story which tells of Jesus Christ is necessitated by the

resurrection, which makes the story relevant to all men and alters their situation (67). The excursus on pp. 314 ff. forms the same circle noted above, between the Gospel narrative and the presence of Christ. It answers the question of how to experience and prove this reality by saying that prayer is the way. This prayer is through Jesus Christ as portrayed in the Gospels, and this procedure leaves no room for turning aside to assess the reliability of those accounts. The argument amounts to an assertion that this is how the story "works" (68).

The next point Barth makes reinforces the circle by affirming both the necessity of the accounts of Christ's life and also ruling out any appeal tp "his remembered form" (69).

Barth goes on to understand the presence of the risen Christ by referring forward to his final parousia (70). But he insists that although the present form of Christ's presence is provisional the completed crucifixion and re-surrection are not (71). One result of his argument here is to forbid any expectation from eschatology of a change in the story's portrayal of Christ:

> "The one crucified and risen Jesus Christ is the object of
> New Testament faith and the content of New Testament hope."(72)

§59 has raised many of the issues with which this book is concerned, and my comments on it are intended to establish in a preliminary way what the issues are. The Gospel narratives, supported by the rest of the New Testament and by the Old Testament, were the court of appeal. The pleading was partly on the basis of literary analysis, most clearly in the exposition of the substitutionary character of Jesus' life on pp. 224 ff., in the companion excursus on Jesus in Gethsemane, and in the five-point discussion of the relation of Jesus' death to his resurrection. The exclusion of criteria from outside the Bible was apparent in the treatment of historicity, of the hermeneutical gap, and of the presence of Christ as a result of his resurrection. The latter event grounds the story's inclusiveness, which is the presupposition for the rest of IV.1. The radicalness of the rejection of external criteria is stressed by the uncompromising statements about our death having already taken place. These suggest a rejection of accepted views of reality in the light of this story such that an imaginative and emotional, as well as intellectual revolution is demanded by Barth.

The next chapter will attempt to give a more coherent form to this chapter's ad hoc and cursory remarks about theology and narrative.

42

(1) For a brief account of what is meant by "central" here, see Bouillard, op. cit., Vol. I, pp. 225 ff.

(2) IV.1, p. 223.

(3) Ib. p. 247.

(4) Ib. p. 320.

(5) Ib. p. 336.

(6) Ib. p. 335, cf. p. 508.

(7) Ib. p. 334.

(8) Ib. p. 313.

(9) Ib. p. 16.

(10) Ib. p. 7.

(11) Ib. p. 316.

(12) Ib. p. 287 ff.

(13) Ib. p. 291.

(14) Ib. p. 249.

(15) Ib. p. 228.

(16) Ib. p. 16.

(17) Ib. p. 16.

(18) Ib. p. 165.

(19) Ib. pp. 175 f.

(20) Ib. p. 183.

(21) Ib. p. 184 ff.

(22) Ib. p. 186 ff.

(23) Ib. p. 188.

(24) Ib. p. 199.

(25) Ib. p. 202 ff.

(26) Ib. pp. 217 ff.

(27) Ib. p. 222.

(28) Ib. p. 223, cf. p. 249 f.

(29) Ib. pp. 224 ff. For a formal analysis of the Gospels that pays tribute to this excursus of Barth, while itself being quite different, see Part IV of The Identity of Jesus Christ (Philadelphia, 1975) by Hans Frei, the reference to Barth being in a footnote on p. 128.

For an analysis of the same excursus that notes the details of Barth's literary treatment of the Gospels and sets it out in six steps, see Biblische Denkform in der Dogmatik. Die Vorbildlichkeit des biblischen Denkens für die Methode der "Kirchlichen Dogmatik Karl Barths by W. Schlichting (Zürich 1971), S. 65-66. The context in Schlichting's book is a collection of instances of Barth's recognition of grammatical, stylistic and syntactical features of the Bible. Although he makes his point well, Schlichting's microscopic approach fails to see in Barth the sort of large-scale literary arguments which I hold to be central to his theological method.

(30) Ib. p. 228.

(31) "Was bietet diese Historie?" Ib. p. 224, S. 246.

(32) Ib. p. 224.

(33) Ib. p. 227, S. 249.

(34) Ib. p. 225.

(35) "in sich selber und durch sich selber bedeutsam". Ib. p. 227, S. 249.

(36) Ib. p. 227.

(37) Ib. p. 227.

(38) Ib. p. 250.

(39) Ib. p. 228.

(40) Ib. p. 224, S. 246.

(41) Ib. p. 238 ff.

(42) "Er gibt sich dazu her, in diesem Geschehen selbst die menschlich handelnde und leidende Person zu sein." Ib. p. 246, S. 271.

(43) Ib. p. 249 f.

(44) Ib. p. 259 ff.

(45) "In der harten Sprache der Tatsachen". Ib. p. 266, S. 293.

(46) Ib. p. 267.

(47) Ib. p. 268.

(48) Ib. p. 268.

(49) This way of interpreting the story is best exemplified in the account
of Jesus and His Father in relation to Judas, see Chapter 5 below,
pp. 84 ff.

(50) Ib. pp. 287 ff.

(51) "Sie ist eine typisch methodologische Frage." Ib. pp. 288-9, S. 318.

(52) Ib. pp. 289 ff.

(53) Ib. p. 293.

(54) Ib. pp. 293 ff.

(55) Ib. p. 356, cf. pp. 300 ff., 342 ff.

(56) Ib. p. 204.

(57) Ib. pp. 334 ff.

(58) Ib. pp. 336 ff.

(59) Ib. p. 337.

(60) Ib. p. 336, cf.

(61) Ib. pp. 336 ff.

(62) Ib. 339-41.

(63) The correspondence between Barth and Bultmann shows their mutual puzzle-
ment over how the other can miss the crucial point. The lengthy exchange at the end of 1952, after the appearance of Kerygma und Mythos
Vol. II, ed. H.-W. Bartsch (Hamburg. E.T. Vols. I and II, London 1972)
with its essay of Barth, "Rudolf Bultmann. Ein Versuch, ihn zu verste-
hen", is especially interesting, all the more so since Barth was at this
time writing C.D.IV.1 (whose forword, with its recognition of the
volume's polemical relation to Bultmann, was written in June 1953).
Bultmann, after reading Barth's contribution to Kerygma and Mythos, in
November 1952 wrote to Barth a full answer (Briefwechsel, op. cit., S.
169-192) and Barth answered on Christmas Eve (Ib. S. 195-201). For
Bultmann talk of the resurrected Christ in himself is mythological (Ib.
S. 180) and Barth is accused of objectifying what cannot be objectified.
Barth sees the objectifying in the N.T. "mythology" as its main point,
claims that Bultmann's method covers up exactly the element of the text
that is for himself the first and decisive thing to be brought to light,
and accuses Bultmann of pointing to a vacuum (Ib. S. 198 f.). Barth
compares himself and Bultmann to a whale and an elephant trying to find

common ground (Ib. S. 196), and his next letter to Bultmann, over their
differences in interpreting Rom 5:21b, gives an excellent humorous example of the different imaginative worlds in which the two men live:

"Im Himmel (als dem obersten Stockwerk des mythologischen Welt-
bildes) suchen wir dann vielleicht - ich freilich erst nach einem
längeren Abstecher zu W.A. Mozart - den Apostel Paulus gemeinsam
auf, um uns von ihm erklären zu lassen wie er es endlich und zu-
letzt selbst gemeint habe." (Ib. S. 203)

(64) Ib. pp. 309, 312.

(65) Ib. p. 310.

(66) Ib. p. 313.

(67) Ib. p. 316. Cf. F.-W. Marquardt, op. cit., commenting on the resurrection in C.D.IV.1:

"Der Auferstehungsrealismus besteht darin, dass Barth sich nicht
begnügt mit einer Lehre vom real verändernden Wort. sondern vor-
wartschreitet zu der Lehre von einer durch das Wort real verän-
derten Situation." (S. 243)

(68) Cf. Chapter 9 below on the spirituality of the C.D.

(69) Ib. p. 320.

(70) Ib. pp. 322 ff.

(71) Ib. pp. 322, 330.

(72) Ib. p. 328.

CHAPTER 4. REALISTIC NARRATIVE

<hr>

"I am dissatisfied because this method (sc. of Austin
Farrer in exegesis) does nothing to illuminate, and indeed
evaporates, St. Mark's sense of what we mean by historical
reality, the "Here and Now" of our daily experience, the
"Then and There" of memory, by which I do not mean detailed
precision of testimony, but the deep sense of "happening".
Surely a literary criticism of the Gospels must take into
account this quality, which has struck, and strikes, reader
after reader. I have in mind here, as a contrast to the
method of interpretation through patterns of symbolic images,
a remarkable piece of literary criticism which illuminates
precisely this: the chapters in which Professor Auerbach
in his Mimesis, or the Representation of Reality in Western
Literature discusses the story of the sacrifice of Isaac in
Genesis and the episode of Peter's denial in the Gospel of
St. Mark. He compares Homer with the Old Testament writer
to demonstrate the difference between legend treated as
poetry and the sacred legend of the Jews, whose historical
reality the writer believed in. After his discussion of
St. Mark's narrative, he declares that he can find nothing
comparable in any antique historian for sense of actuality."(1)

This chapter is intended to explain my approach to the C.D. and especially to suggest how literary criticism of the sort Dame Helen Gardner ap-
proves may illuminate Barth's method.

(i)

Discussions of Barth (as my list of "-isms", above (2), shows) have not
lacked doctrinal and philosophical comparisons and assessments, whereas literary criticism has rarely been employed. Yet the Bible is literature, and
Barth works with a principle of sola scriptura that leads him to take seriously the relation of its form to its content. In particular, as the previous two chapters have shown, he is concerned with biblical narrative, so
an obvious direction to look is to the literary criticism of narrative.
Within this vast field Dame Helen points to the area of realistic narrative
and from among the conflicting voices there she selects Erich Auerbach's.
I am doing likewise, for my simplest contention, supported by this and other
chapters, is that Barth is one of the readers of the Bible who sees what
Dame Helen sees, and that this is an important factor in understanding his
theological method.

Auerbach's work (3) sets part of the Bible in a long tradition of realism
in literature, on which, he claims, it had a powerful influence. His discussion of the nature of realistic narrative is more an analysis of instances
than an attempt to give a theoretical account. There is good reason for this,

since realism is by nature resistant to a general definition of its essence, and its meaning is better clarified by gathering a family of instances. Auerbach's instances, illuminated by his analysis of them, are what I have in mind when I refer to literary realism. Barth is like Auerbach in offering a large number of interpretations of narratives without any satisfactory account of his method. To bring them together in a helpful way it is therefore necessary to be more theoretical than either. In attempting this I will draw on other literary critics, theologians and philosophers, and in particular on works by Peter Stern (4) and Hans Frei (5), both influenced by Auerbach and both offering a more theoretical account of realism than he does.

Besides the intrinsic appropriateness to Barth's method of such comparisons, there is also a larger context in the growing number of works on the importance of narrative within theology (6), philosophy (7), history (8) and life in general (9). I will deal briefly with the issue of philosophy, and then will present a case for making interpretation of the realistic novel the main area of comparison with Barth's interpretation of biblical narrative, before dealing with the main topics of this chapter: the realiability and unity of the Bible in Barth's thought, and the role of the resurrection in his interpretation of the relation of the evangelists' perspective to their plot and central character.

(ii)

Renford Bambrough, pursuing lines begun by Ludwig Wittgenstein and John Wisdom, discusses the philosophy of stories in a way congenial to Barth's position. In particular he champions poets, dramatists and novelists as practical philosophers on the enigmas of life, sees in their work an "important kind of reasoning" inseparable from the forms in which it is presented (10), and says that

> "When we think about life and conduct, just as when we think about knowledge and its grounds, we must engage in that explanation of the similarities and differences between particulars and particulars on which even the more formal and systematic modes of thought are in the end dependent. In Ezra Pound's words, 'Art does not avoid universals, it strikes at them all the harder in that it strikes through particulars' (Literary Essays, p. 440). The literary power of accurate and precise portrayal of complexity, individuality, and particularity, is as much as any human power a power of human thought. Literature is one of the functions of the human reason."(11)

Such a position is a minimum for granting Barth's method of Nachdenken philosophical respectability. As Donald Mackinnon says:

> "There is in Barth's thought a note of positivism. He is always the champion of the concrete against, for instance, the abstract or merely possible..."(12)

Barth saw that it is chiefly through stories that the Bible conveys its thought about God, man, freedom, evil, new developments, time, conflict, promise, growth and other subjects, and his theological method attempts to do justice to these. His point is that of Stern, who limits the role of philosophy in his investigation by appealing to Wittgenstein, concluding:

"What we require for our present undertaking is not a 'definition of reality' at all but a certain kind of description of the world. Such a description, moreover, is not antecedent to or a condition of realism, it is the thing itself. That is what realism is."(13)

The result is not a positivism so much as a descriptive metaphysics (14), and much of his polemics against various philosophers fastens on their prescriptions of positions he finds alien to the stories by which he measures reality (15). He was especially sensitive to other Weltanschauungen presuming to dictate what the Bible may be permitted to say (16) and the philosophical traditions with which he was acquainted all did this in various ways (17).

It is Barth's insistence on the autonomy of the Bible as against threats from the sciences, history, philosophy or natural theology that points to the realistic novel as a parallel. For this genre is especially suited to rendering in realistic narrative a world of meaning on its own terms. Indeed, a case can be made for the plurality of worlds offered by novels being successors in Western culture to the one overarching Bible story (18). Wesley Kort takes four elements of narrative (atmosphere, character, plot and tone), correlates them with elements in religion (otherness, paradigm characters, ritual and myth, and belief) and suggests that

"the elements of narrative stand to the characteristics of religion like two walls of a canyon stand to each others, separated, but with structural matching points."(19)

Then he sums of the matching points as follows:

"What fiction has in common with religion is a fund of resources to constitute an entire world."(20)

To enter a fictional world one needs at least a "willing suspension of disbelief" (21) is perhaps a more accurate description, and for fiction to be called realistic one may need to go on to demand a shared notion of reality (22). Barth certainly does so, for all his theology is written "from faith to faith", thus sealing its autonomy, and avoiding apologetics.

(iii)

Having supported the philosophical legitimacy of Barth's enterprise and the appropriateness of a comparison between his view of the Bible and literary criticism of novels, I now turn to the issue of history and fiction with the aid of a historical perspective proposed by Hans Frei. Frei sees the Protestant Reformation, especially Calvin (23), in the mainstream of Christian hermeneutics as regards biblical narratives, and with the help of Auerbach he

describes their precritical interpretation (24). He then traces the rise
in the eighteenth century in England and Germany of new approaches to the
narrative and their effect in producing a major reversal. The nature of
this reversal is the theme of his book. Precritical reading of the biblical
stories took them both literally and figurally (or typologically), and Frei
draws on Auerbach (25) to show how these two approaches complemented each
other. Figuration, Frei says,

> "was literalism at the level of the whole biblical story
> and thus of the depiction of the whole of historical
> reality. Figuration was at once a literary and a histor-
> ical procedure, an interpretation of stories and their
> meanings by weaving them together into a common narrative
> referring to a single history and its meaning."(26)

The overarching nature of this story meant that it also embraced all
ages and readers. Each reader could take it as his real world of meaning
and by figuration make sense of his own place in it (27). Barth's use of
typology and of the literal sense is in this tradition, though with his own
innovations, as will be shown below in the chapters of analysis.

The reversal of this precritical approach began with "a logical distinction and a reflective distance between the stories and the 'reality' they
depict" (28). What succeeded still tried to do justice to the precritical
concerns for the reliability and unity of the Bible. I will deal with each
of these concerns in turn and relate them to Barth.

The reliability of the biblical stories became the concern of historical
criticism. Instead of realistic, literal reading of the text, there was an
attempt to reconstruct critically the events recounted. Realistic reading
came to mean reading with a view to such a reconstruction, and the importance of the realistic literary form of the stories told in the text was
ignored:

> "The confusion of history-likeness (literal meaning)
> and history (ostensive reference), and the hermeneutical
> reduction of the former to an aspect of the latter, meant
> that one lacked the distinctive category and the appropriate
> interpretative procedure for understanding what one had
> actually recognised: the high significance of the literal,
> narrative shape of the stories for their meaning. And so,
> one might add, it has by and large remained ever since."(29)

One of my tasks, already begun in Chapter 3 above, is to show that the
last sentence does not apply to Barth, who consistently refers his theological
reflections to the literal meaning of the "history-like" Bible narratives.
Yet Barth lived in a post-critical age and was well aware of the challenge
of historical criticism. Rudolf Smend has seen how important this issue is
and has described Barth's solution in the title of an article, "Nachkritische
Schriftauslegung" (30). Smend notes the literary element in Barth's exegesis
and his stress on the main form of the Bible being narrative; and he con-
trasts Goethe's "nebekritische Schriftauslegung" with Barth's "nachkritische
Schriftauslegung". The hallmark of the latter is that it takes note of biblical and historical criticism but then insists that the text must be read

as a whole, the meaning coming from its combination of "das Historische und das Unhistorische" (31). Barth's exegesis is called "wieder naiv" (32), distinguished from the precritical naivety in differentiating between the Bible as a source for ancient history and as material for theological reflection (33).

This is the same as Frei's division of literal meaning from ostensive reference and it raised the central issue of an intense cultural debate, which has continued in its modern form since the Renaissance, on the relation between fact and fiction (34). The inheritor of the precritical synthesis is the novel, and this is another reason why Barth's "wieder naiv" interpretation of the Bible finds such close parallels in literary criticism. Brian Wicker, commenting on our understanding of the Gospels, makes the same point:

> "Perhaps it is only now, as a result of our long experience of reading novels, that is, narratives that once again combine the empirical and the fictional in a mode of narration more complex than either of these can be by itself, are we able to recover the true nature of narratives that were written before that split occurred."(35)

Similar statements could be made about plays, and it is a play which Stern uses as his example for my next problem, which is about the relation of a novel, play or gospel to reality as an historian reconstructs it. Not all fictions have an identifiable historical subject, and in that case their relation to real life needs to be elucidated with all the subtlety that Stern brings to that problem (36); but there is an added complication when, as in Schiller's play about Mary Queen of Scots, there is a clear historical reference. In this connection Stern distinguishes between the qualitative and absolute uses of "real" (37). The absolute use has as its opposite false, inauthentic, an imitation, "not real", and is like the relation of a real to a cultivated pearl or a genuine to a forged pound note. The qualitative uses of real (and of its qualitative opposite, unreal)

> "are readily replaceable by other words, such are 'substantial', 'strong', 'convincing', or again 'shadowy', 'defective', 'feeble'" (38).

Applying this to Schiller's play, Stern concludes:

> "A critic who claims that Schiller's Maria must 'fail to represent what is' or that she 'is not a living reality' is offering the qualitative use of 'real' where what he has in mind is its absolute use. He is claiming that 'the real Mary Queen of Scots' has more reality than Schiller's Maria Stuart, when all he can properly be saying is that, while they have certain things in common, the one is not the same as the other."(39)

Barth holds that the Jesus of the Gospels and the Jesus reconstructed by historical critics are in a similar relation. He never denies that the Gospels refer to historical events, but he does deny that critical investigation of the events should be coordinated with exegesis of the biblical text

in order to arrive at the text's meaning. The meaning of the text and the
meaning of an account of events reconstructed by an historian are not systematically related, and attempts to combine them will only yield a third
account. Theological reflection on one of these accounts will produce different results from reflection on either of the other two, and Barth is
quite clear which he chooses: the biblical text. His fundamental reason
is that he believes Jesus to be risen and alive, and so the ostensive reference of the Gospels is to a living person who is in a position to confirm
their message (40). This circle between the stories and the presence of
Jesus Christ has already been shown in Chapter 3 above, and for Barth it
represents the ultimate in reliability. We are here beyond anything that
plays or novels can parallel, though I shall stretch them to their utmost
in an attempt to illuminate the unique logic of the resurrection according
to Barth (41).

(iv)

I now pass from the reliability to the unity of the Bible. Frei sees
the successor to figural interpretation as "biblical theology" which, like
figuration, tried to show the unity of the Bible, but did so by means of
demonstrating the unity of its religious meaning, whether in its central
concepts or in its developing history (42). This kind of stress on meaning
could act as an alternative to ostensive reference: individual narratives
could be taken as referring to separable moral or religious truths rather
than to events (43). Barth's rejection of this option is also clear in the
C.D., where it is one of the targets of his polemical use of the concepts
of particularity, abstraction and generalisation (44). Attempts to make
biblical narratives meaningful when the literal and figural meaning is rejected have an obvious apologetic ring, and Frei analyses this aspect in a
way congenial to Barth (45). The necessity for elaborate apologetics sprang
from rejecting the overarching story, for now the biblical stories had to
be fitted into other frameworks of meaning, and their importance established
within these -

"By something like figuration in reverse, (Jesus) is now
entered into another story"(46),

whether that of Marx's progressive world, or salvation history or whatever.
In my chapters of analysis of the C.D. I show Barth insisting on a framework which is that of the single narrative woven by typological interpretation, and attacking any standpoint which claims a position "outside" or
"above" this all-embracing world (47).

The unity that Barth proposes is held together by the central character,
Jesus Christ, and the plot of his life. In generalising this man's story
(to embrace not only the O.T. but also the rest of history before and since)
the resurrection plays the vital role, as Chapter 3 has already shown. The
way C.D.IV.1 sums up that role is as "the verdict of the Father", and this
can be clarified with the help of Stern's concept of the "realism of assessment".

Both Barth (48) and Stern would agree that "the resurrection...belongs to another sphere, beyond the reach of realism" (49). When Stern comes to distinguish between the realisms of description and of assessment (50) he concludes by saying that

> "The distinction is bound to be present whenever trans-
> cendental or supernatural phenomena are to be integrated
> into a humanly convincing story" (51).

Since Stern's main later application of the realism of assessment (or eval-uative realism) is to Aeschylus' <u>Eumenides</u> where, he emphasises, the eval-uation is a further <u>action</u> in the drama (Athene's judgement) (52) it is clearly a concept well suited to the resurrection, though Stern does not make the connection. Stern also illustrates his concept's meaning by show-ing that literature that is not realistic can be produced (as by Kafka(53)) by subjecting a realistic description to a non-realistic or fantastic assess-ment. The resurrection can be seen as in Barth's view the opposite of this: it is an act whose verdict on Jesus Christ reveals his history to be the supreme (and even eternal (54)) reality (55). Stern's concept has much in common with one first elaborated by Henry James, that of "point of view"(56), and Barth can be understood as taking the resurrection as God's point of view, and also the evangelists', on the story of Jesus' life, a viewpoint which we must share if we want to have the right perspective on Jesus.

God's verdict on Jesus and his life also ensures for Barth a stable structure of events to which all men's lives are figurally related (57). This is how the problems others find in the hermeneutical gap are overcome: one must simply realise that this story is one's real world, its central character present and helping one to discover one's place in it. Yet it is not just an overcoming of the gap by fiat, for Stern too uses the realism of assessment in this context. His claim is:

> "The structures which display moral and legal assessments
> translate more readily from one language to another and one
> era to another than do the textures of descriptive passages."(58)

His attempt to prove this by means of Aeschylus' <u>Eumenides</u> (59) suggests that the "irreducible minimum of realism" in the play is provided by the structure of the situation which leads up to Athene's verdict; and under-standing this, the heart of the action, is compatible with a great deal of ignorance of the play's <u>Sitz im Leben</u> and even with lack of sympathy for the religious beliefs it portrays. There is here a clue, not only to Barth's concentration on the resurrection's part in the Gospels' narrative structure, but also to the rationale of his interpretation of biblical nar-ratives so as to bring out the structure of God's judgements (60), culminat-ing in his view of Jesus as the judge judged in our place. If Stern is right, then it is Barth's appreciation of this realistic aspect of biblical narratives which is the strongest (human!) argument for an exegesis of them which mostly ignores the hermeneutical gap (61).

Frei's account of the fate of realistic narrative in biblical hermeneutics continues beyond the breakdown of traditional ways of upholding the
reliability and unity of Scripture to the description of another major
change, that marked by Kant's hermeneutics of understanding (62). Schleiermacher is the main subject in this connection, and his hermeneutics, with
its two "moments" (grammatical, and technical or psychological), and the
oscillation between them, is analysed (63). Frei finds the crucial innovation to be the emphasis on the unique stance and spirit of both author and
interpreter. This results in an ambiguity, because

> "'meaning' hovers between the explicative sense of a work
> and its significance for somebody" (64).

To hold the two together a general context of meaning is needed for realistic
biblical narratives as for all other texts, and the context proposed is that
of consciousness. Whereas previously the narrative meaning had been obscured
by searching for the subject matter beyond the text in history or in general
concepts, now

> "it was the quest for narrative unity or continuity in the
> consciousness of the author, or in the inner form as re-
> presented by the characters' consciousness, which prevented
> the descriptive or narrative shape from assuming its right-
> ful place."(65)

Frei's way of elucidating the inadequacy to realistic narrative of this
general hermeneutics (66) is to focus on the issue of continuity in the Gospel narrative. For Schleiermacher continuity

> "does not lie in the narrative sequence of character and
> incident shaping each other through their interaction but
> in consciousness" (67).

His eventually expressed preference for the view that Jesus' death was a
"Scheintod" is therefore perfectly consistent with his hermeneutics, because
the death of Jesus could not be imagined as an element included within his
or the interpreter's consciousness, and the even more awkward problem of the
resurrection is then avoided too (68). Frei here mentions Schleiermacher's
affinities with Bultmann, and my chapter on C.D.IV.1 (a volume written with
Bultmann in mind) has already shown the great emphasis Barth places on the
temporal continuity between crucifixion and resurrection.

Stern offers an even richer concept than continuity for revealing the
danger in the post-Kantian shift. This is "the middle distance", which
supplements the "realism of assessment" in describing "point of view" in
narrative. Stern describes it as follows:

> "There is no valid description of 'the middle distance',
> or indeed of that mixture of meaning and fact and language
> we call realism...except one that is related to 'the purpose
> of the whole' for which the description is intended; and
> any description that takes the notion of accuracy from some

other purpose is bound to be misleading.... 'The purpose
of the whole', or again 'the proper point of perspective'
that determines the middle distance of realism, is the
most familiar thing in all literature: it is the fictional
creation of people, of individual characters and lives
informed by what in any one age is agreed to constitute
a certain integrity and coherence."(69)

Stern's definition of the purpose of realism as the rendering of individuals in their settings includes the warning that a change in perspective
can result in a change in objective: to be too far from a building is to see
it as a blur, to be too near is to lose the ability to see it as a whole(70).

"The middle distance", with its focus on the rendering of persons, is
perhaps the most valuable single concept for clarifying Barth's handling of
narrative. While he does not see the Gospels as biographies of Jesus, their
portrayal of him by his words, acts, sufferings, and by the reactions of
others to him (71), is of great importance for his theology, as Chapter 3
above has already demonstrated, and many of his efforts can be interpreted
as aimed at preserving the New Testament perspective on Jesus. Since, as I
have said, Barth takes the resurrection as determing that perspective, the
middle distance focuses on the further fact that the resurrection is a story
about a particular person, on whom Barth's theology concentrates to an un-
usual degree.

Barth's negative delimitation of valid exposition of the Gospel story
frequently attacks targets which can be interpreted in terms of perspective
(though this does not exhaust their meaning). He objects to any viewpoint
which claims to stand "above" the story and allied to this is his running
battle with "generalising", which stands at such a distance so as to blur
or even change the distinctive meaning of the story. Barth insists that the
sort of interrelationships, sequences and identity portrayal, which can only,
in Stern's terms, be given through the middle distance perspective, are themselves normative (because of the resurrection), and just as C.D.IV.1 showed
him eliciting from them the exchange pattern of the atonement and much else,
so also the exegesis of C.D.II.2, for example, analyses the election and rejection of individuals in the O.T. and N.T. by a similar method (72). Generalising as such is not the target so much as any perspective which fails to
take account of these features of the narratives.

Generalising, and the related efforts to see the Bible as part of an
evolutionary or historical development, or to abstract from it a meaning
which can be formulated apart from the story's content and structure, can
be said, in terms of Stern's visual analogy, to stand too far away from the
people and events. One might see some historical criticism as coming too
near to them, thus missing the wood for the trees. Barth is quite happy
with contradictions and alternative accounts of the same events in the Bible,
and even makes theology out of them (73), but without a certain "middle distance" reliability (especially on the sequence of crucifixion and resurrection) many of his dogmatic arguments would be baseless. The literary judgement implied by the way he treats the Gospel rendering of Jesus as normative,
without being bothered by inadequacies or contradictions, is a recognition
that the meaning of the story is grasped by appreciating it as a literary
whole and accepting a middle distance perspective common to the evangelists.

The most dangeous enemy of his own perspective that Barth sees is, however, that which takes its stand in Christian subjectivity, which is what
Frei identifies as the key to Schleiermacher's and Bultmann's hermeneutics.
Barth believes that they do violence to the sense of the narrative by changing its focus from the person of Jesus to that of the believer, and his own
exegesis is the basis for his recurrent arguments against what he saw as this
perversion in neo-protestantism, Christian existentialism, and, in its own
church-centred way, Roman Catholicism. For him their change in focus was a
change in the proper object of theology, and his concern for the correct
ordering of the Christian in relation to Christ as given in the N.T. has its
parallel in Stern's remarks about the distortion of the middle distance resulting from dominance of the "self" in narrative:

> "Of course, the bits and pieces of experience that go
> into a realistic fiction, too, are chosen and assembled
> by a sentient self, and occasionally both the self and
> the act of choosing are visible in the work; but in
> realism the emphasis is on the things chosen, not on the
> chooser or the choice."(74)

For Barth this remains true even when the resurrection is the thing chosen.
He admits both its intrinsic resistance to realistic depiction and the imaginative element in the accounts of the appearances, but he must find a genre
which does not contradict realism and which does justice to the resurrection
as a real event in Jesus' life. He proposes "Sage" or "Legende" (75), and,
as I have shown, interprets the resurrection's role in the Gospels in a way
which intensifies rather than detracts from their realism. Stern too recognises that the presence of non-realistic elements can enrich the realism of
stories, and he devotes a chapter to showing how realism and religious transcendence can coexist (76). In the appendix to this chapter I show the distinctiveness of Barth's position on the resurrection by comparison with the
positions of some biblical scholars and with the problem of fact and fiction
in Solzhenitsyn's works. The conclusion, a confirmation and elucidation of
Chapter 3 above, is that Barth is claiming a unique status for the stories
about Jesus such that the extra nos objectivity of the resurrection is main-
tained against Schleiermacher and Bultmann and that the guarantee of this is
the presence of Jesus mediated through those same stories.

In this chapter I have shown how Barth's appreciation of the realism of
important biblical narratives is the key to his position on the reliability
and unity of the Bible and to his critique of post-Enlightenment hermeneutics.
I have also suggested that, because the chief source of support for his theology is his interpretation of stories, it is worthwhile drawing parallels
between his handling of them and the insights of literary critics who also
interpret stories. In the chapters to come I will develop these themes with
the help of detailed analyses of parts of the C.D.

NOTES to Chapter 4

(1) Helen Gardner, "The Poetry of St. Mark", in The Business of Criticism (Oxford 1959), p. 118.

(2) P.6.

(3) Op. cit. (Princeton 1969, first published Berne 1946); cf. Scenes from the Drama of European Literature (New York 1959), and Literary Language and its public in late Latin antiquity and in the Middle Ages (London 1965).

(4) On Realism (London 1973).

(5) The Eclipse of Biblical Narrative, A Study in Eighteenth and Nineteenth Century Hermeneutics (New Haven 1974).

(6) E.g. Frei, op. cit.; Wesley A. Kort, Narrative Elements and Religious Meaning (Philadelphia 1975); Sallie Te Selle, Literature and Christian Life (New Haven 1966); Harald Weinrich, "Narrative Theology" in Concilium, Vol. 5, No. 9, May 1973, pp. 84-96; Dennis Nineham, "A Partner for Cinderella?" in What About the New Testament? Essays in Honour of Christopher Evans, ed. Morna Hooker and Colin Hickling (London 1975); Ulrich Simon, Story and Faith in the Biblical Narrative (London 1975); Hugh Jones, "Biblical Theology and the Concept of Story" (unpublished paper, Mainz Univ. 1975).

(7) R. Bambrough, Reason, Truth and God (London 1969); R. Braithwaite, An Empiricist's View of the Nature of Religious Belief (Cambridge 1955); Brian Wicker, The Story-Shaped World. Fiction and Metaphysics: Some Variations on a Theme (London 1975); Robert P. Roth, Story and Reality. An Essay on Truth (Grand Rapids Michigan 1973); A.C. Danto, Analytical Philosophy of History (Cambridge 1965); Dietrich Ritschl, "Notes on the Concept of Story in Relation to the Quest for Human Identity" (Ecumenical Institute, Bossy, 1975).

(8) Danto, op. cit.; G.R. Elton, Political History: Principles and Practice (London 1970); J.H. Plumb, The Death of the Past (London 1969); R. Koselleck and W.-D. Stempel (ed.), Geschichten und Geschichte (München 1972); R. Koselleck, "Historia Magistra Vitae", in Natur und Geschichte. Karl Löwith zum 70.Geburtstag (Stuttgart 1967), S. 196-219.

(9) E.g. from the vast amount of literary criticism on this theme: Stern, op. cit.; R. Scholes and R. Kellogg, The Nature of Narrative (New York 1966); Lionel Trilling, Sincerity and Authenticity (London 1974); Gabriel Josipivici, The World and the Book (London 1971); Frank Kermode, The Sense of an Ending. Studies in the Theory of Fiction (London 1966); Damian Grant, Realism (London 1970); Barbara Hardy, Tellers and Listeners. The Narrative Imagination (London 1975); Miriam Allott, Novelists on the Novel (London 1959); E.M. Forster, Aspects of the Novel (London 1962; first published 1927); James E. Miller (ed.), Theory of Fiction: Henry James (Lincoln, Nebraska 1972); J.R.R. Tolkien, "On Fairy Stories", in Tree and Leaf (London 1964); J.Halperin

57

(ed.), The Theory of the Novel (London 1974). Perhaps the neatest
summary of one major theme of the discussion is by Stephen Crites,
"The Narrative Quality of Experience", in Journal of the American
Academy of Religion, Sept. 1971, whose main point is that it is more
true to say that consciousness is created by story than vice versa.

(10) Op. cit., pp. 117 ff. E.g. p. 121:

   "What is said by King Lear and War and Peace is said through the individuality and particularity of the characters, situations and
   conversations of which the work consist. Above all it is expressed
   in different language from any that can be used in a short summary
   or in any paraphrase, and differences of language amount to differences of meaning - that is to say, to differences of content."

   Cf. p. 122:

   "These points taken together indicate a degree of overlapping in
   scope and function between literature and religion that sets in
   a new light the idea of the Bible 'Designed to be read as
   literature'."

(11) Op. cit., p. 123. Cf. his essay "Literature and Philosophy" in Wisdom.
   Twelve Essays, ed. R. Bambrough (Oxford 1974), pp. 274-292.

(12) "Philosophy and Christology" in Essays in Christology for Karl Barth,
   ed. T.H.L. Parker (London 1956), pp. 283 f. Mackinnon adds:

   "There is...something analogous to that (note) sounded by Bertrand
   Russell when he said, suggesting the application of the methods of
   mathematical logic to the solution of classical philosophical
   problems: 'Whenever possible, let us substitute logical construct-
   ions out of the observable for inferred, unobserved entities.'
   There is in Barth something analogous to this recommended logical
   economy." (p. 284)

   This dissertation aims to show how Barth constructs his doctrines out
   of the "observable" biblical narratives.

(13) Op. cit., pp. 131 f.

(14) I deal with this most fully in Chapter 8 below.

(15) Schlichting, op. cit., gives a thorough, if plodding, account of how
   various philosophical positions violate, in Barth's eyes, the "biblische Denkform", but misses the function of narrative in this.

(16) For a sustained, mature exposition of this see C.D.IV.3, §§69, 70.

(17) Cf. his letter to Bultmann, 24 Dec. 1952, where in reply to what he
   saw as Bultmann's insistence that he be an existentialist he states
   that he had already been trapped by Kant, Schleiermacher and Plato,
   and, having escaped each he will not be trapped again. He stresses
   that his concern in this is for accurate exegesis. Briefwechsel,
   op. cit., S. 196 ff.

58

(18) C.A. Patrides in The Grand Design of God. The Literary Form of the
Christian View of History (London 1972 traces the course of that overarching story from biblical times through the patristic period and the
Middle Ages to its breakdown after the Renaissance as history was
secularised. Patrides stresses the disorientation in men's relation
to time that followed the breakdown, and the various attempts, especially by historians, poets and novelists, to deal with this. Lionel
Trilling suggests that nineteenth century narrative history was one
attempt to answer this problem: "'To write the history of England as
a kind of Bible' - this was the enterprise that Carlyle urged in a
time of crisis and anxiety. 'For England too (equally with any Judah
whatsoever) has a History that is Divine; an Eternal Providence
presiding over every step of it...'" (Op. cit., p. 138). (The Nazi
German version of this helps to explain why Barth was so insistent
on the uniqueness of Judah.) But Trilling notes the failure of such
history to convey "authenticating power", and its rejection by historians too. A persuasive analysis of the twentieth century novel as
filling the role of the biblical story (especially in its structuring
of time) is given by Frank Kermode (op. cit.). Georg Lukács calls
the novel "the epic of a world that has been abandoned by God" and
sums up the substitution of novel for Bible by saying that the former
"raises the individual to the infinite heights of one who must create
an entire world through his experience and who must maintain that
world in equilibrium - heights which no epic individual, not even
Dante's could reach, because the epic individual owed his significance
to the grace accorded him, not to his prime individuality." (The
Theory of the Novel: A Historico-Philosophical Essay on the Forms of
Great Epic Literature (Cambridge, Mass. 1971), pp. 88, 83.)

(19) Op. cit., p. 111.

(20) Ib., p. 111.

(21) The phrase is Tolkien's, op. cit., p. 36, and he extends the religious
parallel in talking of fiction as "sub creating" a "secondary world".

(22) George Levine, "Realism Reconsidered", in Halperin, op. cit., pp. 233-
56 argues for this.

(23) This is of interest as regards Barth, on whose exegesis after his
Commentary on the Epistle to the Romans Calvin had an increasing influence, though it is not part of my task to trace this.

(24) Op. cit., Chap. 2.

(25) For Auerbach's own definition of figuration see his essay "Figura" in
The Drama of European Literature (New York 1959), where he sets it
between allegory (which is the literary personification of abstract
qualities), and the description of earthly, personal existence (which
does not "mean" anything else - it just is what it is). "Figura"
both is itself and points beyond itself to something that it prefigures,
and as he says of the Divine Comedy: "For Dante the literal meaning or
historical reality of a figure stands in no contradiction to its pro-
founder meaning, but precisely 'figures' it; the historical reality

is not annulled but confirmed and fulfilled by the deeper meaning."
(p. 73).

(26) Op. cit., p. 2.

(27) Ib., p. 3.

(28) Ib., p. 5.

(29) Ib., p. 12.

(30) In Parrhesia. Karl Barth zum 80. Geburtstag (Zürich 1966), S. 215-237.

(31) Ib., S. 232 f.

(32) Ib., S. 218, cf. S. 233.

(33) Ib., S. 229 ff. Smend convincingly suggests G. von Rad's distinction between historical reconstruction and "Nacherzählung" as a parallel to and influence on Barth's thought here. The passage in Barth that supports Smend's point most clearly is in IV.2, pp. 478 f. where Barth introduces an excursus on Numbers 13, 14 as follows:

> "We call it a 'history' and this calls for a short hermeneutical observation which applies in retrospect to the three preceding excursi as well. The term history is to be understood in its older and naive significance in which - quite irrespective of the distinctions between that which can be historically proved, that which has the character of saga and that which has been consciously fashioned, or converted, in a later and synthetic review - it denotes a story which is received and maintained and handed down in a definite kerygmatic sense.... To do justice to this sense, we must either not have asked at all concerning these distinctions, or have ceased to do so. In other words, we must still, or again, read these histories in their unity and totality.... When the distinctions have been made they can be pushed again into the background and the whole can be read (with this tested and critical naivety) as the totality it professes to be."

(34) For an account of its origins, with a look forward to its continuation in debates on the novel, see William Nelson, Fact or Fiction. The Dilemma of the Renaissance Storyteller (Cambridge, Mass. 1973).

(35) Op. cit., p. 105.

(36) Stern's attempt to define the word "realism" concludes that it has a unique "amphibian existence" (p. 37) in literature and life, and much of the rest of his book is about ways in which the two are related. He is at pains to attack Plato's idea "that, in as far as it is 'mimesis' or 'imitation', literature is inferior to 'life', its ontological status is of a lower kind of 'reality'" (p. 60). He attempts to show its falsity by giving a transcript of a conversation and asking about its reality as an event on the one hand, and considered as a transcript and then as part of a hypothetical novel on the other. He concludes that there are gains and losses in the change from speech

to writing, and that it is not proper to argue that the transcript or
the novel gives something "less real" (pp. 66-7). This leads into the
discussion of the qualitative and absolute uses of "real". Cf. Rene
Wellek and Austin Warren, Theory of Literature (London 1949), Chapter
XVI, "The Nature and Modes of Narrative Fiction", for its discussion
of the ways in which fictional and empirical worlds overlap, and the
conclusion: "The soundly critical approach is to the whole fictional
world in comparison with our own experienced and imagined world, commonly less integrated than that of the novelist." (p. 272)

(37) Op. cit., pp. 68 ff.

(38) Ib., p. 68.

(39) Ib., p. 69.

(40) This is where Barth's constant stress on the objective reference of the
biblical narratives is relevant, and also where one should speak of
philosophical realism. What I have in mind is a well-argued unpublished
Cambridge doctoral dissertation by Alan Millar, Realism and Understanding: some problems in the Philosophy of Religion (1973). He relies
mainly on Tarski and Quine in arguing for a correspondence theory of
truth in which acceptability is not the criterion of truth. He con-
trasts this "realism" with "naive realism" in which the object of knowledge (or of faith) is characterised in terms of the way in which it
can be known. (This is a philosophical version of Barth's distinction
between dogmatics and apologetics, and in my present context it distinguishes between, on the one hand, having faith that Christ is resurrected and is the same person rendered in the Gospel stories, and, on
the other hand, knowing how to prove this.) Millar devotes Section 12,
pp. 81-95 to an approving analysis of Barth's realism, and, drawing on
Donald Mackinnon, he sums up Barth's method in a way which my dissertation corroborates: "Barth's theology amounts ot a translation of all
sentences in which the word 'God' occurs into sentences which a) are
known to be true only if certain statements about Jesus Christ are
known to be true, and b) do not contain the word 'God' as a singular
term but as what Russell called an incomplete symbol." (pp. 90 ff.)
One might add that "man" is also an incomplete symbol for Barth.

(41) See below in this chapter and its appendix and Chapters 8, 10.

(42) Op. cit., pp. 8, 165 ff. See pp. 173 ff. for Frei's account of the
differences between figural interpretation and the Heilsgeschichtliche
Schule, by which criteria Barth is clearly not a member of that school.

(43) See ib. pp. 261 ff.

(44) For more on this see below my discussion of "the middle distance".

(45) See especially ib., Chapters 6 and 7.

(46) Ib., p. 230.

(47) A specially good example is his verdict on the debate between Supra-
lapsarians and Infralapsarians, below, Chapter 5.

(48) See above, Chapter 3, and below, Chapters 8 and 10.

(49) Stern, op. cit., p. 47.

(50) Ib., pp. 129 ff. The phrase "realism of assessment" is Ian Watt's in
The Rise of the Novel (London 1957).

(51) Ib., p. 141.

(52) Ib., p. 171.

(53) Ib., pp. 135 ff.

(54) See below, Chapter 8.

(55) Though to many, of course, it is unreal and fantastic as an event and
assessment.

(56) See Miller (ed.), op. cit., Ch. XII, where James' own statements on this
are collected.

(57) Cf. my use of Brian Wicker's binary structure at the end of Chapter 8,
below.

(58) Op. cit., p. 131.

(59) Ib., pp. 169 ff.

(60) See Chapter 5 below.

(61) The stress on verdict, or decision, also calls to mind the centrality
of this idea for Bultmann, and my discussion shows how sharply he differs from Barth on it. For Barth links it inextricably with an event
in the story and with the whole logic and sense of the story; whereas
Bultmann locates it in the subjectivity of the disciples responding to
the crucifixion, and the historical status of the resurrection as an
event that happened to Jesus is irrelevant.

(62) Op. cit., Chapters 15, 16.

(63) Ib., pp. 290 ff.

(64) Ib., p. 304.

(65) Ib., p. 313.

(66) But he does not deny its validity for certain genres and certain aspects
of narrative interpretation:

"One may feel that one understands how a particular text makes ex-
plicative sense, i.e., what its subject matter or formal structure

is, without relating it to the author's spirit and without paying
heed at the same time to its changing meaning over a long stretch
of time - and yet this does not mean one denies that the other
things are also true!" (Ib., p. 322)

Cf. Stern's criticism of Karel Košik's "dialectics of concreteness"
which is full of echoes of what Barth has to say about the interpretation of the Bible in neo-protestantism and Roman Catholicism:

"Where the survival of the work is explained exclusively in terms of
its 'life' - that is, in terms of its ever renewed effectiveness in
and relevance to ever new historical situations - there the question
of how to distinguish between a true and a false interpretation
receives no convincing answer. It is true (as Košik observes) that
'the effective function of the work' - its capacity to emanate illum-
inations which are themselves factors in the changing reality of
the world - is not 'a quality of the work analogous to the way that
radiation is a quality of radium, for that would mean that the work
would live, that is, be effective, even if no human subject were to
"take it in".' But to infer from this that 'the life of the work
cannot be understood from the work itself' because 'whatever happens
to the work is a manifestation of what the work is', is to place not
only the possibility of interpretation but also the limits of an
authentic interpretation in the social reality outside the work.
(What happened to the poets of the 1920s at the hands of the Soviet
critics is not a manifestation of the works of Yesenin, Pasternak,
Mandelshtam; nor is what happened to the literature of classical
Weimar at the hands of the National Socialist critics a manifestation of the works of Goethe, Schiller, Kleist and Hölderlin)...
The works of realism live, often without any manifest relevance to
our own situation. They draw on our 'spontaneous capacity for understanding others' which is a factor in relative freedom from the
trammels of our historical situation. Košik's argument underestimates
that capacity and that freedom...." (Op. cit., pp. 181-3)

(67) Op. cit., p. 310.

(68) A striking twentieth-century parallel in fiction is in D.H. Lawrence's
two works The Woman who rode away and The Man who died. Of the former
Brian Wicker writes: "(Lawrence) cannot, as narrator, put himself
above the white civilisation he himself belongs to. The woman must
remain, for him, the 'central intelligence' from whose viewpoint everything is told. Once that intelligence is extinguished, everything goes
black..." (op. cit., p. 130). In the other story Wicker notes the ambiguity about whether the man actually died, and the half-hearted natural-
istic explanation offered. He sees Lawrence's evasion of the problem
of his hero's death as characteristically "modern" (ib., pp.132 ff).

(69) Op. cit., pp. 120 f.

(70) Ib., pp. 120 ff.

(71) Elements which can be seen as just the ones which in the first century
A.D. were "agreed to constitute a certain integrity and coherence" in
character portrayal. Cf. Graham Stanton, Jesus of Nazareth in New

<u>Testament Preaching</u> (Cambridge 1974) on the relation of the Gospels to biography of their time. Especially relevant to my point is Chapter 5, pp. 117 ff.

(72) See below, Chapter 5.

(73) E.g. Judas' death, see below Chapter 5, and the Genesis creation stories, below Chapter 6.

(74) Op. cit., p. 150.

(75) See above Chapter 3, below Chapters 6, 8.

(76) Op. cit., Chapter 3.

Appendix to Chapter 4

Aesthetic Exegesis, Fiction and the Resurrection

(i)

James Barr in The Bible and the Modern World (1) has given one recent
account of the problems of using Scripture in modern theology. In his chapter
on "The Bible as literature" he gives a triangular diagram of three possible
procedures: referential (the study of the entities referred to), intentional
(the study of the mind of the writer) and poetic or aesthetic (the study of
stories and images as given in the text) (2). Barth is mentioned later as
giving the referential approach its "most towering restatement" in modern
times (3). My interpretation of Barth suggests a more complex assessment(4).
His exegesis is referential, but, because a person (Jesus Christ, whether
prefigured, incarnate or resurrected) is its reference and no extra-biblical
sources are admitted, the process of exegesis is nearer to Barr's "poetic or
aesthetic". On the "intentional" approach, the present chapter has shown
how Barth, parallelling certain types of literary criticism, rules out this
area from providing data for reflection on the text. As Chapter 5 below
will show, the category of intention is essential to his exegesis, but the
intention is that of God, and the identification of God's intention with his
action is such that there is no room for appeal to an intention different
from or fuller than that which is evident in the biblical stories of election
and rejection. Barth's rejection of the notion of a decretum absolutum (5)
behind revelation is the theological equivalent of a literary rejection of
the "intentional fallacy". Thus the way Barth handles both reference and
intention is "transcendental", but in such a way that the third of Barr's
approaches, the poetic or aesthetic, becomes more important.

Barr admits the possibility of Barth's project in a pregnant comment:

> "It may well be asked, however, whether the time is now
> coming when a more fully literary study of the Bible will
> begin to assert itself, a study which will really concern
> itself with the imagery and structure of the text as it
> stands, probably ruling out as irrelevant for this purpose
> the historical and intentional concerns which have dominated
> technical biblical scholarship."(6)

Barr recognises the "reactionary" potential of such an approach in supporting
prejudices against historical criticism, but also the possibility of its being
theologically neutral (7). He does not, however, discuss the value for theology of the literary meaning when this differs from a historical reconstruction. The two examples of the literary approach which Barr gives are the works
of Austin Farrer and D.E. Nineham. He accepts Dame Helen Gardner's criticisms
of Farrer's understanding of realistic narrative (8). Barr's criticisms of
Nineham are also relevant to Barth. First, he shows the ambiguity of Nineham
towards the unitary meaning of the Bible and the accompanying ambiguity about
"an appeal to the crassly supernatural" (9). It is clear that this is not an
area of ambiguity in Barth, whose position involves a doctrine of providence
(10). Secondly, Barr takes issue with Nineham's cultural relativism: if
ancient texts may perhaps have no meaning for us today in our very different
context, does this not contradict the principle of following the analogy of

literary appreciation? (11) In order to define Barth's position by comparison, I will pursue this point with reference to a lecture by Nineham, New
Testament Interpretation in an Historical Age (12).

The lecture is based on an argument for cultural relativism which yet
admits that it is possible to try to reconstruct and enter imaginatively into
cultures of the past. J.S. Dunne's concept of "passing over" into the lives
of other people and ages in order to return enriched by the experience is
Nineham's approved model (13). The lesson which he draws is the need for
a reconstruction which presents

> "New Testament Christianity displayed in its pastness,
> with its various doctrines, rituals and commandments
> exhibited in the sort of unity they seemed to form in
> the context of first-century cultural assumptions."(14)

This gives the reality into which we can "pass over", with results which it
is "impossible to specify" (15).

The implied answer to Barr's objection is that it is not a matter of
there being a contradiction between cultural relativism and literary appreciation, but that the reconstruction, when appreciated, is not systematically
related to any meaning for our time, and such a meaning may not (such is the
diversity of cultures) be assumed.

Nineham's remarks dismissing Barth for allowing "faith" formulated in
the categories of patristic and Lutheran (sic) orthodoxy to dictate the interpretation of texts (16) may seem to rule out any reconciliation between the
two; and in fact Barth refuses to attempt the reconstruction urged by Nineham. Yet I have argued that Barth's categories are not primarily fifth century or sixteenth century, but are those of action, time and personal identity, all referred to realistic narratives of the first century and earlier.
The question then becomes a matter of the importance of historical reconstruction for understanding those narratives. Are they, as Nineham suggests,
so alien to our culture? Or do they, as Auerbach, Gardner, Stern and Barth
suggest, render character and event in interaction and thus portray a world
of meaning which is largely intelligible? Stern's discussion of the realisms of description and assessment, of literary works as "stepping-stones"
and as "monuments" and of the dangers of the Rezeptionsästhetik of Karel
Košik and other Marxist critics is especially relevant here (17). Stern
never denies the need for illumination by historians (and neither does
Barth), but in view of the prevailing orthodoxies is more concerned to assert that:

> "The works of realism live, often without any manifest relevance
> to our own situation. They draw on our 'spontaneous capacity
> for understanding others', which is a factor of our relative
> freedom from the trammels of our historical situation."(18)

There is a difference of opinion between Barth and Nineham over the
issue of historical reconstruction which could only be settled by Nineham
demonstrating that particular interpretations of Barth are wrong because of

66

failure to appreciate the <u>Sitz im Leben</u>. Yet as regards their approach to
using the Bible in theology there is some similarity between them. This is
in their common rejection of approaching the text with a question which is
"apologetic" or seeking to show its relevance to a modern situation. This
is at the root of Nineham's reservations in his lecture about The Interpreter's Bible (19), and I have remarked on it in Barth (20). Likewise, in the
impossibility of specifying what will result from "passing over" there is a
formal parallel with Barth's refusal to make any systematic connection between understanding the biblical narratives and coming to faith. There is
here, however, a profound difference in the substance of their positions.
Barth's main reasons for rejecting apologetics are that the narrated world
of the Bible is all-inclusive (21), and that it does not make sense to try
to "prove" someone who is alive and able to speak for himself - the freedom
of the living Jesus Christ rules out any method for coming to faith. There
is no hint of such considerations guiding Nineham's approach, and for Barr
too they would be "crassly supernatural". Barth draws from the biblical
narratives, and in particular from the resurrection narratives, conclusions
which, by focussing on the presence of the risen Christ, give him his distinctive hermeneutical position. Expressed in its simplest form his position
is that, because of the presence of the living Jesus Christ witnessing to
himself through the text of the Bible, that text, despite its imperfections
and errors, can convey all the truth that we need for faith. This opens up
the whole area of literary analysis as one in which his conclusions are
necessarily vulnerable, and this gives him his common ground with Barr and
Nineham; but he goes further, claiming that this particular story is unique
in demanding a decision about whether Jesus is alive today, a decision which
can only be taken in faith which is the result of Jesus' initiative. Neither
Barr nor Nineham allow such a logic in the story leading to a unique mode of
proof, and Barr explicitly gives the resurrection as his example of the
limits of the literary approach:

> "Granted that the resurrection is the central symbol of a
> Gospel, does it have existence only within the text of the
> Gospels, as Setebos has existence only within the text of
> The Tempest, or does it also stand for something in the out-
> side world?" (22)

(ii)

There have been many analyses of Barth's position on the historicity of
the resurrection (which changed between the <u>Römerbrief</u> and the C.D.). One of
the most acute on the validity of his arguments is Van A. Harvey's in <u>The
Historian and the Believer</u> (23). Harvey's conclusions appear to me to be
sound insofar as they show that Barth's arguments in C.D.III.2, pp. 437 ff.
do not succeed in establishing anything to a historian's satisfaction (24).
In the face of the positions of Barr and Harvey what is the best that can be
said for Barth? I want to suggest that Barr's reference to Setebos and
Harvey's deprecation of Barth's position on the "imaginative-poetic" status
of the saga of the resurrection oversimplify the relation between literature
and historical truth (25).

I will make this point with the aid of a contemporary parallel, the

works of Alexander Solzhenitsyn. He is a writer whose works constantly pose
the problem of historical truth, and by dealing with subjects of fundamental
importance to the most widespread secular faith of our century he has in
addition aroused many of the passions that have surrounded the study of the
Bible. With themes of such power and scope the question of the form in which
to convey his meaning is acute. Michael Scammell writes about Solzhenitsyn's
book on Lenin as follows:

"Nevertheless Lenin in Zürich is not, in the last analysis,
history, nor is it biography. For not the least of Solzhenitsyn's
audacities is the proud claim that he is making for the art of
fiction. History, he seems to be saying, is not up to this
job, has made a hash of it in the past. Biography likewise.
Now it is time for the artist to take a hand."(26)

Lenin in Zürich is extracted from his serial novel, the first part of which,
August 1914, has evoked similar comments to Scammell's. The problem has been
the subject of a study by an American historian, Dorothy Atkinson. After
assessing August 1914 against historical sources and authorities, she concludes as follows:

"Some years ago a scholar discussing historical novels
wrote, 'The historian and the novelist work on parallel
lines which never meet, the former telling us what happened
and the latter helping us to see it happen.' In August
1914 the lines converge." (27)

Similar statements could be made about the autobiographical novels A Day
in the Life of Ivan Denisovich, The First Circle and Cancer Ward (28). The
Gulag Archipelago is nearer than the novels to "reporting", and it contains
a mass of pericopes gathered from eyewitnesses, but here too the problem
of the relation of literature to history is raised. Alexander Schmemann has
taken the subtitle of The Gulag Archipelago, "An experiment in literary investigation", as his theme for discussion of the book (29). He discussed
the failure of history and of literature, both inside and outside Russia, to
convey the truth about the Russian labour camps, and the significance of the
conjunction of "literary" and "investigation": it is a union of history and
art which is a "challenge to the accepted categories and classifications"(30).

Most historians would agree that the Jesus of the Gospels is, as a historical problem, nearer to Lenin or Kostoglotov than to Setebos. Since there
are four different Gospels it is clear that the authors and their traditions
are engaged in "fiction" (in the sense implied by Scammell) to some degree.
The question is to what extent one considers this procedure legitimate in
trying to do justice to their subject. One consideration in answering it
must be the added difficulty in conveying a vivid character by means accept-
able to historians; and, when a character such as Kostoglotov or Samsonov
has been rendered in a way which takes into account the available informat-
ion about his historical counterpart, there is the difficulty of specifying
in what falsification might consist, short of giving an alternative portrayal
which would raise the same problems. If one concludes that some such approach
as Solshenitsyn's is necessary to convey his meaning, and that there are
parallels between his solution andthat of the Gospel writers, then one will
be more likely to be favourable to Barth's policy of taking the Gospels in

their integrity as literary works and reflecting on them as pointing to the identity of Jesus. So far as that identity is concerned, it is generally agreed that the crucial events are those of the passion, death and resurrection, and it is here both that Barth centres his christology and that the convergence of the Gospels is greatest. One thing that the fixing of the canon and doctrines of biblical inspiration could be seen as saying is that we may trust that the rendering of Jesus given in these stories is the best available and so may confidently begin our theological reflection from them. It seems to be the practical function of Barth's doctrine of scripture to support such a view, enabling him to get on with the business of <u>Nachdenken</u>.

Yet for all the surprises in his works, Solzhenitsyn does not claim that any of his characters rose from the dead. One may try to imagine the consequences for <u>Lenin in Zürich</u> were he convinced that Lenin had been resurrected and was actively present rather than merely embalmed in a mausoleum and ubiquitously present in Russia in sculptures, paintings and references, but the incongruity defeats the effort. Somewhat nearer might be the status of Solzhenitsyn in relation to his autobiographical works. Among many efforts to cast aspersions on them, there has been a suggestion that his works were compiled by the K.G.B. for their own reasons, and, unlike the case of the <u>Penkovsky Papers</u> (which U.S. Senate investigation has revealed, were fabricated by the C.I.A. after Penkovsky's death), the main protagonist himself can be called to testify and his word trusted or not. But Barth's doctrine of revelation and <u>sola scriptura</u> will not allow Jesus to testify independently of the Bible, and his way of understanding faith in the Gospel coming through grace (rejecting any appeal to religious experience) leads to the concept of the self-authentication of revelation with its hermeneutical circle between the story and the presence of Jesus. This seals his story world and he then proceeds to generalise it by means of his doctrine of time, which is also exegetically focussed on the resurrection (31).

The resurrection, therefore, is where Barth's perception of the logic of the Gospel story cannot be parallelled in Solzhenitsyn. Yet on the basis of my analysis of Barth's exegesis (32) one can see how his position depends on a literary analysis. The resurrection is an integrated part of the story, even though not described, and the continuity of Jesus' identity through death is indicated. The narratives do seem to stutter in places, but even that helps to express the strangeness of their ending. There is a good case for seeing this ending itself as the <u>raison d'être</u> for their narratives. The way the Gospels are told (<u>spirant resurrectionem</u>) poses the reader the problem of the present status of the central character, and offers a solution in the telling. They suggest that the fact of the present individual identity of Jesus is a crucial part of the New Testament message, and in the way they are told pose a unique epistemological problem. They both inescapably raise the question: Did this actually happen? and at the same time describe what is claimed to have happened in a way which makes verification inseparable from faith in the presence of Jesus - an intensification beyond its limit of the difficulty of verifying the characters of Solzhenitsyn. "Pure saga" is Barth's name for the way the Gospels indicate the event of the resurrection, and he rests his theology on that event, seeing in it the convergence of the logic of the story with the necessity for the gift of faith. Thus the vulnerability of his theology is greatest here, and the decision about the validity of it must include a verdict on his literary insight (33).

NOTES to Appendix to Chapter 4

(1) London 1973.

(2) pp. 61 ff.

(3) Ib., p. 91.

(4) This is not to suggest that Barr's presentation of Barth in the course
    of the book is so simple, but my main concern is the omission of Barth
    in discussing the Bible as literature.

(5) See below Chapter 5, pp. 73 ff.

(6) Op. cit., pp. 63 f.

(7) p. 65.

(8) Cf. above p. 47.

(9) Ib., p. 71.

(10) See below, Chapter 5.

(11) Ib., p. 73.

(12) London, 1976. The same points are made at greater length in his work
     The Use and Abuse of the Bible (London 1976).

(13) p. 20 ff.

(14) Ib., p. 21.

(15) Ib., p. 21.

(16) Ib., pp. 15 f.

(17) Op. cit., pp. 178 ff. Cf. above p. 63.

(18) Ib., p. 183.

(19) Op. cit., pp. 4 ff.

(20) E.g. above pp. 52 ff.

(21) As explained above, Chapter 3, and below, especially in Chapters 5, 6, 8.

(22) Op. cit., p. 74.

(23) London 1967, pp. 153 ff.

(24) Cf. C.F. Evans, Resurrection and the New Testament (London 1970), pp.
     174 ff.

70

(25) Cf. with what follows, Stern op. cit., Chapter 5 on the relations between literature and life, history and fiction.

(26) T.L.S. No. 3867, April 23, 1976, pp. 489-490.

(27) Aleksandr Solzhenitsyn. Critical Essays and Documentary Materials, ed. John R. Dunlop, Richard Haugh, Alexis Klimoff, second edition, London (1975), p. 429.

(28) On their relation to their author's life see Solzhenitsyn by David Burg and George Feifer (London 1972), Chapters VII-XVII.

(29) "Reflections on The Gulag Archipelago", in Dunlop, Haugh and Klimoff, op. cit., pp. 515 ff.

(30) Ib., p. 516.

(31) See below, Chapter 8.

(32) See especially above Chapter 3, below Chapter 8.

(33) Frei has attempted to show the uniqueness of the resurrection in a way which supports the argument of this paragraph, in The Identity of Jesus Christ, op. cit.

CHAPTER 5.   ELECTION AND REJECTION

This is the first chapter of three devoted to the analysis in turn of
parts of the C.D. treating the three major doctrines: of God, of creation
and of reconciliation. This is the longest of the three chapters, for it is
an attempt to follow my theme through the whole of one locus. The doctrine
of election is especially suited to this. It is relatively short and compact,
and its main conclusions appeal to stories with a directness that corresponds
to the simplicity of the basic issue: how the stories tell about election and
rejection. The doctrine also represents a new turn in Barth's theology, in
which he is most conscious of being original, and therefore he must go to
great lengths to support his position by Scripture; and in the course of this
he uses many of his characteristic methods of narrative interpretation, culminating in the forty-eight page treatment of Judas Iscariot. Besides, the
doctrine of election has been called "the heartbeat of Barth's theology"(1),
and I consider that it is where the interrelations of the main topics of
Barth's theology are laid out most clearly. It is a part of the doctrine of
God (2); it is the raison d'être of creation and reconciliation; it shows
how Jesus Christ, Israel, the Church and the individual Christian are related;
and it also includes Barth's most important proposal for understanding the
problem of evil. In short, it is an ideal test case for examining Barth's
method.

(i)

The doctrine of election is given in C.D.II.2, §§32-35, and in the opening section of the volume, under the heading of The Orientation of the Doctrine, Barth states the broad lines of his doctrine. He emphasises that its
only source is Scripture, which is the "human form" ("menschlich bezeugt")(3)
of what God says about his own knowledge and reality. In Scripture is given
an account of that history which plays out ("abspielen") the primal history
("Urgeschichte")(4), and

> "Everything happens according to this basic and determinative
> pattern ('Urbild'), model and system."(5)

The next section, §32.2, The Foundation of Doctrine, reiterates that
Scripture is the sole foundation for dogma, and goes on to rule out four
other possibilities: tradition, concern for didactic or pastoral value, our
experience of those we judge to be elected or rejected, and "the concept of
God as omnipotent Will" (6). The first three of these come under the heading
of Barth's habitual strict distinction between the story in the Bible and
that of the later Church and Christians. The fourth is about different ways
of seeing the biblical story in relation to God, and this is the bulk of the
section.

Under the fourth heading the main point Barth makes is that the doctrine
of election should not be a part of the doctrine of providence. He says that
this is "critical...for the methodological question which here concerns us"(7)

He argues that before we speak of the concept of a World-ruler

"we must know first who this Ruler is and what He wills and
does in that rule."(8)

This guards us against applying inappropriate concepts to him. According to
Scripture, Barth says, the question of God's identity is answered in Jesus
Christ:

"In this name we may now discern the divine decision as an
event in human history and therefore as the substance of all
the preceding history of Israel and the hope of all the
succeeding history of the Church."(9)

After describing the incarnation as the carrying out of God's decision he
then claims that this story is ultimate for knowledge of God:

"There is no greater depth in God's being and work than that
revealed in these happenings and under this name."(10)

There follows an exegetical excursus which aims to demonstrate that the lines
of the O.T. converge on Jesus Christ. Adam, David, Solomon, Jeconiah and
Zerubbabel all prefigure Jesus Christ; as types they are concentrated and
surpassed in him (11). This is how he is shown to be the substance of Israel's history. In answer to the demand that reasons be given for this particular sequence, Barth says that:

"always there is only one answer to such a demand, and that
is the event as a fact ('das faktische Ereignis'), the
existence of the cases as such.(12)

There is no wider realm of meaning in which these events can be comprehended, there is no standing outside them, and they must be understood in
cumulative sequence leading to Jesus Christ. That is how we know who God is.
The fundamental objection to election as pars providentiae and to a decretum
generale or decretum absolutum is that they claim to know something independently of the biblical story, a general will of God which is not wholly concentrated in Jesus Christ as revealed in his history. Likewise, tendencies
towards Pelagianism presuppose an election not completely determined by Jesus
Christ (13).

§32.3, The Place of the Doctrine in Dogmatics, locates election in the
doctrine of God, where the transition is made from knowledge of God to knowledge of all his work (14), and states its relationship to the doctrine of reconciliation and the rest of dogma. This section includes Barth's discussion
of the problem of dealing with this doctrine, and in §33, The Election of
Jesus Christ, he begins his own presentation of it.

§33.1, Jesus Christ, Electing and Elected, identifies the object and the
content of the eternal decree of election with Jesus of Nazareth (15). The
electing God is identical with him, and to know both we look to the cradle,
cross and resurrection of Christ (16). The only decision of God is the one
he revealed in Christ, so that is his decretum absolutum (17). We know who

God is and who the elect is by following the events of the Gospel (18). Jesus Christ is "the type of all election" ("exemplarisch für alles Er- wähltsein") (19).

This way of focusing on Jesus Christ is signified at the beginning of the section by his exegesis of Jn I,1, where ὁ λόγος is seen as a stop-gap concept to be elucidated by the ensuing story of Jesus (20). As regards his biblical interpretation the most important statements come in his discussion of Infralapsarianism and Supralapsarianism. He states agreements with and differences from both positions, but his qualified preference for Supra- lapsarianism is decided by its way of seeing the biblical story.

> "The history of Israel and of Jesus Christ and of the Church is not played out within the framework of a prior and already preceding history of nature and the universe. That is not the picture of the world and history as it is given us in the Bible. According to the Bible, the framework and basis of all temporal occurrence is the history of the cov- enant between God and man, from Adam to Noah and Abraham, from Abraham and Jacob to David, from David to Jesus Christ and believers in Him. It is within this framework that the whole history of nature and the universe plays its specific role, and not the reverse, although logically and empirically the course of things ought to have been the reverse. At this point the Supralapsarian had the courage to draw from the biblical picture of the universe and history the logical de- duction in respect of the eternal divine decree. The Infra- lapsarians did maintain the sequence of the picture in respect of the realization of salvation, but they shrank from the deduction."(21)

Within this framework there can be arguments of faith (22), and entering it means bursting out of the framework of a general divine world order which "had been a limiting concept from the time of Thomas onwards" (23). The importance Barth ascribes to the biblical narrative framework is seen in his tracing of the bad effects of natural theology and the Enlightenment to its breakdown:

> "The theological Enlightenment was nothing more than the exhaustion of thinking upon a basis of faith, for as such thinking was exhausted it was inevitably replaced by think- ing upon a basis of unbelief." (24)

Barth's own use of the biblical framework is his attempt to reverse the Enlightenment reversal. His perception of this issue in the Supralapsarian controversy is one of the five instances of support for his position that he finds in church history (25), and the only one of them that gives support for his understanding of the biblical framework. Frei's interpretation of bib- lical hermeneutics in the 18th and 19th centuries (26) agrees with Barth on the fact of the reversal. The lesson that Barth draws from it here is that any attempt to supplement or even support the biblical narrative by extra- biblical evidence is an invitation to such reversal, and so he goes back through theological history and attempts to purify it, judging its issues in the light of later developments.

In §33.2, The Eternal Will of God in the Election of Jesus Christ, Barth defines his break with traditional doctrines of predestination as being his affirmation that

> "at the beginning of all things God's eternal plan and
> decree was identical with what is disclosed to us in time
> as the revelation of God and of the truth about all things."(27)

He later defines this more precisely:

> "According to the Bible this was what took place in the
> incarnation of the Son of God, in His death and passion,
> in His resurrection from the dead. We must think of this
> as the context of the eternal divine predestination."(28)

What is given in that story is the identity of the God who predestines and man who is predestined: both are "identical with Jesus Christ" (29). This is the sole epistemological basis for the doctrine (30) and the reference to Christ is the hermeneutical principle for arriving at that knowledge (31).

Barth therefore understands election through the events of the story. Election is to suffering at Golgotha (32), where Jesus substituted for men and revealed the divine wrath in his suffering (33). Barth's main exegetical support for this comes in C.D.IV.1 (34).

The other side of election is the overcoming of evil and death. In terms of the story, evil is there and so must have been permitted by God(35), but its function is to occasion the cross as the

> "unavoidable point of transition to the glory of the
> ascension and session."(36)

The relation of evil to good is given by that sequence of events:

> "The order proclaimed in the work of revelation and atonement
> must be regarded and respected as also the order of the divine
> predestination."(37)

The problem of evil will recur in the discussion of Judas, and I will treat it there and in an Appendix to this chapter.

§33.2 shows in another way how Barth systematically focuses on the story of Jesus Christ. For he holds both that predestination is revealed at one point in history and also that it includes all history (38), and so he must make

> "the controversial assertion that predestination is the
> divine act of will itself and not an abstraction from or
> fixed and static result from it."(39)

This in turn necessitates a doctrine of time and eternity, for predestination must comprise past, present and future, being

> "the principle and essence of all happening everywhere...

a work which still takes place in all its fulness today."(40)

There is a denial of "the separation of the temporal from the eternal" (41) with momentous implications for the role of the story, whose events are to be understood as "quite literally ('unmittelbar') the divine predestination"(42), revealing the secret of God's will and so of all history. Predestination is

"an act which occurs in the very midst of time no less than in that far distant pre-temporal eternity" (43),

and so involves the doctrine of time analysed in Chapter 8 below, and also sets the seal (44) of ultimate reality on the story in time. Further, there is explicit recognition of the narrative as the only means of expressing election, for Barth says that his

"activist understanding of predestination depends wholly and utterly upon the identifying of it with the election of Jesus Christ",

and this means recounting a story:

"Who and what Jesus Christ is, is something which can only be told, not a system which can be considered and described."(45)

(ii)

§34 is on The Election of the Community and attempts to show how the christological pattern of §33 is reproduced in Israel and the Church. §34.1 states this correspondence briefly, but says that recognition of it depends upon faith:

"The bow of the covenant over the two (sc. Israel and the Church) is not a neutral area and observation point between Israel and the Church. The way of this history is, however, the way of the knowledge of Jesus Christ."(46)

The relationship of this judgement of faith to literary analysis of the stories will be noted later in this chapter.

In §34.2, The Judgement and Mercy of God, the correspondence between Christ and the community of Israel and the Church is worked out in greater detail with special reference to Roms. 9,6-29. It is summed up thus:

"The Church form of the community stands in the same relation to its Israelite form as the resurrection of Jesus to His crucifixion, as God's mercy to God's judgment."(47)

In the discussion and exegesis there are two connected Barthian characteristics relevant to my thesis. First there is the usual centring of the meaning in Jesus Christ, which is clear throughout, culminating in saying:

"The vessel of mercy (prefigured in the patriarchs, in Moses,

76

in David and in the Prophets) is primarily the Lord Jesus Christ risen from the dead, and secondarily the apostolic Church called and gathered by Him through the Gospel."(48)

Secondly, there is the way of perceiving this, mentioned in the previous quotation, that of figuration, with Barth's own discernment of an overall pattern:

> "The circle of the elect grows continually smaller, or at least continually less visible, in the course of Israel's history, until it is ultimately reduced to the person of one man, Jesus of Nazareth. Strictly speaking, the pre-existent life of the Church in Israel consists only in the light which, without changing its character, is provisionally cast on the history of Israel by this one man, who is Israel's future and goal, making visible within this history certain individual, fragmentary, contradictory and transitory prefigurations of the form of the community which will be revealed in and with the appearance, death and resurrection of Jesus Christ." (49)

Pharaoh prefigures Paul as Saul the persecutor, and is the "dark prototype" of all the rejected in Israel (50), and these are "taken up into the teleology of (God's) merciful willing", heading for their embodiment in Judas Iscariot (51). The position of the Gentiles in the O.T. is also reinterpreted in the light of the events at Golgotha (52).

The main argument of the section is that Paul's defence of God's predestining is correct because the story of Jesus Christ lets us see that rejection and election are not in equilibrium but in an "irreversible sequence (53) which overcomes rejection. This involves giving to Paul's statements a more precise reference. In particular, by taking "vessels of wrath" as singular and referring to Christ, Barth relativises the phrase "made for destruction": now, because of Christ's crucifixion and resurrection, which gives us full knowledge of God's will, the election of all Israel is decided. There is a merging of the identities of Israel, the Church and Jesus Christ:

> "Israel lives by the grace of God, and living in this way it is identical with the offspring for whose sake it was chosen, and in turn identical with all who believe in this offspring, with the totality of those who will be called to faith in this offspring. In this mission of Israel, and ultimately in this its identity with Jesus Christ and His Church, lies the justification of God with respect to what He has willed and done, and still wills and does, with this people."(54)

This assertion of identities in the analogia gratiae needs of course to be supplemented by the stress on their hierarchical ordering, which is a central concept in Barth's theology and which I deal with in my commentary on IV.2(55).

§34.3, The Promise Heard and Believed, is based on Roms 9,30 - 10,21, and deals with Israel's hearing of the Gospel and the Church's believing and proclaiming of it. The Church confirms Israel's election by justifying

77

Israel's history: "its teleology is revealed" (56). Even though Israel as a whole does not believe the Gospel, its "sterile hearing" (57) is an important witness, because it does point to the fact of God's promise and cannot reverse it (58). The exegetical side of this is

> "the Israelite (Jewish) regard for sentence, word and
> letter." (59)

The way in which Barth attempts to affirm this Jewish attitude and also go beyond it could be seen as the theme of this thesis (60).

§34.4, The Passing and the Coming Man, based on Roms 11, continues the discussion of Israel and the Church. Again Barth makes the cross and resurrection the master pattern:

> "As the crucifixion of Jesus is a divine benefit in its
> association with His resurrection, so also is Israel's
> history of suffering in its association with the pre-
> history of the Gospel enacted within it."(61)

It is the resurrection which is overlooked by those who see only a historical succession between Israel and the Church, because:

> "In the resurrection of Jesus Christ God has cancelled
> both the finis of the Jewish rejection of Christ and also
> that of the rejection of the Jews, acknowledging, against
> the will of Israel, His own will with Israel, the Messiah
> of Israel as the Saviour of the world, and therefore also
> and all the more fully of Israel itself." (62)

The overruling of evil in the resurrection is the "concrete omnipotence" of God, and Barth distinguishes his position from that of apokatastasis by appeal to this concreteness (63). Likewise the way in which God remains true to Himself (not by displaying the immutabilitas, incomprehensibilitas and independentia of a philosopher's supreme being, but by the death and resurrection of Christ), and the "objectivity" which Barth invokes (64) are to be defined with reference to that central story. In line with this objectivity he suggests that in Roms 11,1 Paul is thinking not of his personal experience of conversion but of its typological significance, and, even more, of his apostolic office; and, later, that

> "when Paul bases his own approach to the Gentiles on his
> repulse by the Jews, which is so much emphasised in Acts
> (13^{46}, 18^6, 28^{28}), he sees a parallel and illustration of
> the greater event which came on Jesus Christ Himself."(65)

In that event evil clearly has a role to play, and the conclusion is that the divine hardening of some is not an interruption of the salvation-history(66); that those who were blinded, embodied in Judas Iscariot,

> "managed to break open in this way the door between the
> Israelite and non-Israelite world to effect the solidarity,
> both of sin and of grace between Israel and the Gentiles"(67),

and that the precedence of Gentiles over Jews is necessary (68).

The main conclusion of the section is this justification of the ways of
God to man by taking the resurrection as the last word in a providential history, and seeing Israel and all it stands for as a demonstration of the relevance of the Gospel (69). The whole of §34 has thus continued by various
means to order all of biblical history and experience towards the central
story of Jesus Christ.

(iii)

§35, The Election of Individual, includes the most important exegeses
of biblical narratives in the volume, and I will treat these in some detail.
The introduction, §35.1, Jesus Christ, Promise and its Recipient, repeats
themes already stated, chiefly that the relationship between rejection and
election shown in Christ's death and resurrection is the norm for all thought
about individual election (70).

§35.2, The Elect and the Rejected, again identifies Christ as the type
of the elect and rejected (71). The material in support of this is taken from
the O.T., and the overriding concern is to discern "the one absolute hand of
God" (72) revealing the relativity of the contrast of election and rejection.
The two are seen as lines running through the biblical history, with the
elect and rejected being complementary in a binary structure until finally
they meet in one person, Jesus Christ. In the light of this others can only
be elect or rejected "figuratively ('uneigentlich') or secondarily" (73).

The excursus, after surveying the blessings given to the rejected in the
O.T., thus showing that they are not absolutely rejected, has three important
exegetical essays: on Leviticus 14, 16, on Saul and David, and on I Kings 13.

On Lev. 14, 16 Barth's first step is to juxtapose the two as being

"very different but obviously related in general structure"(74).

Secondly, he says that sacrifice in the O.T.

"accompanies the history of Israel (as does prophecy its
own manner) as a sign and testimony of the divine intention
which underlies it and guides it to its goal, and therefore
of the meaning of the events and sequences of events in
which this history proceeds."(75)

This makes two points: there is a further juxtaposition of both chapters
with some O.T. stories; and both stories and sacrifices are seen as expressions of the divine intention - they are the media of revelation.

Barth next treats the common form of the chapters and sees it corresponding to those of the Genesis stories of Abel and Cain, Isaac and Ishmael,
etc. The common aim of the chapters is purification. He then discusses the
special features of Lev. 16, and says that while the reference of the sacrifice is single (to Israel, which is both sinful and the recipient of life

from God), this is

> "an identity which the picture itself cannot reproduce, and
> which is also not to be seen in its historical counterpart,
> that is, in the history of the distinguishing choices as
> such."(76)

This duality is therefore to be seen as an expression demanding completion,
so there is to be a search for unity. His comments on the details of Chapter
16, as on Chapter 14, provide backing for his claims about the prefigurative
nature of the content.

On Lev. 14 Barth is explicit about his interpretative model, the central
Christian story:

> "This bird undoubtedly signifies the resurrection...."(77)

That model also suggests his emphases:

> "The one (bird) has necessarily to die in order that
> the other may live. And this is the real point of the
> differentiation in the stories of election. The purpose,
> and the only purpose, in the death of the one bird, the
> separation and reservation of the one man, is that the
> other may live."(78)

A comparison of the two rituals leads Barth to

> "see at once the whole inscrutability of the reality
> which is attested by both passages" (79).

He assumes that there is such a reality, and that it is "the one complete
man", but because no one man could yet bear both the death and life he has
to be expressed in picture prefigurative of Christ. Barth then explicitly
applies his demand for unity to the chapters, this time from the reader's
point of view:

> "The question still remains how we are to recognise
> ourselves simultaneously in both the one and the other.
> If a man may die by the grace of God, how then can he
> still live, whether in the realm of Azazel or in the
> realm of freedom?...."(80)

Thus he manufactures his problem out of the double inscrutability of the
chapters (81) by applying a model of unity to them.

Yet he immediately grants that there may be no such unity. The O.T.
may have "no subject at all", and the pictures and stories may point to nothing (82). On the other hand, his exegesis has shown it possible that Jesus
Christ is the subject. The choice between the two is

> "a question of faith. It is, therefore, to be disting-
> uished from exegesis. But it is inescapably posed by it;
> and in the answer to this question, whatever it may be,

exegesis is forced (even in the form of a <u>non liquet</u>)
to speak its final word." (83)

This implies the neutrality of exegesis: that the analysis of form and content of Lev. 14, 16 are open to verification in the text. Thus literary analysis of the chapters has been fulfilling a role similar in some other systems to natural theology or apologetics as a <u>praeparatio evangelica</u>: it is
a way of posing an enigma which faith in the Gospel answers. Barth here
stresses his own originality in relation to "the older exegesis" which came
to the same conclusions, but by a different method. Their exegesis explicitly looked to Christ from the start, whereas he claims that he begins by
letting the text "speak by and for itself" (84). The move from his literary
analysis to the "necessary" judgement that the texts are prophecies of Christ
is decided by faith. The practical effect of faith is that Lev. 14, 16 are
seen as part of a providential history leading to Christ, and that correspondences between the two (which are open to neutral observation) are not
accidental. This teleological perspective enables the Christian to "specify
the theme of the passages" (85).

Noteworthy in this method is the lack of any systematic connection between the literary analysis and the judgement of faith (86). The analysis is
admitted to be inconclusive, and there is no attempt by exegesis to prove
anything more than the possibility of a christological interpretation. When
this is given, no arguments are added. The literary analysis is merely extended by explicit juxtaposition with the N.T. story (87). The twofold concern is to observe "the multiformity of historical appearances" and to see
them as types of Christ. This "cannot be reduced to a formula", but depends
on a separate assessment of each correspondence (88). The procedure relies
on an implicit doctrine not so much of revelation as of providence; these
stories are part of the same divinely ordered sequence as the Gospels, and
so correspondences are not fortuitous.

Because the chapters from Leviticus are not stories, it is important to
note their role in the theological argument. They are not put in the same
category as the stories, but are taken as commentary on them (89). Barth
sees them doing what his own commentary aims to do, elucidating the patterns
of meaning common to the stories of election and rejection, and thus helping
to show that all refer to "a single reality" (90). In particular, the relativity and connection of rejection and election are illustrated in a purer
form by the parallelism of the sacrifices, due to the fact that it is two
pairs of identical animals which are offered (91). The rituals are a model
of God's ways with men, and their function, as commentary on the O.T. stories
and as prophecy of Christ, depends on their patterns being verified in those
events. These patterns can be seen as giving the structure of God's way of
judging men, and in order to decide in which of the possible directions God
intended the pattern to point the Christian looks to his final verdict in the
crucifixion and resurrection, and discerns the same pattern there. The procedure here, too, can be related to the "realism of assessment". Barth uses
the pattern of the sacrifices to highlight the element of decision in the
stories with which he links them.

The second exegetical essay is on Saul and David. Much of this is a rich
reflection on both kings as portrayed in the incidents of their lives. This
must be convincing in detail in order to support Barth's claim that it

clarifies "the problem and solution of the differentiating choice of God" here where

> "it re-emerges historically with a distinctness which
> in contrast gives all the corresponding material in the
> patriarchal narratives of Genesis the appearance of mere
> intimation."(92)

Whether the details do add up to Barth's pattern is a decision to be made continually in reading him, and, as he says, there is no formula for deciding. But if one wants to be arguing at least on the same ground as him one has to accept that the story of Saul and David is to be read as the text gives it, and that the only answer to Barth is an alternative literary analysis which does justice to the same text. In line with this assumption, any reflection which begins from a historical reconstruction of Saul and David and their age has no basis for agreement or disagreement with Barth, since the dat a for reflection differ. This becomes especially important in assessing the questions Barth asks of the text. When he has done his analysis of the similarities and dissimilarities between Saul and David, and has pointed to the new orientation in the Bible that their story represents (93) his main question is about the will of God in Israel's history. The series of questions he poses in order to illustrate the obscurity of the story and of its continuation in the succeeding kings is based on the assumption that the will of God is the decisive element in the story (94). His speculation about the human motives for including the story in the canon are not only of dubious value (e.g. the suggestion that there were "in the last resort...no historic, aesthetic or pedagogic reasons" for inclusion (95)) - but irrelevant to his main argument from the text itself, as he himself says later (96). The main point is that the story is perplexing if we want to understand it as under God's will:

> "Is the will of God for this monarchy - assuming that He
> has a will at all - a single will or a twofold? And what
> is His true and proper will when in this twofoldness He
> apparently wills that which is self-contradictory?" (97)

So by deducing logical consequences from God's will as expressed in the story, Barth sets up the story of the kings as a problem which the Gospel answers. If his demands on the text, even in setting up the problem, seem to go beyond the literary analysis, Barth might appeal to the peculiarity of this text in having the will of God as one of its elements, and in this he would have the support of Erich Auerbach (98). That element is one which Barth interprets in the light of what he knows about it from the rest of the Bible, and so

> "the ultimate exegetical question in relation to these
> passages - the question of their subject - is identical
> with the question of faith: whether with the apostles
> we recognise this subject in the person of Jesus Christ,
> or whether with the Synagogue both then and now we do not
> recognise Christ." (99)

But the non-systematic relation between the text and the judgment of faith is again stressed. Jesus Christ is not to be accepted because the story of his life is the best available answer to the enigma of the kings,

82

but because he is convincing in himself as the revelation of God's will.   So
the typological exegesis with which the discussion of Saul and David concludes (100) is not presented as proof of anything.   It portrays the unity
of God's will in history and how particular events go together to express
its many sides.   It is the justification of Barth's insistence on the necessity of all the elements in the story, in particular the rejected Saul
alongside the elect David, and in this way it supports the theological conclusions.   In Stern's terms, God's will would be seen as the ultimately realistic assessment of the story, expressed in a later set of events, and always
through the interaction of people seen in "the middle distance" perspective.

The third essay, on 1 Kings 13, is another example of a literary analysis
discovering a pattern which connects it with Barth's conclusions on election.
There are three crisis points with role reversals (101), "manifold inter-
sections" and two double-pictures (102), and the details are marshalled in
a masterly way.

The crucial question is again about the unity of God's will:

> "We therefore go on to ask how far these two double-
> pictures belong to one another, and how far they are
> opposed, not merely mutely but eloquently - speaking of
> what in all its distinction is in itself the one will
> of God for Israel, of that which makes divided Israel
> more than ever His people." (103)

He then goes back over the story of the man of Judah and the prophet of Bethel
to show how

> "in their union as elect and rejected they form together
> the whole Israel, from which the grace of God is not turned
> away." (104)

Because this is embodied in a story the two are

> "not just numerical units, which as such are interchange-
> able, but two sharply and antithetically differentiated
> individuals";

and the unity has in it an "irrevocable and irreversible order" parallel to
that of Saul and David, and Lev. 14, 16 (105).   Barth finally notes that this,

> "perhaps the most expressive and at any rate the richest
> and most comprehensive prophetic story in the Old Testament"

ends with both prophets in a common grave, and he says that

> "this story too, does point to one real object if Jesus
> Christ is also seen in it, if at the exact point where
> this story of the prophets breaks off a continuation is
> found in the Easter story." (106)

Again he repeats his challenge to see it another way if possible, confident
that he has at least shown that his way does justice to the text.   This

exegesis of I Kings 13 has been examined in detail by an O.T. scholar, Martin
A. Klopfenstein, in his article, "1 Könige 13" (107). It is not my intention
in this thesis to compare Barth's individual exegeses with the manifold proposals of other exegetes (108), and in this case I will not attempt to discuss Klopfenstein's detailed criticism of Barth. The point of interest for
me in his article is that his chief point is a literary one, claiming that
instead of Barth's three role reversals the text supports only one (109) and
that several other conclusions of Barth are likewise not drawn from the text.
The only point at which non-literary arguments are important for his criticism
of Barth is on the meaning of the lion (110) but this is not essential to
Barth's argument. Thus the two differ on the pattern of the meaning of the
narrative. Klopfenstein suggests that Barth's "dialektische Denkschema" has
made him read this into the text (111), and even that this endangers its nature as "echte Geschichte" (112). At present, however, what is most important for me is not whether Barth has distorted the meaning of the text but his
method of going about finding the meaning.

The last paragraph of §35.3, The Determination of the Elect sums up its
content:

> "To what does God elect a man? The New Testament
> answers this question with a portrayal of the existence
> of the apostles; their calling, appointment and mission.
> It is in them, in their being and their deeds, that the
> Church can and should recognise itself as the assembly
> of the elect for all time. It is in them that each in-
> dividual member of the Church can recognise the meaning
> and purpose of his own election. He who is elect of God
> is select in Jesus Christ." (113)

His first decision is therefore to use the story of the apostles' relationship to Jesus as the material from which to draw conclusions. He treats
Paul and other parts of the N.T. briefly, then concentrates on the ministry
of Jesus. He divides it into three stages: the story of the resurrection
(114), the last journey to Jerusalem and the passion (115), and the first
part of Jesus' ministry.

The exegetical method is reflection on the details and patterns of the
story as it is given in the text, with the central concern being their relationship to Jesus. In this case his identity is described by setting him
against the foil of the apostles at each stage of his ministry, for what all
three stages have in common is "the standing and falling of the apostles
with Jesus" (116).

(iv)

The culminating, and most important, exegesis of narrative in §35 is in
§35.4, The Determination of the Rejected. The determination of the rejected is

> "that from being a reluctant and indirect witness he should
> become a willing and direct witness to the election of Jesus
> Christ and His community." (117)

What determines this is Jesus Christ as the Rejected on Golgotha substituting
for all others and making their ultimate rejection inconceivable:

> "With Jesus Christ the rejected can only have been
> rejected. He cannot be rejected any more. Between him
> and an independent existence as rejected, there stands
> the death which Jesus Christ has suffered in his place,
> and the resurrection by which Jesus Christ has opened up
> for him His own place as elect." (118)

In supporting these conclusions the only evidence Barth gives is an interpretation of Judas' role in the Gospel story:

> "There can be no doubt that here at the very heart
> of the New Testament we are confronted by the problem
> of the rejected.... And we meet this question at the
> same central place where the New Testament raises and
> answers the question of the elect." (119)

This way of posing the question at once limits the argument to the meaning
and logic of the Gospel story. In the excursus on Judas Barth's typological
exegesis reaches its greatest concentration. Judas and Jesus stand opposite
each other at the heart of the New Testament. Judas represents the sin of
Israel, of the apostles and of the world (120. He also prefigures Paul and
the Church (121); he is essential to God's plan to elect men through Jesus
Christ, and his betrayal reflects the eternal decree of God that His Son be
incarnate and be handed over to sinful men; and Jesus Christ is Himself
Judas' (as well as Paul's) "Urbild" (122).

With all this representation Judas is still not just a representative
symbol. The other side of Barth's typologising is an insistence on Judas'
own identity as a character in the story. If figuration is not to become
what Barth understands as allegory or myth then Judas must not be identical
with his representative function. Rather, that function must emerge from
considering the pattern of his action as real in its own right at its own
time in the story. One danger with figurative exegesis is that the earlier
prefigurative element will fail to hold its place in the story, that it will
be rendered unreal and cancelled out because the whole meaning is seen in
the later element. The way Barth sees Judas, the rejected and elect, in
confrontation with Jesus, the rejected and elect, makes this danger serious.
Barth must insist in many ways that he does not succumb to it, that the meaning gleaned from typology is in harmony with the literal meaning of the
story. So he says that the contrast of Judas with Jesus is "unresolved"(123),
but finds a clue to its resolution in the divine παραδοῦναι and in the correspondence of Judas with Paul. He denies that Judas' repentence is valid
(124), he insists again on his sin, his lack of a future, his real rejection
by God, the impossibility of finding in the N.T. any glimmer of hope for his
personal salvation (125): in short, on the terrible fact of Judas' παραδοῦναι.
Yet he also wants to express what Jesus' death and resurrection mean for
Judas, that he is elect, and that it is possible both to see how terrible
his sin is, and also to find hope for him in how the story continues, because the continuation shows that God's will was done in him. Barth wants
to keep both sides: the gravity of the sin and the overwhelming power of the
salvation. The problem is, can the narrative sustain this conclusion?

The working hypothesis of typology is God's providence guiding the story (126). This makes it normal for one event in the story to resemble and help to interpret another regardless of the intentions of the actors or of the human author. There can be "objective correspondence" (127) because God is the unifier of the parts and the author of their meaning. It is when Barth speaks of God's providence in relation to Judas that the issue of his role in the story is posed most sharply.

> "The paradox of the figure of Judas is that, although
> his action as the executor of the New Testament is so
> absolutely sinful, yet as such, in all its sinfulness,
> it is still the action of that executor. The divine and
> human παραδοῦναι cannot be distinguished in what Judas
> did, as they can be in the genuine apostolic tradition,
> where the human is related to the divine as to its content
> and subject. In the case of Judas, the apostle who per-
> verted his apostleship and served Satan, the two coincide.
> As the human παραδοῦναι takes place, the divine takes
> place directly, and the divine takes place directly as the
> human takes place. It is to be noted that there is this
> coincidence where the human can only be regarded, and is
> undoubtedly regarded by the New Testament, as conscious
> and deliberate sin, as sin with a high hand. In this
> case sin is made righteousness and evil good.... God
> wills this conclusion to His history as the history of
> the man Jesus, and He Himself reaches this conclusion in
> Him.... When God abandoned Himself, it pleased Him so to
> confront this man (Judas) who was also abandoned that he
> of all men became His servant, not indirectly but directly
> and in his blatant rejection, as not even Paul and Peter
> were his servants. That is, he became the servant of
> the work of reconciliation itself, in which these others
> shared only later and as witnesses." (128)

That passage is, as it were, the apotheosis of typology. The divine παραδοῦναι coincides with its antitype, Judas' παραδοῦναι. This interpret- ation is an answer to the problem of divine providence and evil. That the two coincide in one event means that what Judas did and represented (the sin of Israel, of the apostles and of the world) met with God's eternal decree of election. What happens in this conjunction is that the literal meaning (sin) is given a new meaning (righteousness) while the literal meaning still remains. This is only demonstrable because of the employment of typology. And it is crucial that what Barth means by the divine is "necessarily" enacted in history (129). Indeed the divine παραδοῦναι is seen in the whole incarnation (130). Judas' παραδοῦναι bears the meaning it does because it is not an isolated event (131), but part of a cumulative sequence. It is a point in the story where Barth discerns a new direction, Christ ceasing to be the active, free protagonist and becoming subject to what his captors do to him. It is the "deprivation of the freedom of God Himself" (132) - the miracle of divine condescension:

> "But the real nature of this miracle only emerges when
> when we observe how from the very beginning the life of
> Jesus moves towards His arrest and crucifixion, how from

the very beginning it stands under the shadow which will
finally be utter darkness when He has to be arrested, and
to suffer and die." (133)

This is the "form of his life" which leads him into "the place of a man as a
sinner rejected by God" (134). How this form of the story anticipates the
substitutionary death on the cross has been discussed in Chapter 3 above.
Here, where the focus is on Judas, the betrayal is seen as the point of convergence of the patterns of God's and Judas' παραδοῦναι, the exchange between
them being acted out on the cross.

The special interest of §35.4 is in the determination of the rejected,
but there is no direct evidence in the N.T. for Judas' ultimate fate. Barth's
main contribution to a solution is to see Judas as a negative type of Paul.
A statement that sums up the exegetical judgement on which the theological
conclusion of the section is based is:

"It is by the death of Jesus that the Judas in Paul dies."(135)

The move from their typological identification to the general theological conclusion is direct:

"When we consider the question of the determination
of the rejected, in view of Judas and Paul we have to
bear in mind that the elect alwaysoccupies what was
originally the place of a rejected, and that the work of
the elect can only be the amazing reversal of the work
of the rejected." (136)

When Barth juxtaposes Judas and Paul he finds a number of parallels(137),
summing up these by saying that the form of their action is the same:

"For although the act of Judas cannot be justified
in itself, it does actually have the form which found
its positive disclosure in the acts of the faithful
apostles, and in the transmission of his successor
Paul. What justifies Judas is the fact that Paul, too,
is what he is by the grace of God in the activity of
handing-over." (138)

The main conclusion of the section depends on this insight into a formal correspondence. The method used here has no rules of procedure except the maxim
to look for such parallels. When corresponding patterns are found they are
not seen as randomly linked, but as significantly related in a providential
order. It is teleological exegesis, because it discovers that part of the
earlier events' meaning is that it is part of the divine plan which intends
the later event. In fact, the major use is to show the unity of meaning in
the divine plan: while a literal reading leaves Judas and Jesus in "unresolved contrast" (139), the "objective" correspondence of the παραδοῦναι of
Judas with that of Paul (140) demonstrates that it did "in fact have another
meaning" (141) which shows its relation with the death and resurrection of
Jesus and the birth and future of the Church. There can be no proof of this
except a judgment about how convincing each correspondence is as a piece of
literary analysis. Appeal to the intention of the author is irrelevant, e.g.

"Whether the Acts of the Apostles really intended to say
this implicitly is another question." (142)

So also is appeal to the intention of human actors, e.g.

"It was obviously not his own will or work if his (Judas')
act had another meaning and content than the 'delivery'
which was to serve the monstrous lie of the devil." (143)

Nor is there any question of appeal to a chain of historical causality between type and antitype, even though in this case (unlike e.g. that of Ahi-
tophel and Judas (144)) there is no large temporal gap between the two. Nor
is the prefiguring taken as predictive. We are left simply with the discovery by literary examination of real resemblances in a providential
scheme. Judas is like "a planned figure in a planned role" (145), and the
correspondences with God's and Paul's roles reveal the patterns of meaning
in the narrative. The above general remarks also apply to the interpretation of Zech. 11 in relation to Judas, where Barth follows up Matthew's hint
and gathers meaning from it which likewise is independent of the author's
and actor's intentions, of historical causal connection and of predictive
content (146). The latter is noteworthy in how it interprets Matthew's
claim to fulfilment (147). The governing of providence even extends to the
errors of the Bible, for when Matthew gets his Old Testament references con-
fused, Barth searches for meaning in the newly juxtaposed texts, and concludes:

"We have here another example of how even in its mis-
understandings and confusions, the Bible is usually
more instructive than other books in their accuracy."(148)

In all his exegesis of narrative in this section, Barth ignores the
question of their historical reference. He goes straight from understanding
the lexical meaning, without any intermediate stage of historical assessment.
In other words, he chooses as his datum for reflection the element which history books and novels have in common: the cumulative description of character
and circumstance in interaction with each other. The frontier between fact
and fiction is not discussed, since the text's literary meaning is the same
no matter where it lies. The contradiction between Acts and Matthew over
Judas' death is not seen by Barth as a problem to be solved by trying to
discover "what really happened". Rather, each is a description whose details
give its meaning, and the meaning of each is to be reflected upon as a contribution to our understanding of Judas and the story. Harmonisation of the
two does not take place by writing a third account which tries to do justice
to the evidence of each. Their convergence is rather seen in their similar
contribution to one pattern of meaning in the story: that both show "the
utter absence of any future ascribed to Judas himself" (149). Their divergence contributes by enriching our understanding both of Judas himself and of
his representation of Israel, for each account has different O.T. resonances.
This method refuses to assume any higher inclusive viewpoint on the events
from which to compose a synthesis, but insists that the way to gather the
meaning is by following in the footsteps of each author in turn. As Barth
remarks about another set of contradictory accounts, about the anointing at
Bethany:

"The historical complications in which we may find ourselves because of this discrepancy are of little consequence compared with the instruction which is yielded
by the inconsistency." (150)

The instruction Barth receives in the case both requires that the differences
in detail be taken literally (i.e. that the anointing should be objected to
by Judas, by some disciples, and by all, respectively) and also that this be
taken as evidence for the representative role of Judas in his sin, which is
important for Barth's understanding of the logic of the story.

Barth's method here can be contrasted with an historian's. The latter
would take the meaning of the passages to be their reference to certain historical events. So he would distinguish the narratives from their referent,
try to determine the referent, and then reinterpret the passage on that
basis. For Barth the historical referent is not the meaning of the passages,
and even when there are clear contradictions they can yield a unified meaning.
The ultimate basis of this unity is the will of God, and in §35.4 all the
typology and other exegesis surrounding the παραδοῦναι is referred to that of
God.

"All other delivery looks to or from this. It has its
reality in what happened here. It is impossible to interpret it apart from its connection with this event." (151)

It is "the original and authentic παραδοῦναι " which is "from the very beginning, from all eternity, and therefore necessarily in history" (152).

In such a view minor contradictions and mistakes in the text are of
little interest compared with the question of how Judas' sin can be comprehended in God's plan. If the latter is possible, then errors in the Bible
can also be comprehended in it! The central issue in §35.4 is therefore
how God's will includes Judas. The answer is that his act coincided with
God's: the two deliveries intersected in one event whose meaning is shown
by the continuation of the story.

"The more profoundly and comprehensively we attempt
to formulate the sin and guilt of Judas, the more
nearly his will and deed approach what neither he himself willed and did, nor the people of Israel, nor the
Gentiles at whose head he finally appears - the more
nearly his will and deed approach what God willed and
did in this matter...." (153)

I have already pointed out how necessary Barth's discernment of types and of
the shape of the story is for this conclusion: it is the literary-analytical
side of thinking "more profoundly and comprehensively". So the answer to the
problem of how evil and God's will can be reconciled is to read this story
and note how Judas' election (seen in his being one of the twelve and also
in typological exegesis of the continuation of the story),

"excels and outshines and controls and directs his rejection: not just partly but wholly; not just relatively but absolutely" (154).

Barth's description of the apostolic role after Pentecost emphasises the once and for all nature of Jesus' life, death and resurrection, their primacy over all other events:

> "The context of their message, the subject of their
> tradition, is quite simply the name of Jesus Christ,
> the 'account of the things which have been fulfilled
> among us'.... Enclosed in his name, as the declaration
> of His name, as the record of His story and work -
> these statements declare the truth, not abstractedly,
> but as a fact and therefore as revelation." (155)

The apostles give an echo (156), a repetition and reproduction (157), they correspond to the situation objectively created by Jesus' death, they portray ("abbilden") it.

> "As the bondage and torment of the rejected is not a
> new or strange thing, an independent reality, in relation
> to what Jesus Christ suffered, and suffered on their
> behalf, so also the saving apostolic tradition is not
> a new or a strange thing, an independent reality....
> It is not a productive, but only a reproductive activity
> ...a human repetition and imitation of the divine
> original." (157)

The lines of the O.T. converge in Christ, and that climax does not need completion by the Church. As Barth says of the suffering of the rejected:

> "Their suffering is, as it were, only a prelude ('Vorspiel')
> and postlude ('Nachspiel') to the suffering of Jesus Christ."(158)

The primary story is clearly set apart and given unrivalled importance as the narrative corresponding to the decisive events, and the O.T., Church history and our lives today are ordered in relation to it. The connection of these with the primary story is, on the one hand, that of temporal sequence, and, on the other, that of figurative correspondence. In the temporal sequence something irreversible has happened, so that:

> "The story of God's faithfulness and Israel's faith-
> lessness, the story of Judas Iscariot and what follows
> at Gethsemane and Golgotha, will not be repeated. All
> apparent repetitions of these stories are only formless
> phantasmagoria. What cannot be reversed is the fact
> that Jesus is the Victor." (159)

Yet there is the apostolic repetition which, as with Paul's apostolate, relates figuratively to the primary story, where it finds its prototype.

(v)

How is all this to be assessed? My analysis of the exegesis with which Barth supports his doctrine has shown how it is inextricably tied up with literary methods: a use of typology which presupposes a certain sort of providence, and positions on the identity and will of God, on the framework of history, on evil, on time, on an equivalent of natural theology, and on the irrelevance of historical criticism. All of this is groundless if his literal and typological exegesis fails to support it. There are clearly many openings here for those who want for whatever reason to part company with Barth, but my aim is not to criticise him by taking an alternative view of, for example, providence or historical criticism. Rather I wish to assess him (while granting his method) using the tools I have employed in my analysis, asking whether Barth's literary criticism is sound enough to support his conclusion.

First I will enlist Stern in helping to develop the insight of Auerbach, quoted above, about discerning the will of God in biblical stories. Stern suggests that what in "real life" are the purposes and intentions of characters become the meanings of a work of literature:

> "Purpose, then, stands in the same relation to realism in life as does meaning to realism in literature: they are not the same but they are closely related (they have the same 'logical form')." (160)

What a character says is determined by his ends; and the author's selection of words and characters is determined by his ends:

> "What is being established are two distinct but analogous hierarchies of ends." (161)

What the present chapter has shown is Barth's God as the author who takes up the intentions of individuals and nations and, using his unrivalled supremacy in the hierarchy of ends, brings about his own ends and so creates the meaning of history, expressed in the Bible. The way Barth explains the relationship of Judas, Jesus and the Father in παραδοῦναι is his supreme example of trying to show the purposes of man being given meaning by God, and since the purposes of both God and man must be understood from the stories alone, there are obvious affinities between Barth's method and the sort of examination Stern applies mainly to novels.

Yet this does mean that the purposes ascribed to God must ring true with the stories. Many of Barth's conclusions seem to me to do so given his presuppositions, but one that is important for his doctrine seems not to do so, and an examination of it is instructive.

The conclusion in question is the suggestion of Judas' election. There seems here to be a misuse of typology which spoils the realism of the literal story for the sake of trying to know more of God's purposes than can properly be elicited. In his desire to support the possibility of an ultimately favourable verdict on Judas Barth presses his method to the point of producing contradictions. How can one say both that we must leave the question of Judas' "personal justification" to God (162) and also that he is wholly elect?(163) Is his thinking not bound to lead to such nonsensical concepts as

> "a limit which encloses even that which is boundless in itself, eternal fire"? (164)

The drive behind the distortion of the story is clearly the desire to enclose
all rejection in Jesus' death and so see it all overcome in his resurrection.
But in the way in which he insists on the central character dominating the
meaning of the whole Barth implies that the story's proper analogy in fiction
is not the sort of realistic novel which Auerbach or Stern define, but rather
another, less realistic, type, the "Entwicklungsroman" (or "Bildungsroman").
This is a genre which has predominated in German novels, and Stern sees its
influence in the final work of the greatest German novelist of this century,
Thomas Mann. Commenting on Mann's "Joseph" tetralogy, Stern writes:

> "I have already mentioned that in the figure of Joseph,
> especially in the last part of the tetralogy, that game
> of selfconscious insights was played out to its most
> problematical conclusions. By this I mean that both he
> and several of the other characters see themselves not
> only as agents in living historical situations, but also
> as actors in a biblical or mythological or cosmic play -
> they see themselves (and occasionally each other) as
> parts of a preordained whole. The peculiar effect of
> this kind of knowledge is of course to deprive the novel
> of some of its dramatic quality. As happens in the
> classical Entwicklungsroman, the sting of finality is
> taken out of their lives. Linear time is curved into
> a circle, it becomes a sort of joyful eternal recurrence.
> A man's exposure to the consequencesof his acts, of his
> final and irrevocable decisions, is avoided. The results
> of his decisions are known to him before he has actually
> taken those decisions, and so is the cosmic plan his life
> is to follow. Thomas Mann is intent on circumnavigating
> the question of faith but, given the expectations aroused
> by the biblical story in its readers, this proves to be
> an impossible undertaking. The question of religious
> faith is not really avoided - it is deflected into a
> literary faith, a sort of 'pan-literariness'. Not
> Jehovah is the God of the Israelites, but a God-novelist.
> The oneness in which God and the novelist merge and which
> the characters share is no unio mystica but a sort of
> literary knowingness, a consciousness, a consciousness
> in excess of the story." (165

In the C.D. it is not the Bible's characters who see themselves in this
way but Barth who takes God's viewpoint and sees them so, laying claim to "a
consciousness in excess of the story". The result is that "the sting of
finality" is taken out of Judas' life - however terrible his sin, Barth
wants to make a case for his salvation, of which the N.T., with its two
stories of his death, both smacking of the most bitter finality, gives no
hint. Barth's bias towards stressing "objective" atonement and salvation
here leads him into an interpretation which is bound to devalue subjective
responsibility and faith.

It is no accident that Barth calls up comparisons with the "Entwicklungsroman", of which Stern says that in it the hero "eats up the background" -
the whole world yields before him and is organised around him (166). One
can see Barth's great temptation to this sort of interpretation, for he does

92

believe that all creation is ordered through and for Jesus Christ. Yet the Gospels do not reflect this in the manner of an "Entwicklungsroman", but are stubbornly realistic. So Barth's tendency is to interpret them as more christocentric than they are. The virtual enveloping of Judas in salvation despite himself, the language of "primary" and "secondary", and other features which will emerge in later chapters all suggest the importance of a picture of Jesus which plays down the reality of other people in a way the stories themselves do not support.

Nor is it an accident that such a fault should appear in a doctrine which integrates so much of Barth's theology. He is straining to put in place the keystone of his structure, the christocentric interpretation of election which will let it retain the importance it had for Calvin while avoiding the objectionable aspects of "double predestination". He had been impressed by the rightness of such an interpretation by reading the work of Pierre Maury (167) but had to justify it by his own methods (168). Yet the method and the conclusion are incompatible, and Barth misuses the method in the service of a system. I say "system" deliberately, for despite his aversion to the term Barth was not immune to the attraction of a theology having something of the beauty and integration of Mozart's music, an attraction which had deep roots in the Germanic culture which he shared. Stern, discussing Mann's Doktor Faustus, remarks that the period and culture of Mann's floruit, before 1945, was one in which

> "people believed in and acted on systematized tenets
> and convictions to a degree unprecedented" (169),

and sees it reflected in Mann's "attempting a 'total' novel of interconnections and allegorical correspondences" (170). Barth too has in his doctrine of election proposed a totality of correspondences. It is one which is fundamentally a matter of the relation of literal to typological sense, and it must at the very least be corrected from within by his own method (171).

NOTES to Chapter 5

(1) Von Balthasar, op. cit., p. 145. Besides von Balthasar the most helpful
commentators on this doctrine are Eduard Buess, "Zur Prädestinationslehre Karl Barths", in Theologische Studien, Heft 43 (Zürich 1955),
especially S. 45 ff., 58 ff., with whose criticism of von Balthasar I
agree; and H. Bouillard, op. cit., Vol. II.

(2) Its appeal to stories in this context is the major sustained illustration of the integration of Deus revelatus and Deus in se referred to in
Chapter 8 below.

(3) C.D.II.2, p. 3, S.1.

(4) Ib., pp. 8 f., S. 6 f. On "Urgeschichte" see E. Jüngel's extended note
on Barth's use of the term from The Epistle to the Romans to C.D.II.2
in op. cit., S. 88 f.

(5) Ib., p. 8, S. 7.

(6) Ib., p. 44.

(7) Ib., p. 45.

(8) Ib., p. 51.

(9) Ib., p. 53.

(10) Ib., p. 54.

(11) Ib., p. 58.

(12) Ib., p. 58, S. 62.

(13) Ib., pp. 63-76.

(14) Ib., p. 88.

(15) Ib., p. 116.

(16) Ib., pp. 110 f.

(17) Ib., p. 100.

(18) Ib., p. 125.

(19) Ib., p. 117, S. 126.

(20) Ib., pp. 95 ff.

(21) Ib., p. 136.

(22) Ib., p. 135.

(23) Ib., p. 144.

(24) Ib.

(25) Ib., pp. 154 ff.

(26) See above Chapter 4.

(27) Ib., p. 156.

(28) Ib., p. 161.

(29) Ib., p. 149.

(30) Ib., pp. 146 ff.

(31) Ib., pp. 150 ff.

(32) Ib., pp. 164 f.

(33) Ib., p. 167.

(34) See above, Chapter 3.

(35) C.D.II.2, p. 170.

(36) Ib., p. 173.

(37) Ib., p. 174.

(38) E.g., ib., p. 184.

(39) Ib., p. 181.

(40) Ib., p. 183.

(41) Ib., p. 185.

(41) Ib., p. 185.

(42) Ib., p. 185, S. 203.

(43) Ib.

(44) The expression of which is the resurrection. Cf. Chapter 4 on the realism of assessment.

(45) Ib., p. 188.

(46) Ib., p. 200.

(47) Ib., p. 211. The stress, throughout Barth's treatment of the relation of Israel to the Church, on the resurrection (e.g. pp. 208, 221, 227,

237 f., 266, 291) as the decisive novelty can be seen as an example of
the "realism of assessment", see above, Chapter 4.

(48) Ib., p. 228.

(49) Ib., pp. 212 f.

(50) Ib., p. 220.

(51) Ib., pp. 212 f.

(52) Ib., p. 229.

(53) Ib., p. 224.

(54) Ib., p. 233.

(55) Below, Chapter 7.

(56) Ib., p. 239.

(57) Ib., p. 236.

(58) Ib., pp. 236 f.

(59) Ib., p. 234.

(60) The fact that Jews and Christians have a book in common pointed Barth
towards literary criticism as the presupposition of dialogue: "I have
never denied that if we have to explain texts, that criticism - literary
criticism - must have its place; and certainly if this dialogue (i.e.
between Jews and Christians) should take place, we would have to under-
take very earnest common research." Later he talks of the "necessity
of having such a discussion". (Barth answering questions in Chicago,
1962. Published as "Introduction to Theology. Questions to and Discussions with Dr Karl Barth", in Criterion. A Publication of the
Divinity School of the University of Chicago, Vol. 2, No. 1, Winter
1963, p. 20.)

(61) Ib., p. 266.

(62) Ib., p. 291.

(63) Ib., p. 295.

(64) E.g. ib., p. 278.

(65) Ib., p. 279.

(66) Ib., p. 275.

(67) Ib., p. 279.

(68) Ib., p. 301.

(69) Ib., pp. 260 ff.

(70) Ib., p. 320. On p. 309 Barth has a brief excursus remarking that he
      does not see his order of treatment, from the election of Jesus Christ
      to that of Israel and the Church and then of the individual, as ir-
      reversible. The only essential point is the connection of the indiv-
      idual's election to that of Jesus Christ and the community. In §35.4
      it becomes clear that the reason the order is not important is that
      there is ultimately a convergence of Jesus Christ, Israel, the Church,
      the rejected Judas and the elect Paul in a literal and typological
      understanding of the role of Judas.

(71) Ib., p. 347.

(72) Ib., p. 350.

(73) Ib., p. 353, S. 389.

(74) Ib., p. 357.

(75) Ib., p. 357, cf. pp. 363, 366.

(76) Ib., p. 359.

(77) Ib., p. 361.

(78) Ib.

(79) Ib., p. 362.

(80) Ib.

(81) Ib., p. 363.

(82) Ib.

(83) Ib., p. 364.

(84) Ib.

(85) Ib.

(86) Cf. Arnold Come's comments on Barth's exegesis of Lev. 14, 16 in An
      Introduction to Barth's Dogmatics for Preachers (London 1963), pp.
      196 f.

(87) Op. cit., pp. 364 ff.

(88) Ib., p. 366.

(89) Ib., pp. 358, 363, 366.

(90) Ib., p. 366.

(91) There is no question of one animal being more "worthy".

(92) Ib., p. 366.

(93) Ib., pp. 367, 384.

(94) Ib., pp. 384 ff.

(95) Ib., p. 393.

(96) Ib., p. 393.

(97) Ib., p. 388.

(98) In Mimesis, op. cit., Chapter 1, Auerbach analyses the story of Abraham and Isaac (pp. 8 ff.) and applies his insights also to that of Saul and David (pp. 12, 19 ff.). "Fraught with background" (p. 12) is the phrase he uses to suggest the distinctiveness of these stories when compared with Homer's, and he connects it with the O.T. stories' "insistent relation - a relation constantly redefined by conflicts - to a single and hidden God, who yet shows himself and who guides the universal history by promise and exaction, (which) gives these stories an entirely different perspective from any the Homeric poems can possess" (pp. 16-7). He sees the unity of the groups of O.T. stories in this "vertical connection" (p. 17), suggests that in this background the truth claim of the stories is found, with their realism a means to this end (p. 14), and on the subject of doctrine writes: "Let no one object that this goes too far, that not the stories, but the religious doctrine, raises this claim to Absolute authority; because the stories are not, like Homer's simply narrated 'reality'. Doctrine and promise are incarnate in them and inseparable from them; for that very reason they are fraught with 'background' and mysterious, containing a second, concealed meaning" (p. 15). It is such an insight that Barth's story-based doctrine of election expresses.

(99) Op. cit., p. 388.

(100) Ib., pp. 389 ff.

(101) Ib., pp. 395 ff.

(102) Ib., pp. 398 ff.

(103) Ib., p. 404.

(104) Ib., p. 406, cf. p. 408.

(105) Ib., p. 408.

(106) Ib., p. 409.

(107) In Parrhesia Karl Barth zum 80. Geburtstag, herausg. E. Busch, J. Fangmeier, M. Geiger (Zürich 1966), S. 639 ff.

(108) It is, however, noteworthy that it is O.T. scholarship which provides most support for Barth's attitude to the biblical narratives; cf. the essay by James A. Wharton, "The Occasion of the Word of God. An unguarded essay on the character of the Old Testament as the memory of God's story with Israel", in Austin Seminary Bulletin, Faculty Edition, Vol. LXXXIV, No. 1, September 1969, pp. 3-54. The author, himself an Old Testament scholar, acknowledges in the preface his debt to others in his discipline, as well as to Karl Barth: "Those who are familiar with recent theological literature will recognise a host of ideas which in their germ, at least, go back to such Old Testament men as Gerhard von Rad, Walther Zimmerli, Hans-Joachim Kraus, John Bright, Brevard Childs, James Barr, Claus Westermann and others. My stealing from Karl Barth will be forgiven by him..."(p.5).

(109) Ib., S. 668.

(110) Ib., S. 660 ff., 669.

(111) Ib., S. 670.

(112) Ib., S. 671.

(113) Op. cit., p. 449.

(114) Ib., pp. 432 ff.

(115) Ib., pp. 435 ff.

(116) Ib., p. 446, cf. pp. 435, 437, 439.

(117) Ib., p. 458.

(118) Ib., p. 453.

(119) Ib., p. 471.

(120) Ib., p. 472.

(121) E.g. ib., p. 484.

(122) Ib., pp. 480, 503.

(123) Ib., p. 476.

(124) Ib., pp. 466 ff.

(125) Ib., pp. 466 ff.

(126) Cf. above, p.

(127) Cf. ib., p. 488.

(128) Ib., pp. 502 f.

(129) Ib., p. 491.

(130) Ib., pp. 490, 492.

(131) Cf. the many statements that he is not "selbständig", that he is a "Schattenbild", e.g. ib., p. 504, S. 561.

(132) Ib., p. 492.

(133) Ib.

(134) Ib.

(135) Ib., p. 501.

(136) Ib., p. 480.

(137) Their representation of Israel, ib., p. 478; their closeness to Jesus, ib., p. 479; their mutually determinate "deliveries", ib., p. 483.

(138) Ib., p. 484.

(139) Ib., p. 476.

(140) Ib., p. 488.

(141) Ib., p. 482.

(142) Ib., p. 478.

(143) Ib., p. 482.

(144) Ib., p. 469.

(145) Ib., p. 460.

(146) Ib., pp. 463 ff.

(147) Cf. esp. ib., p. 464.

(148) Ib., p. 468.

(149) Ib., p. 467.

(150) Ib., p. 471.

(151) Ib., p. 489.

(152) Ib., p. 491.

(153) Ib., p. 501.

(154) Ib., p. 504.

(155) Ib., p. 449.

(156) Ib., p. 499.

(157) Ib., p. 497.

(158) Ib., p. 494, S. 549.

(159) Ib., p. 500.

(160) Op. cit., p. 81.

(161) Ib., p. 81.

(162) Op. cit., p. 484.

(163) Ib., p. 104.

(164) Ib., pp. 486 f.

(165) T.L.S., No. 3822, 6 June 1975, p. 622.

(166) On Realism, pp. 101 f.

(167) Barth wrote in the preface to Maury's La Prédestination (Genève 1957): "on peut certainement dire que c'est lui qui, alors, a contribué d'une manière decisive à donner à mes recherches sur ce point leur orientation fondamentale. Avant d'avoir lu son étude (i.e. Maury's contribution to the Congrès calviniste de Genève, 1936), je n'avais encore rencontré personne qui eut traité la question avec tant de fraîcheur et d'audace" (p. 6).

(168) Barth's exegetical method is not in Maury, even in this later work.

(169) History and Allegory in Thomas Mann's Doktor Faustus (London 1975), p. 8.

(170) Ib., p. 10.

(171) There is a fascinating further parallel with Doktor Faustus, for there too, as Stern says, the "perplexing and shocking" thing is that "There is more than one sign, in the last two chapters especially, that Adrian Leverkuhn (who sold his soul to the devil) will be saved" (ib., p. 11). But at least Mann could write such signs into the text!

Appendix to Chapter 5

Barth's Doctrine of Nothingness

In C.D.III.3 §50, <u>God and Nothingness</u>, Barth treats the problem of evil under the concept of "das Nichtige".

> "Under the control of God world-occurrence is
> threatened and actually corrupted by the nothingness
> which is inimical to the will of the Creator and
> therefore to the nature of His good creature. God
> has judged nothingness by His mercy as revealed and
> effective in Jesus Christ. Pending the final revelation
> that it is already refuted and abolished, God determines
> the sphere, the manner, the measure and the subordinate
> relationship to His Word and work in which it may still
> operate."(1)

Barth takes as his main category in the discussion that of "Geschichte". Theology must always be "broken utterance" because it is the record of a history which nothingness interrupts, though nothingness is "no more than an alien, disrupting and retarding moment" (2). He insists therefore that theology must not attempt to unify or systematise or tidy up where the history does not permit it: theology's "aim must simply be to make the right report" (3).

I want to show the connection between what Barth says in §50 and what he says in II.2 on election. There too his main category was history, and the role of evil in it was an issue, with the question of God's responsibility for it being posed sharply by such statements as that about election being "the principle and essence of all happenings everywhere" (4) and also by the interpretations of biblical stories. In §50 Barth recognises the dependence of his doctrine of nothingness on that of election (5) and his main focus is again on the story of Jesus Christ. A typical statement is:

> "The true nothingness is that which brought Jesus
> Christ to the cross, and that which he defeated there.
> Only from the standpoint of Jesus Christ, his birth,
> death and resurrection, do we see it in reality and
> truth, without the temptation to treat it as something
> inconclusive or relative, or to conceive it dialectically
> and thus render it innocuous. From this standpoint we
> see it with fear and trembling as the adversary with
> whom God and God alone can cope." (6)

This is my justification for carrying over the results of Barth's II.2 exegesis, especially of Judas through whom Barth there considered what it was that "brought Jesus to the cross". That discussion made it clear the extent to which Barth's conclusions depend upon a certain type of literary analysis, the crisis point being the convergence of the intentions of the Father, Jesus and Judas in the handing over of Jesus to be crucified. From that crisis the verdict that emerged was the resurrection, which showed that

Judas' action was overcome and had "no future".

§50 elaborates on the temporal ontology (7) suggested there. When Barth is defining the reality of evil he places it on a hierarchy of levels: God, creatures and nothingness, the latter being real in a "third fashion peculiar to itself" (8). One way he describes this peculiar reality is as what God rejects when he elects, the activity of God on his left hand (9). His account of what this means builds up to his "final and decisive insight that nothingness has no perpetuity" (10). His final definition is, therefore, that

> "Nothingness is the past, the ancient menace,
> danger and destruction, the ancient non-being which
> obscured and defaced the divine creation of God but
> which is consigned to the past in Jesus Christ, in
> which death it has received its deserts, being destroyed
> with this consummation of the positive will of God which
> is as such the end of His non-willing." (11)

It is therefore in terms of this temporal ontology based on the story of Jesus Christ that Barth conceives the reality of nothingness. In short, the reality of God is eternal, with past, present and future coinciding in pure duration; the reality of creation is historical, with past, present and future in succession; and the reality of nothingness is only past.

Such statements about nothingness are sharply opposed to common-sense, as Barth admits:

> "The aspect of creaturely activity both as a
> whole and in detail, our consciousness both of
> the world and of self, certainly do not bear them
> out.... The only valid presupposition is a backward
> look to the resurrection of Jesus Christ and a for-
> ward look to His coming in glory." (12)

The originality of Barth's doctrine of nothingness therefore lies in the thoroughgoing and distinctive way in which it takes as the sole criterion of reality the story of Jesus Christ. Consistent with this, when he talks of ontology he uses the temporal language of the story: Because Judas' παραδοῦναι is overcome and succeeded by the resurrection (which reveals that this story reflects the "Urgeschichte" in God) therefore evil is seen to be overcome from all eternity, and so always "past" in this sense. An-other way of expressing it is that the story of Jesus Christ is taken as the all-inclusive story of world history; all history is figuratively re-lated to it, and all evil is "figured" into it in the person of Judas; and so faith, knowing the outcome of his action, sees that evil is past, and only waits for this to become clear to all at Jesus Christ's coming in glory.

My criticisms of such a doctrine have already been suggested in Chapter 5, and more will be said in future chapters (13).

NOTES to Appendix to Chapter 5

(1)   C.D.III.3, p. 289.

(2)   Ib., p. 295.

(3)   Ib.

(4)   II.2, p. 183.

(5)   III.3, p. 351.

(6)   Ib.,p. 305.

(7)   For my discussion of this see below, Chapter 8.

(8)   Ib., p. 350.

(9)   E.g. ib., p. 351.

(10) Ib., p. 360.

(11) Ib., p. 363.

(12) Ib., p. 363.

(13) For the criticisms of others see especially Wolf Krötke's excellent
      study Sünde und Nichtiges bei Karl Barth (Berlin 1970) which has the
      advantage of taking account of what critics up to a recent date have
      said of Barth's doctrine of evil, and which also has excursus dist-
      inguishing Barth's position from those of Hegel, Plato and Plotinus;
      also Kurt Lüthi, Gott und das Böse. Eine biblisch-theologische und
      systematische These zur Lehre vom Bösen, entworfen in Auseinander-
      setzung mit Schelling und Karl Barth (Zürich-Stuttgart 1961);   and
      John Hick, Evil and the God of Love (London 1968).

In the traditional Christian scheme the creation story was the beginning of the overarching story and accepted as an accurate account of what happened (1). With the growth of modern biblical scholarship and of sciences such as geology and biology this world-view became generally untenable, and there resulted not only a crisis over how to understand Genesis 1 and 2 and how to conceive of creation, but also a deep disorientation as regards the place of man in time and history. To Barth, a theologian who wished to avoid apologetics, this situation posed a special problem when he came to his doctrine of creation. His solution of it offers a good illustration of the role of this dissertation's theme in his thought. He draws attention to it in his preface to C.D.III.1:

> "It will perhaps be asked in criticism why I have
> not tackled the obvious scientific question posed in
> this context. It was my original belief that this
> would be necessary, but I later saw that there can be
> no scientific problems, objections, or aids in relation
> to what Holy Scripture and the Christian Church under-
> stand by a divine work of creation. Hence in the cen-
> tral portion of this book a good deal will be said
> about 'naive' Hebrew 'saga' but nothing at all about
> apologetics and polemics, as might have been expected.
> The relevant task of dogmatics at this point has been
> found exclusively in repeating the 'saga', and I have
> found this task far finer and far more rewarding than
> all the dilettante entanglements in which I might
> otherwise have found myself." (2)

As will be shown, his repetition of the saga includes many of those previously noted features which draw attention to the novel-like characteristics of the Bible, and the overall story which he describes differs in important respects from the traditional one.

I will now comment on Barth's exegesis of Genesis 1 and 2 as he presents it in C.D.III.1 (3).

(i)

§41.1 makes several claims about the form and content of the creation narratives, and is the justification of Barth's hermeneutical method in the exegesis of §41.2, 3.

The main claim about the form is that it is saga, which Barth defines in distinction from history and myth (4). The basic definition is:

> "an intuitive and poetic picture of a pre-historical
> reality of history which is enacted once and for all
> within the confines of time and space." (5)

Saga is part of the larger category of biblical narrative. §41.1 continually stresses what the two have in common, in particular in being "pure narration without any after thoughts" (6), whose "truth is identical with the historical picture which is presented by it" (7).

> "It does not merely use narrative as an accepted
> form. It is itself narrative through and through.
> It has no philosophical system as an accompanying
> alter ego whose language can express abstractly what
> it says concretely. What it says can be said only
> in the form of its own narrative and what follows."(8)

It is this concern to assimilate as far as possible the creation accounts to other biblical narratives that is dominant in his naming them "saga", and I have already referred to this as Barth's search for a genre that recognises both an imaginative element and realistic depiction (9).

Barth's inclusion of "Geschichtswirklichkeit" in his definition of saga might lead one to think that he makes truth claims on the basis of his definition. He is careful not to do this. In his arguments for accepting the creation narratives as descriptions of reality he relies on two related propositions: that their content is God (10) (and only the Holy Spirit can confirm this (11)); and that they are in harmony with the rest of the Bible (12). His concern in §41.1 could be summarised as that of giving directions on how to read Scripture theologically (13). He always concludes that the Holy Spirit is indispensable for this, but this does not exclude a defence of his reading on literary-critical grounds. His aim, like that of a literary critic (at least part of the time), is to

> "let the text say what it wants to say, and thus to
> mediate any profitable perceptions" (14).

This leaves no room for historical criticism (15) or science (16) to provide data for theological reflection on the text. He concentrates on that meaning of the text which can only be given by the narrative, and §41.2, 3 give his exposition of Genesis 1, 2 and his reflection on it.

The most important thing that he finds when he reads the narrative of the creation is that it does not just tell of happenings but of God who made them happen. Here Barth's literary reading focuses on the character of the Actor in the narrative. His first reason for distinguishing these sagas from the ensuing history is that they do not tell of "creaturely occurrence in its creaturely context", but that their "only content is God the Creator" (17). That the meaning of the narratives is the knowledge of God as Creator is crucial to Barth's exegesis, and is the main point of §41. This is his way of avoiding seeing the content either as meaningless or as a "revealed cosmosophy" (18) (and thereby avoiding the major modern controversy over Genesis).

It is by pointing to God as the subject of the creation narrative, the "Lord and Ruler of this history" (19) (and then later in the volume, in §42.1, 2 and 3, making basic God's affirmative verdict on all creation as it is given by the saga) that Barth can claim that that history "encloses all other history" (20), and that "even as I exist I find myself at the centre of this history" (21). Thus the narratives evoke a sphere outside which we cannot go to have a vantage point (22), and which

> "has a genuine horizon which cannot be transcended...
> (which is the divine will and utterance and activity)."

The function of the creation narratives in telling who God is by what he does and says is also Barth's way of connecting them with the rest of the Bible for God is common to many genres. "The one and only thing" that the creation saga seeks to exhibit is God and his activity, and so the natural context for interpretation is the whole Bible (23). Barth sees a turn away from this to allegedly more general contexts of meaning taking place since the close of the 17th century (24). His reversal of this trend once again offers the Bible as the overarching world of meaning, and this functions as an exegetical equivalent of Anselm's "quo maius cogitari non potest", the subject of both the Bible and Anselm's definition being God (25).

"World" and "sphere" do not, however, do justice to the temporality of the Bible.

> "No less than everything depends upon the truth of the
> statement that God's creation takes place as history
> in time." (26)

This is "the overflow of his inner glory", and Barth's contention that the narratives which tell us about God are irreducibly temporal is reflected in his understanding of God's temporality. His principle of sola scriptura together with his recognition of the temporal nature of biblical truth leave him no option but to state that

> "God in His eternity is the beginning of time.... If
> we are not prepared to venture this statement, we will
> have to take back all that has been said about the
> historicity of creation." (27)

He even says that God's eternity, which is the unity of the past, present and future, and the source of our time, is "the essence of God Himself"(28). But our time is now "lost time" (29), and real time is the time of grace, "the true prototype of all time" (30).

> "Real time, in this case, is primarily the life-
> time of Jesus Christ, the turning point, the trans-
> ition, the decision which were accomplished in His
> death and resurrection, together with the time pre-
> ceding and following this event in the history of
> Israel and the existence of the Christian Church." (31)

The time of creation is the reflection of the time of grace, even though it precedes it, and so it too is "real time in the supreme sense" (32).

So Barth has a hierarchy of times, and therefore a hierarchy of stor-ies, with the lifetime of Jesus Christ at the top, and other time deriving its reality from this. This is where the essence of God enters history, where the character of God is revealed in Christ, and so the goal of all exegesis. Time is unified in one story centred in Christ, the Lord of time, and this unity is Barth's answer to the temporal disorientation of modern man.

I have summarised the role of Barth's discussion of saga as being to justify his way of reading the biblical narratives, and in the process to:

> rule out scientific data and historical criticism as ir-
> relevant, thus limiting which questions may be asked of
> the text and claiming that the text tells its own story;

> point to the rendering of God in temporal form as the aim
> of the creation saga and therefore a positive guide to
> questions to be put to the text;

> claim that this gives a horizon of truth, in irreducibly
> temporal form (33), which cannot be transcended and which
> rules out a mythical interpretation;

> and to connect the creation saga with the rest of the
> Bible on the basis of form and content.

There is, however, one further role which the discussion of saga plays: it suggests the way in which the truth of the saga may be appropriated. The indispensability of the Holy Spirit is understood throughout, and Barth underlines in a remarkable way the importance of subjective appropriation:

> "It may well be said that it is in the Holy Spirit that the
> mystery of God's trinitarian essence attains its full pro-
> fundity and clarity.... We may say in a word that it is in
> God the Holy Spirit that the creature as such pre-exists."(34)

The discussion of saga, however, points to a particular means of appropriat- ion, the use of one's imagination. He makes an epistemological claim for the imagination against

> "a ridiculous and middle class habit of the modern Western
> mind which is supremely phantastic in its chronic lack of
> imaginative phantasy" (35).

That bad habit must be given up in order to have a chance of understanding the creation sagas.

> "Imagination, too, belongs no less legitimately to the
> human possibility of knowing. A man without an imagin-
> ation is more of an invalid than one who lacks a leg."(36)

"Spiritual invalids" should not be allowed to dictate in which form the Bible may express its truth. Imagination is clearly necessary if I am to wake up to the fact that the world of the Bible is the real world, and that

> "even as I exist I find myself at the centre of this
> history" (37).

Barth's defence of the imagination both in composing (38) and under- standing saga is an important recognition of both the logic of his literary analysis and the importance of cultural conditioning. It calls to mind what Wicker says about novels helping us to understand the Bible (39), and suggests again that Barth's literary criticism acts as a praeparatio evangelica in a way similar to natural theology in other systems.

My final point about §41.1 is that it also deals briefly with two applications of his way of reading the Bible which Barth treats at length elsewhere: the problem of the two accounts of creation (40), and the comparison and contrast of the creation and resurrection narratives (41). He says of the two accounts of creation that

> "seen from the point of view of the other, each of
> these accounts reveals painful omissions and ir-
> reconcilable contradictions",

and that they cannot be harmonised to reveal a "historical" substratum (42). Barth, as usual, concludes from the fact of contradiction not that either account is untrue, but that it is wrong to suppose that the truth of these narratives is to be measured by an alleged historical reference. Rather they are reflected upon as in §41.2, 3, and their structure provides the form in which he presents the whole relationship of creation and covenant.

He thinks that the nature of creation rules out any historical account at all - it is pure saga; but for the resurrection he does allow that "the historical ('historische') element is not wholly extinguished" (43). This grading of the historicity of events (miracles, in turn, are taken to be more "historical" than the resurrection) (44) I interpret as the result of literary discrimination, not of any critical historical consideration. Most New Testament miracles are recounted in a realistic manner (45); the resurrection itself is not described at all, but is an event in the course of a realistic narrative; but creation can have no context of human characters and events in interaction. Yet the creation narrative does present God acting, and Barth seizes on this in order to employ his exegetical method of showing what sort of person is portrayed in a story.

Furthermore, the saga form of the accounts of creation is, like that of the resurrection, significant for men primarily through its serving the "realism of assessment" in relation to the story of the covenant. For example, in the first account, God's verdict is given both by his saying that creation is good, and by his act of resting on the seventh day (46). This verdict is the justification of the transition to the rest of the doctrine of creation. So just as the resurrection is The Verdict of the Father in §59.3 and necessitates the inclusive christology of the rest of C.D.IV.1 (47) so §42 is called The Yes of God the Creator, and leads into the anthropological discussion in the rest of C.D.III.

§42 indeed shows how closely Barth's doctrine of creation is bound to his method of exegesis. For its major theme is that creation is justified only by God's self-revelation (primarily in Jesus Christ, but prefiguratively in creation) (48). Barth even denies that there is any other proof of the reality of creation than God's self-disclosure (49). The proof, however, is of course given through Scripture, which must, in order to support such theology, be construed as disclosing the self of God, and also as giving a world of meaning which nothing in creation can challenge. Barth's resulting des-

cription of the self of God as an identity involving a decisive verdict on
the nature of reality is his great weapon in §42 for reversing the post-
Enlightenment man-centred world-view. Descartes' God, he says, is "hope-
lessly enchained within the mind of man" (50). For Descartes' thinking self
(and for all the other subject-centred epistemologies since Descartes) Barth
tries to substitute the self of God, and he bends his literary exegetical
skills to describing this self and the world of meaning of which God is the
centre (51).

(ii)

When Barth in §41.2, <u>Creation as the External Basis of the Covenant</u>,
does detailed exegesis of the first creation saga his most general principle
is to take literally what the saga says, and then to reflect on it theologically. An example is the celestial ocean (52). Barth praises 17th century
orthodoxy for taking the ocean literally but criticises it because it had not

> "understood theologically the individual data which it
> had correctly established and maintained exegetically" (53).

Orthodoxy's mistake was to try to see the statement in Genesis as natural
science, but Barth is interested only in

> "what function is ascribed by Gen. 1 and the rest of the
> Bible to these waters <u>supra firmamentum</u>..." (54).

The issue is where one is to look for the meaning referred to in the text.
Barth claims that its only context of meaning is the Bible, and so, apart
from pointing to its function in the Bible, he rules out attempts to justify
the literal meaning. In the case of the celestial ocean Barth can therefore
grant that the saga uses "the view of myth, or of ancient natural science"
(55), but he sees the meaning elsewhere, on two levels: that the world is
threatened by a dangerous higher power; but

> "to be precise, however, the sage is not interested in
> this metaphysical danger as such, but in its repulsion
> by God's creative Word, and therefore in the fact that
> man and the lower cosmos are protected and guarded
> against it...that there is no infinite threat" (56).

In this way the focus is changed from orthodoxy's empirical celestial ocean
to an assurance of God's providence. The ocean has been taken literally in
both interpretations, but for Barth it is enough that it is a real element
in the saga, and beyond this no further verification is needed in order to
understand its truth. The meaning of the text is not that the ocean exists
in some real world behind the saga. The saga's world must be seen in its
integrity and theological conclusions drawn from what is seen there.

The preservation of the integrity of the saga's world makes Barth insist on admitting even its more unlikely features as the data for his reflections: creation in seven days; creation of light and vegetation before
the sun and stars; the decree of vegetarianism; and the rest of God on the

110

seventh day. There are frequent pleas to let the saga say what it wants to
say (57).   The saga, however, is brief, and its implications must be extended by following the history of its key words in the Bible: darkness,
light, heaven, earth, waters, the heavenly bodies, fish, fowl, animals,
leviathan, the image of God, are all treated in this way.

One question about this procedure is whether it does from a different
source what Barth accuses apologists and historical critics of doing: reading
alien elements into the story. Barth's claim, as becomes even clearer in
§41.3, is that his are the only external elements which are not alien, because the saga and the history of the covenant are intimately related within
the same world of meaning. The unity of the Bible is that it reveals God.
The saga is proclamation, not scientific or philosophical theory (59). As
he said in §41.1, its content is God. His theological conclusions do not
therefore depend on adding together the results of his study of the words
and images of the saga, and it does not jeopardise his theology if there
are mistakes in his philology. The only fatal danger would be if it could
be shown that the saga intends a different God. The answer to the question
about reading alien elements into the saga is therefore that Barth sees himself drawing on other stories about the same person in order to illuminate
his character in this saga. The details of the saga are as important for
understanding the character as is the portrayal of speech, action and in-
cident in a novel or play. That is why, in our opening example, Barth would
not think he was generalising or reading too much into the celestial ocean
by taking it as referring primarily to God's providence.

Granted that Barth sees the account of creation in Gen. 1 being theologically meaningful only as the external basis of the covenant, it is not
surprising what he emphasises.

The main focus is, as I have said, on God, and discussion of the Word
of God, of the incarnation and of the trinity arise out of exegesis of the
saga (59).

The works of God are reflected upon in their role in the covenant history, and one theme which is important for Barth's theological method is
that creation guarantees that certain signs and images important in the covenant history are inherently suited to their role. "Waters" are not merely
an image, but

> "they fully participate as an image in the actuality of a
> higher order which is the theme of the history of Israel"(60).

And on the heavenly bodies:

> "The cognitive relationship obviously present in the Old
> Testament corresponds to an ontological and factual dis-
> closed in Gen. 1.14f. in connection with Gen. 1.26 f." (61)

Barth means that God creates in the foreknowledge that his works are to
function as meaning-bearers in the covenant, and so that story (and not
science or comparative religion or common sense) is the court of appeal
for the meaning of the saga's terminology.

Besides God and the works of God, special attention is paid to time.
It occurs in discussing the first, fourth and seventh days. "Everything
depends on the fact that what is in question in this passage (Gen. 1.3) is
concretely our time." (62) But the way in which everything depends on this
is not that it might conceivably be proved that creation took more than a
week and thus that Genesis is right or wrong in an empirical assertion, but
that Gen. 1.3 is "a proclamation of the meaning of history" (63). Time is
the form of God's work (64), a sequence of particular events leading up to
a climax, and the whole is God's form of self-expression in creation. When
Barth deals with the Sabbath as the climax of creation he notes that hte
narrative form is especially suited to this mode of God's self-expression:

> "What the biblical witness has to say is not a
> contribution to an abstract concept of God but a
> narration.... What God was in Himself, and had done
> from eternity, He had now in a sense repeated in
> time, in the form of an historical event, in His
> relationship to His creation, the world and man;
> and the completion of all creation consisted in the
> historical event of this repetition." (65)

This is what makes it meaningful to speak of God's immanence (66), and
the exposition in the following pages argues that the Sabbath is the hinge
of the relation of nature to grace, the link between creation and covenant,
the summing up of creation and the prefiguring of the resurrection. That the
climaxes of the creation and reconciliation should be related figuratively
shows the role of the interpretation of biblical narrative in determining
the relationship of these two major doctrines.

Inherent in the concept of time is that of sequence, and several of
Barth's reflections on the saga come from treating its order of events as
a way in which it gives its message: that light is created before the
heavenly bodies; that animals and man are created in the same day, but with
man as the climax of the first six days (so that all creation has man as its
goal but it also has an independent life of its own); that the Sabbath is
the completion of creation and man's first day.

Barth's focus is thus on introducing the biblical world of meaning
(God, creatures, language, time), and in particular on the nature of that
world as a continuous history, the truth of which is conveyed in narrative.
It conceives that world as, in Stern's phrase, a "total novel" whose divine
authorship guarantees its coherence and invites such tasks as the search for
thematic images.

The two chief factors in the biblical history are God and man, and where
the saga touches their relationship and nature Barth finds its chief message:

> "The phrase 'in our image' is obviously the decisive insight
> of the saga, for it is repeated twice." (67)

Barth's controversial exegesis amounts to finding confirmation of a structure
of relationship which he also finds in less controversial places. He decides
that:

"The tertium comparationis, the analogy between God and
man, is simply the existence of the I and the Thou in
confrontation. This is first constitutive for God and
then for man created by God." (68)

The control on his exegesis is explicitly what the rest of the Bible
says about God. He looks for the content of the image of God in the history
of Israel:

"The image of God, and therefore the divine likeness of
man, is revealed in God's dealings with Israel and therefore in the history of Israel." (69)

The goal of this history is Jesus Christ, who is the image of God made visible:

"The invisible God Himself has become visible in Him.
In Him we have the image in face of which the question
of the original is finally answered." (70)

Barth's discovery of multiple patterns of meaning in the O.T. which all point
to Jesus Christ will play a greater role in §41.3.

Now I wish to make one comment on his interpretation of "image". A
convincing argument can be made against his conclusion that the image of God
is the relationship between man and woman, and most commentators differ from
him (71). Yet Barth's typological hierarchy ensures that an attack on those
of his theological conclusions which appeal to Gen. 1.27 would have to include far more than a rejection of this piece of exegesis, and this is in
line with the lack of doctrinal weight given to the creation narratives as
a whole.

My final point about §41.2 takes up a criticism already made in Chapter
5 above and continues my critique of Barth's method by internal criteria.
One danger of Barth's method is that the literal content of a text will be
violated by the figurative meaning or by being inappropriately pressed into
service to show the nature of God. Both of these appear to happen in what
he says about the problem of a "Golden Age" in Gen. 1. Barth says that the
saga tells of a "Golden Age" only "between the lines" (72). In face of the
"it was so" of the saga he relies on his distinction between pre-history and
history. He claims that because the saga describes pre-history the "it was
so" cannot refer to any activity of the creature (which would be history),
but must only refer to God's permission and command that it be so. The pre-
historical era is one

"in which strictly speaking - and the saga confines itself to this - the question can only be that of God's
permission and command and not of the corresponding
activity and existence of the creature, so that it cannot be the object of a pictorial representation" (73).

Pictorial representation of post-history is permitted, as in Is. 11.6b, Hos.
2.18 and Is. 65.25 (74). The distinction here seems to be that whereas post-
history must portray the redemption and perfection of the creature (in which

the creature is to participate) in order to give a prophetic picture as an
object of hope, pre-history is not so much a picture of events (that might
move "the reader to homesickness instead of hope, and therefore to an optim-
istic view of human origins" (75)) as a "reminder of God's original will"(76).
This reminder does not mean that the saga

> "intends to speak of an original excellence of the existence
> of the creature. Like the sayings about the divine likeness
> of man and his rule on earth, this permission and command
> with the involved prohibition, and therefore the prospect
> of creation as the kingdom of peace, will have to be under-
> stood decisively as a promise whose fulfilment is to be
> sought beyond the immediate horizon of the passage."(77)

Barth here deduces the intention of the saga from his reading of the
rest of the Bible, and has nothing at all in the saga's words to go on. He
appears to ignore what he has said about the nature of saga being to portray
real events in time, and instead to see this saga as a way of telling us the
original will of God. Whereas the category of pre-history was earlier used
only as a way of letting the saga speak for itself without the hindrance of
historicist prejudice, now it is used to make a new distinction between the
saga and the rest of the Bible. Without this change of meaning Barth would
have to grant that the saga speaks in the form of recollection, not of promise, and seems quite prepared to risk homesickness. There is nothing in the
text to justify the theological conclusion that Barth wants to draw (i.e.
that it is really intended as a promise), and so he falls back on an appeal
to its genre which his previous definition does not support. In this case
the pre-history told by the saga has been assimilated completely into a
description of God and his will, and the saga's function is dictated by the
rest of the Bible and not by its own text.

(iii)

The nature of Gen. 2 with which §41.3 deals, makes it an extreme test
case of Barth's method of handling biblical narrative. It is a narrative,
but temporality is not important. (Barth says it must be presupposed(78).)
Its details make a composite picture whose meaning is partly symbolic (e.g.
the four rivers from one) and Barth says that it should be called sacramental,
in contrast to the prophetic view of Gen. 1 (79). Its claim to particularity
is strained by what Barth grants: That Eden, for example, is a "semi-concrete" geographical location (80), and that it is imaginative construction(81).

Yet being extreme it is also instructive about what is essential to
Barth. The theological conclusions which he draws from the narrative are
about the nature of God, the nature of man (this turns out to be the nature
of Jesus Christ), the importance of the I - Thou relationship (seen supremely
as God's relationship with man in Christ), and various statements about freedom, sex, marriage, good and evil and man's dependence upon grace. He arrives
at them after literal and typological exegesis. It is crucial for this process that the particularities of the text should be real in their own right
as well as being prefigurative. So Barth is concerned to uphold the particularity of Eden as a place on the same level of reality as other places (82),

while eliminating any concern for its verifiability (the question must be dropped as soon as it is raised (83)). Symbolism (84) and allegory (85) are also ruled out, so that one is left with a picture that is composed imaginatively and grasped imaginatively, and which refers primarily to the covenant history, but which is yet held to refer to a particular, though inaccessible, place. In other words, Barth insists that the saga be allowed to dictate its own realm of reality called pre-history, in which there can be semi-concrete reality, and whose meaning is missed if it is taken as being in a different realm from other places. As to his criteria of reality, his combination of literal and prefigurative exegesis is crucial. He says that the saga's reality can only be tested against that of the covenant history and especially of Jesus Christ. Jesus Christ is the supreme particularity and gives that concept its justification in Barth's theology. The prefigurative particularities of creation are only shown to be "real" when they correspond to those of reconciliation, but in this light their reality is assured:

> "If the Christian reading of the paradise saga is valid,
> its reference - and therefore the reference of the history
> of Israel prefigured in it - is to a reality." (86)

This way of assessing the reality of the saga goes with seeing the unity of the Bible in a certain way. In his literal exegesis he argues about the sense of the words, and a frequent reason for his rejection of other theologians' interpretations is that they are "foreign to the passage" (87). Yet for important theological conclusions the context is always the whole Bible, and his arguments show how he sees it s unity.

In my Appendix to this chapter I present the rest of my detailed analysis of Barth's exegesis of Genesis 2. There I show how Barth unifies the discordant accounts of Gen. 1 and 2 by reference to their common subject, God. This bias towards seeing the stories on the model of an "Entwicklungsroman" is supported by the use of patterns found in the narrative to show God's identity and so go beyond the literal meaning to the "objective" content. Barth's typological method is revealed as a device for maintaining the perspective discussed above in Chapter 4. This methodological centring of exegesis on the master pattern, Jesus Christ, in whose story the literal and deeper meanings coincide (and so the "exegetical buck" stops there) is Barth's way of maintaining the function of the O.T. in a christocentric theology. In place of a "systematic principle" he uses a method which involves continual literary discernment.

In the course of this chapter many points from previous chapters have been confirmed and developed, in particular Barth's use of the same methods for understanding the Genesis sagas and the realistic narratives used in C.D.IV.1 and II.2. Yet signs of strain in the method were plain. Barth's weakness for the "Entwicklungsroman" tendency of the main character to "swallow up the background" was abetted by the lack of human actors in the story; his equivocation over the "Golden Age" was about whether the narrative represented a promise present only in the will of God or a concrete recollection; and the extraordinary concept of "semi-concreteness" was said to derive its reality somehow from the central character identical with God, Jesus Christ. In the event, however, little theological weight was placed on the "concreteness" of the saga: it served on the one hand to help render a picture of God which needs the evidence of other parts of the Bible and emerges far more naturally there, and on the other hand as material for the lowest level of a typological hierarchy.

Finally, what is the effect of Barth's exegesis of Genesis 1 and 2 on our perception of his overarching story? The creation sagas have an obvious function: they give the necessary introduction to the story of the coven- ant, even though they are of a different genre and are composed imaginatively and retrospectively from a position within the covenant history. Yet Barth's presentation of them greatly weakens the "sense of a beginning" which they had in the traditional Christian scheme. His emphases are not on anything intrinsic to the sagas but on their correspondence with God's will and with the history of Jesus Christ. These indicate where Barth relocates the sense of a beginning: in election (which, as Chapter 5 showed, is supported by stories other than those of creation) and in its historical consequence, the incarnation (cf. his understanding of Christmas (88)). The first of these points to the beginning in the Author of the story, the second to the begin- ning of the realistic story in which all other stories have their figural place. This concentration is Barth's innovation in the traditional world of meaning.

(1) Cf. Patrides, op. cit., passim.

(2) pp.ix-x.

(3) The most comprehensive critique of Barth on this is by J.-F. Konrad, Abbild und Ziel der Schöpfung. Untersuchungen zur Exegese von Gen. 1 und 2 in Barths Kirchlicher Dogmatik III.1 (Tübingen 1962).

(4) For an assessment of the literature on saga in Barth see Helmut Zwanger's unpublished Tübingen dissertation of 1974, Sage und Mythos in Karl Barths Kirchlicher Dogmatik. Ein Beitrag zum Verständnis Barthscher Hermeneutik.

(5) III.1.81. ("Ein divinatorisch-dichterisch Bild einer konkret einmaligen, zeitlich-räumlich beschränkten praehistorischen Geschichtswirklichkeit" - S. 88.)

(6) Ib., p. 84.

(7) Ib., p. 86.

(8) Ib., p. 87.

(9) See above Chapter 4, p.

(10) E.g. ib., pp. 78, 86, 87, 90, 92.

(11) Ib., p. 93.

(12) Ib., pp. 43 f., 86, 92.

(13) Cf. ib., pp. 79, 90.

(14) Ib., p. 64.

(15) Ib., p. 79.

(16) Ib., p. 64.

(17) Ib., p. 78, cf. p. 64.

(18) Ib., p. 61.

(19) Ib., p. 44.

(20) Ib., p. 60.

(21) Ib., p. 65.

(22) Ib., p. 65.

(23) Ib., pp. 65, 86.

(24) Ib., p. 65.

(25) Cf. on the reversal, above Chapter 4, pp. 49 ff. and Chapter 5, p. 74.

(26) Ib., p. 69.

(27) Ib., p. 68.

(28) Ib., p. 67.

(29) Ib., p. 72.

(30) Ib., p. 76.

(31) Ib.

(32) Ib.

(33) Cf. Chapter 8 below.

(34) Ib., p. 56.

(35) Ib., p. 81.

(36) Ib., p. 91.

(37) Ib., p. 45.

(38) Cf. his comments on saga and invention in C.D.IV.2, pp. 478 ff.

(39) Above, Chapter 4, pp. 51 f.

(40) Ib., p. 80.

(41) Ib., pp. 78 f.

(42) Ib., p. 80.

(43) Ib., p. 79, S. 85.

(44) Ib., p. 78.

(45) Cf. Frei, The Eclipse of Biblical Narrative, op. cit., p. 14.

(46) III.1 pp. 213 ff. Barth in fact sees the Sabbath as corresponding to the resurrection (p. 228, cf. C.D.III.4, pp. 53, 57).

(47) See above, Chapter 3.

(48) E.g. II.1, pp. 378 ff.

(49) Ib., pp. 344 ff.

(50) Ib., p. 360.

(51) Yet the God of Scripture too must be safeguarded from imprisonment in
      the mind of man, and Barth later states Scripture's origin and history
      to be specially providential - C.D.III.3, pp. 200 ff.

(52) III.1, pp. 137 ff.

(53) Ib., p. 138.

(54) Ib.

(55) Ib., p. 139.

(56) Ib.

(57) E.g. ib., pp. 125-6, 221.

(58) Ib., p. 126.

(59) Ib., pp. 114 ff., 191 ff.

(60) Ib., p. 168.

(61) Ib., p. 164.

(62) Ib., p. 126.

(63) Ib.

(64) Ib., p. 130.

(65) Ib., p. 216.

(66) Ib.

(67) Ib., p. 183.

(68) Ib., p. 185.

(69) Ib., p. 200.

(70) Ib., p. 202.

(71) The best refutation, combining exegetical and theological points, which
      I have found is by John McIntyre, op. cit., pp. 109 ff.

(72) III.1, p. 210.

(73) Ib., p. 211.

(74) Ib., pp. 211-2.

(75) Ib., p. 212.

(76) Ib., p. 211.

(77) Ib., p. 212.

(78) Ib., p. 240.

(79) Ib., p. 233.

(80) Ib., p. 252.

(81) Ib., p. 253.

(82) Ib., p. 252.

(83) Ib., p. 253.

(84) Ib., p. 317.

(85) Ib., p. 319.

(86) Ib., p. 276.

(87) Ib., p. 325.

(88) See above, Chapter 2, p. 25.

Exegesis of Genesis 1 and 2

The unity Barth seeks is not one which requires that Genesis 1 and 2 be harmonised in detail. Barth is content that the second saga

> "does not contradict the first and that it has the same
> pre-historical event in view; that it deals with the
> same God on the one hand and the same man and world on
> the other; thus the same relationship exists between
> the Creator and the creature in the act of creation, and
> the same connection of this act with the purpose and
> work of God after creation." (1)

The key phrase there is "the same God", and in what follows creation is seen as an expression of who God is:

> "This is creation to the extent that it makes the
> creature the exponent, sign and witness of the divine
> meaning and necessity." (2)

This revelation of who God is is also the ground for unity with the rest of the Bible, and Barth says that the use of the name Yahweh Elohim in Genesis 1.6b is "decisive for all that follows" (3). This name is "the key to the peculiar orientation of this creation saga", of which the theological explanation is that it embraces creation and covenant, the law and mercy of God, the foundation of the world and of Israel, man and elected man, and in each case

> "in the first of those elements we have pattern of the
> second" (4).

Barth here has passed from claiming that the same God is at work in both to discerning this identity in a similarity in the patterns of his works.

In Genesis 2 he finds various patterns corresponding to patterns in the covenant history and in the N.T. One is that of God giving life to Adam in two stages (selecting and forming the dust, and then breathing in life) which corresponds to the election of Abraham and the gift of a prophetic spirit to his seed, and to Ex. 37, which is fulfilled in Christ's resurrection.

This exegesis is part of an excursus supporting an argument which concludes with the christological meaning of the creation of Adam. The importance of the patterns as a way of going beyond literal exegesis is clear there. Barth can grant that the saga gives "a childlike description of human existence" and that it is a childlike "magnifying of the state of the husbandman, his divine election and call", but he continues:

> "It is inherently improbable, however, that these
> themes explain the origination or even the adoption
> of this account into the Old Testament sphere. Behind

these prefigurative pictures, which have their own
meaning as such, there stands the whole of Old Testament
anthropology." (5)

Barth is not, however, suggesting that a general anthropology is given,
and the corresponding patterns in Israel's history are (as the excursus
shows) crucial in proving that

"behind this anthropology as such there stands directly -
conditioned and predestined by the will and act of Yahweh
Elohim - the election and calling of Israel, its existence and position within the world of nations to which
it belongs..." (6)

This he claims to be the "subjective content" of the passage (7), which means
that the author was writing from within the covenant history, and so had such
things in mind. But he wants to go beyond this to the "objective" meaning of
the passage: that it points to Jesus Christ. He says that to see this is a
matter of faith:

"If we do not deny but believe this we shall have to
press on to a final and deepest meaning of the content
of the passage." (8)

Yet faith does have something in the text to go on, and the way in which
Barth sees the connection is in the twofold pattern of Jesus' life: fulfilling
Genesis 2 and Israel's hope by being fully a creature and fully for God,
humiliated and exalted, a pattern basic in C.D.IV.1, 2.

Another part of Genesis 2 which turns out to have "a final, objective
christological meaning" (9) is Eden with its two central trees. Again, a
subjective meaning in relation to Israel and, secondarily, to general
anthropology, is given. Eden is the type of the Promised Land, and the two
trees are

"the type of the order in which Yahweh Elohim and His
revelation will encounter man, and in which man will
always and everywhere encounter Him." (10)

But in Israel's history the two trees have their unity divided into the two
components of Gospel and Law, and

"everything now seems to be designed for the man who
has eaten of the tree of Knowledge" (11).

Israel's history leads to death, and, if it is taken as self-enclosed, does
not appear to correspond to Eden. Eden is either a "grandiose illusion"(12)
or else it is shown by the Christian answer to correspond to Israel's history.
Apart from Jesus Christ

"we really have to doubt the unity and therefore the
reality of the whole" (13).

In Christ the covenant is fulfilled and there is "only one tree instead of two". What Barth has done is to see the trees as part of a unified story whose end was envisaged at its beginning, and the patterns of Genesis 2 are discovered, concealed and distorted, in Israel's history only because that history is taken as fulfilled by Christ.

The main example of a pattern in Genesis 2 being found in Israel's history and the N.T. is the relationship of man and woman. Barth notes a common denominator between Genesis 2 and the Song of Songs: that both deal with the delight of man and woman with each other without mentioning parenthood (14). The Song (with Genesis 2) is not treated as symbolic (15), nor as allegorical - "It says exactly what it says" (16), - nor as a love song that has strayed into the Bible. A place is found for it in the context of Israel's history because it is in the Bible and exhibits a pattern of relationship between man and woman which corresponds to that of Genesis 2, to that between God and Israel as seen by the prophets, according to God's election (the last mentioned is "the unattainable prototype of what is realised in the human sphere between husband and wife" (17)), and finally to that between Christ and the Church. The concept of an ordo essendi is important here: God's election of Israel, which includes that of Jesus Christ, is the primary reality, and is the raison d'être for love and marriage, whose "total form" is expressed in Genesis 2 and the Song. That expression of the total form is itself prophetic of its realisation in Jesus Christ. In between comes the history of Israel, and

> "the covenant which in its historical reality was
> broken by Israel" (18).

There the pattern is violated, and Barth contends that it would seem totally irreconcilable with Genesis 2 were it not for Jesus Christ. Barth says of Eph. 5.32:

> "If this is accepted, it cannot be denied that even the
> obscure language of the creation saga takes on a wholly
> different form and colour acquiring indeed a very con-
> crete meaning." (19)

He proceeds to interpret the statements of Genesis 2.18 ff., with aspects of Christ's life and work being seen as their raison d'être. This is an unusually detailed example of prefigurative interpretation, and its message for the ordo essendi is hammered home soon afterwards:

> "The fact that everything essential in the Old
> Testament along the lines of Gen. 2.18 f recurs in
> supreme concretion at the central point in the New
> is a clear indication that this is also the focal
> point of these Old Testament lines, and that they
> and their origin in Gen. 2 are really to be under-
> stood from this angle. If the man Jesus Christ is
> the fulfilment of what is prophesied in the Old
> Testament in respect of the husband of Yahweh, the
> questions which crowd in upon O.T. exegesis as such
> are not unanswerable.
>
> "When the O.T. gives dignity to the sexual re-
> lationship, it has in view its prototype, the divine

likeness of man as male and female, which in the plan
and election of God is primarily the relationship between Jesus Christ and His Church, secondarily the relationship between Yahweh and Israel, and finally, although very directly in view of its origin - the relationship between the sexes." (20)

Prefiguration is part of Barth's perception of this order in the biblical texts, his chief clue being the "lines" passing through Israel's history to Christ. Such lines are found by him in the most diverse O.T. texts,
but he sees the search especially justified in Genesis 2. There the creation of man and woman is

"the climax of his creation. But this irreversible
declaration is the quintessence of the whole history
of the covenant and salvation in both Old and New
Testaments. It is quite out of the question that
there should be no significance in the fact that,
wholly irrespective of its concrete content, it
forms the climax of the whole history of creation.
It is thus quite out of the question to read and
expound these verses properly without taking this
significance into consideration." (21)

That argument offers the form of the narrative and its position in the Bible
as the reason for beginning the search for other strata of meaning. The
decision to give great weight to the results of this search is crucial for
Barth's theological method, and in his exposition of Genesis 1 and 2 it is
the chief way in which he integrates creation into the structure of the
C.D.

(1)   III.1, p. 229.   But cf. p. 80 on the "irreconcilable contradictions"!

(2)   Ib., p. 230.

(3)   Ib., p. 234.   Cf. p. 267.

(4)   Ib., p. 240.

(5)   Ib., p. 238.

(6)   Ib., p. 228.

(7)   Ib., p. 239.

(8)   Ib.

(9)   Ib., p. 273.

(10) Ib., pp. 272 f.

(11) Ib., p. 274.

(12) Ib., p. 275.

(13) Ib.

(14) pp. 312 f.

(15) Ib., p. 319.

(16) Ib., p. 319.

(17) Ib., p. 318.

(18) Ib., p. 316.

(19) Ib., p. 321.

(20) Ib., p. 322.

(21) Ib., p. 326.

The central problem of traditional christology is the relation of divinity to humanity in Jesus Christ. Barth's conclusions on this are impec-
cably Chalcedonian, but his way of reaching them is his own, and this is the
subject of this chapter. Barth's fullest treatment of the two natures is
in C.D.IV.2, §64 The Exaltation of the Son of Man, and my analysis focuses
on that section.

Before I begin that, however, I want to draw attention to an important
recent study which supplements and supports mine, that by David Kelsey. He
has devoted part of a chapter of his book The Uses of Scripture in Recent
Theology (1) to Barth's §64.3 The Royal Man. He draws, as I do, on the work
of Hans Frei, and demonstrates how Barth has interpreted the Gospels as

> "having the logical force of identity-description of
> Jesus" (2).

Of particular relevance is his discussion of the role of the teaching and
miracles of Jesus in Barth's theology. He shows how they play their part
in describing Jesus' identity; they are not constitutive of it in the way
the passion, crucifixion and resurrection are, but they are, for Barth,
rather like anecdotal illustrations of what Jesus was like, they fall into
patterns which harmonise with the rest of the story in O.T. and N.T., and
they can be interpreted in a two-sided way as both human and (especially as
regards their sovereign freedom) divine. Kelsey's use of Frei also leads
him to the insight that for Barth the Bible is like

> "one vast, loosely-structured non-fictional novel",

so he endorses my attempt to draw out that parallel.

(i)

Kelsey's work leaves me free to confine myself now to showing how
Barth's arguments about the two natures of Christ are circular within the
Gospel story. Barth says that the novelty of his own christology lies in
his "actualizing" of the doctrine of the incarnation (3). This turns out
to mean a concentration on the event, or history, of Jesus Christ, which is
defined as his "birth and life and death" as "revealed in His resurrection",
but which also "takes place in every age" (4). I will argue that the effect
of the "actualization" of christology is not so much to solve as to by-pass
the traditional problems of the distinction and unity of the two natures of
Jesus Christ.

Whereas most traditional theologians had criteria of divinity and
humanity and applied them to the story of Jesus Christ, Barth refuses to
do this. He denies the possibility of humanity as such and of Godhead as
such, and so both must be found together in the story.

The existence of Godhead as such is denied from the sides both of election and of incarnation. In the doctrine of election the denial is in the form of a rejection of the idea of a λόγος ἄσαρκος (5): the human history is included within the divine election, and the humanity of Christ is said, like his deity, to be integral to the whole event (6). In the doctrine of the incarnation Barth preserves the divine initiative by accepting the <u>anhypostasis</u> of the human nature of Christ (7), and then, in support of the <u>unio hypostatica</u>, he says that "God himself speaks when this man speaks in human speech..." (8). But who is the God who thus speaks? Barth denies that "the human essence" is the subject of Jesus Christ's history, but also denies that the divine essence is, because

"The Godhead as such has no existence. It is not real. It has no being or activity." (9)

The subject therefore is Jesus Christ as presented in the New Testament (10). It is the denial of the Godhead as such which means that the story must be the highest court of appeal, with no other criterion of who God is.

Likewise, any independent norm for humanity is rejected (11). Barth can assert "the <u>humanum</u> of all men" (12) is in Jesus Christ brought into unity with God, but no criterion for the <u>humanum</u> is allowed except Jesus Christ, e.g.

"It is indeed unique that the existence of a man is this history and has this character. But it is not the case, and we must not state or complain, that it contradicts the concept of man which embraces us too. It only contradicts all other actualizations of this concept." (13)

The rejection of independent norms does not rule out making distinctions between humanity and divinity within the story, as in the list of human characteristics on p. 73. But these characteristics are immediately identified with the Son of God who became the Son of Man (14); in other words, the <u>communicatio idiomatum</u> is seen as the whole event of Jesus' life from birth to resurrection (15). This is typical of what is meant by "actualization": there is a refusal to try to define how the two natures affect each other, and instead one is directed to their unified action. Jesus Christ exists only in his act, and that act is an obviously human history (16), but in faith one also recognises it as the act of God (17), revealed by the resurrection (18).

The concept which Barth uses to explain how God and man can meet in Christ without divinity or humanity being violated is that of grace. Here again the problem of the two natures is by-passed by defining grace in terms of the story. Thus on the <u>communicatio gratiarum</u> he says:

"In the existence of this man we have to reckon with the identity of His action as a true man with the action of the true God. The grace which comes to human essence is the event of this action." (19)

The humanity is not violated because it has already been defined to suit the conclusion:

> "It is genuinely human in the deepest sense to live by
> the electing grace of God addressed to man. This is how
> Jesus Christ lives as the Son of Man." (20)

Grace is therefore used to explain the relation of Christ's two natures, but,
because it is defined in terms of the story which poses the problem, the
arguments are circular (21).

The communicatio operationum (22) is the culmination of Barth's doctrine
of the two natures of Christ, and there we see the expected result of the
method I have described, the exclusive focus on the history of Jesus Christ
as the eternal enactment of the natures of God and man.

Barth's way of interpreting the Gospel story strongly affirms the unity
of the two natures of Jesus Christ, and there is a necessary postscript to
this later in §64.2. On pp. 140 ff. Barth takes the resurrection and ascension as events in time and space, but denies that they add to Jesus' identity.
The reason, presumably, is that there would still be a danger of the separation of the two natures if Jesus' identity were to change after his death. So
Barth sees the resurrection and ascension as affirming that Jesus still lives
as the same person. Just as the rejection of the λόγος ἄσαρκος ensured that
the story's portrayal is valid from all eternity, so this interpretation ensures its validity to all eternity.

If the unity of Jesus Christ is in no danger, what of the distinction
between his divinity and humanity? Barth's arguments, as I have shown, do
not try to define two essences and then explain how they unite, but define
each essence by reference to the same story. The story is, however, seen
from different angles in each case, the main thrust of C.D.IV.1 being to
show how it identifies Jesus Christ as the Son of God, and of IV.2 being to
show him as the Son of Man. From each angle one looks at the same acts, but
sees them as the humiliation of God or as the exaltation of man. This involves a particular way of understanding action: that it can be seen as the
unity of two ordered levels. This is Barth's equivalent of primary and
secondary causality, but he does not argue for it philosophically (23); he
simply interprets the story from two sides. What looks like traditional
theorising on the two natures turns out to be an exhortation to interpret
the story in this way.

When Barth does this he finds not only two distinct natures but also
the absolute superiority and priority of the divine nature. This ordering
is clear when he writes about the communicatio operationum:

> "The one will of Jesus Christ is the eternal will
> of God and it is also - absolutely conformable for all
> its dissimilarity - the motivated human will ('der be-
> wegte Menschenwille') which determines the way of the
> human life as such." (24)

> "The divine will is still above and the human
> below." (25)

128

Barth's characteristic expression of the distinction of the two natures
is, therefore, through the concept of ordered levels discerned in acts in
which

> "the divine acquires a determination to the human, and
> the human a determination from the divine" (26).

This means that the understanding of humanity is dominated by a concept expressed variously as reflection, repetition, correspondence, echo, copy,
image or analogy, and this is upheld by exegesis which relies heavily on
the discernment of patterns.

Barth's whole theological structure depends upon such "ordnungsana-
logien". E. Jüngel's article "Die Möglichkeit Theologischer Anthropologie
auf dem Grunde der Analogie. Eine Untersuchung zum Analogieverständnis
Karl Barths" (27) shows this well in an exegesis of parts of C.D.III.2.
He lucidly sets out a system of correspondences: the relations within the
Trinity correspond to those between God and the man Jesus; those between
the man Jesus and man in general correspond to those of men to each other;
the latter in turn correspond to the relations within the Trinity, which
themselves again correspond to the relations between God the creator and
man in general; and within creation there are "Ordnungsverhältnisse" which
are related to Jesus' humanity. Two statements of Jüngel are especially
relevant to my argument: he warns against understanding the concepts of
order and analogy "antigeschichtlich" (28); and he says that the "Grund-
satz" is

> "Das sein des Menschen Jesus ist der Seins- und
> Erkenntnisgrund aller Analogie." (29)

The methodological correlate of these statements is the sort of exegesis I
describe in this thesis, finding correspondences within the "Geschichte"
and relating them all to the central "Geschichte" of Jesus Christ, understood as itself corresponding to the Urgeschichte in God.

(ii)

Barth's method of arriving at the irreversible ordering of God and man
poses problems about God and man. To the basic problem of how the union of
the two is possible at all Barth simply asserts that it is a mysterious fact,
inconceivable apart from our knowledge of its history (30). This very concentration on the story (or this actualisation of the doctrine of the incarnation) has consequences for what Barth can say about God. The absolute priority of divinity over humanity is expressed by the doctrine of election. That
too, as has been shown by Chapter 5 above, and by Barth's denial of a λόγος
ἄσαρκος , is dependent on the discernment of God's identity in certain stories: there is no decretum absolutum. As in II.2 Barth in IV.2 draws the consequences for the being of God, e.g. for his immutability (31), thus rejecting a traditional rule of thumb for distinguishing God in Jesus Christ. The
practical effect on Barth's method is to exclude non-literary bases for arguing: his theology stands or falls with his literary method of identifying
God.

As regards man, Henri Bouillard sees Barth's way of interpreting God as the prime agent as endangering man's true agency. He accuses Barth of "monoactualisme", the actionalist equivalent of monophysitism (32). His criticism (based on other volumes of the C.D. than IV.2) can be summed up as maintaining that Barth does not distinguish adequately between the orders of nature and grace, so that real human action is inconceivable in Barth's terms. But Barth's very definitions of "real" and "act" include two levels. For they only receive their content from the central character of a story who can be interpreted as fully God and fully man. This is not to refute Bouillard (which is only to say that it is not an answer to the whole problem of free will!) but to suggest that Barth's exegesis needs to be assessed here. His ontology of primary reality, secondary reality and nothingness(33) is supported by conclusions about the biblical stories and above all about the role and identity of Jesus Christ in them. The only proof (other than the invocation of the Holy Spirit) which he offers for his concept of action is that it is true to the Bible.

I will give an example of the sort of assessment possible by my criteria in order to test Bouillard's criticism. On pp. 184 ff. Barth interprets Jesus' compassion as being κατὰ θεόν : "He was on earth as God is in heaven" (34) - obviously with no suggestion of dichotomy. At the same time Jesus' relation to men's sufferings is described as follows: their misery

> "was more His than that of those who suffered it.
> He took it from them and laid it on Himself. In the
> last analysis it was no longer theirs at all, but His.
> He Himself suffered it in their place. The cry of
> those who suffered was only an echo. Strictly speaking,
> it had already been superseded. It was superfluous.
> Jesus had made it His own." (35)

This goes well beyond the meaning of ἐσπλαγχνίσθη , reading into it Barth's doctrine of the atonement. The dependence of human action and suffering on Jesus for their reality is an application of Barth's ontology. He does not mean to take human suffering less seriously, but to relate it to the "real world" told in the story of Jesus, where its significance is shown by comparison with what Jesus suffers, and where what Jesus suffers is also suffered by God. The comparison is not in terms of inherent or "natural" properties of the suffering, but by assigning different instances of suffering to places in an ordo essendi expressed in the metaphor of sound and corresponding echo.

This stands on its head a commonsense reading of the stories of Jesus having compassion, because they tell of Jesus as the one who responds, and although they were written in the knowledge of the crucifixion they do not try to relate themselves to it as Barth does. The difference between Barth's and the Gospels' viewpoints is clearest in how they treat time: "Strictly speaking, it had already been superseded." The apparent violation of the integrity of the narrative is completed by adding: "It was superfluous." This impression is supported by the phrase "only an echo".

Barth seems to be making a paradox and "scandal" where the Gospels have none. He wants to see Jesus' compassion as his action κατὰ θεόν and also as fully human, but apparently sees no way of doing this without

130

seeming to devalue human suffering other than Jesus'. There is no hint of
this in the Gospels. It is hard to conceive of any statement which one could
put into the stories of Jesus' compassion that would count as evidence that
the human sufferings are not superfluous. Barth's method of abstracting the
eternal identity of Jesus Christ from the Gospels is therefore invulnerable
to disproof from passages in those same Gospels. It thus is something with
the characteristics of those "general concepts" which he so often attacks.
For the trouble with general concepts is that they refuse to be governed
by the particularities of the story, and now Barth has made it impossible
to understand particularities such as Jesus' response to human suffering
in the way the narrative presents them. Bouillard could with justice complain here. Yet the criticism is different from Bouillard's, for I am
granting that Barth does wish to affirm genuine human action but fails to
prevent the literal sense of a text from being swallowed up by the typological. There have been similar instances in previous chapters and they
all represent distortions of his own method.

One further point before my conclusion is on Barth's decision in the
debate about the Lutheran emphasis on the communio naturarum and the Reformed
emphasis on the unio hypostatica (36). Barth gives qualified preference to
the Reformed position. In the terms of my discussion, what Barth does is to
accept the Reformed view in his insistence that the acting subject, whose
identity the story gives, is God in all his sovereignty, but he incorporates
the Lutheran concern by denying the Godhead to exist in abstraction from the
history of Jesus Christ. The Reformed were more concerned about the ordering
of man and God, the infinite qualitative difference in which all the initiative is on God's side; the Lutherans more about the unity of God and man in
Jesus Christ. It is perhaps because the method is biassed towards the Lutheran side (they were accused of monophysitism just as he is of "monoactualisme", and his use of the story as a portrayal of God's identity in human
terms makes difficult the distinction of humanity from divinity in action)
that he compensates by stressing with the Reformed the sovereignty of God
and his choosing to assume humanity.

If this chapter has given a sense of fuzziness about Barth's distinction
between humanity and divinity in Jesus Christ then it has reflected my view
of what is the case. His exposition cries out for equivalents of the traditional distinctions between God and man to be applied systematically, but this
is not done. Yet there is such a distinction, that between time and eternity,
which is implicit throughout. It is crucial for the distinction between
election and incarnation, for Barth's position on the λόγος ἄσαρκος for the
doctrine of analogy, for the degrees of reality (37), and for the Lutheran-
Calvinist dispute; and time was also an issue in the discussion of Jesus'
compassion. Chapter 2 has shown how far back a deep concern for this distinction goes in Barth's theology, and subsequent chapters have referred to
it too. It is a theme which Roberts' massive dissertation rightly sees to
be so central to the C.D. as to justify talking of a "temporal ontology" (38).
What Barth says in C.D.IV.2 takes for granted the fact that he has already
written his doctrine of God in II.1 and II.2 and his anthropology in III.2,
in each of which the theme of time and eternity was central. This suggests
itself as the chief structural principle of the C.D. and in particular as a
help in penetrating the fuzziness of IV.2; for Barth can define humanity as
temporality (39) and God as eternity (40). Further, he can say that the
resurrected Christ is where a man is revealed in the mode of God (41) and

where the paradox of time and eternity is resolved (42), and so we are directed back to the resurrection and so to our subject of biblical narrative interpretation. This leads in to the next chapter.

(1)   Philadelphia, 1975, Chapter 3, pp. 39 ff.

(2)   Ib., p. 45.

(3)   IV.2, pp. 105 ff.

(4)   Ib., p. 107.

(5)   Ib., pp. 33 ff.

(6)   Ib., p. 35.

(7)   Ib., pp. 44-50.

(8)   Ib., p. 51.

(9)   Ib., p. 65. ("Die Gottheit als solche ist eben kein Existierendes,
      kein Wirkliches, kein Seiendes und also auch kein Handelndes, das sich
      mit einem anderen Existierenden, Wirklichen, Seienden (aber das ist
      ja eben auch das menschliche Wesen nicht!) vereinigen könnte." - S.70)

(10) Ib., pp. 65 f.

(11) Ib., p. 26.

(12) Ib., p. 49.

(13) Ib., p. 95.

(14) Ib., p. 73.

(15) Ib., p. 75.

(16) E.g. ib., pp. 27-30.

(17) Cf. Barth's earlier rejection of Ebionite and Docetic christology
      because they miss this correct starting point:

> "But the starting point of synoptic thought which finds God in
> Jesus is the fact, disclosed to certain men, of the divine emis-
> sary as such, the unambiguous fact of the man, who was in their
> midst, teaching and healing, dying and rising again, as a reality
> which, as divine, did not first require to be opened up and inter-
> preted and asserted, but which called to their lips the confession,
> Thou art the Christ, the Son of the Living God! (Matt. 16.16)
> immediately, not as a synthetic but as an analytic statement.
> And the starting point of Johannine thought, which finds God in
> Jesus, was the fact, disclosed to certain men, of the divine mis-
> sion, message and revelation, which they found in Jesus 'grace
> and truth', 'resurrection and life', becoming events...." (I.1,
> p. 463).

(18) E.g. pp. 100, 107, 250, 299, 310. Cf. his approval of Bengel's verdict on the Gospels: _spirant resurrectionem_ (p. 132). Perhaps the clearest statement of the role of the resurrection in relation to the two natures is in _Jesus, Lord of Time_ in C.D.III.2. E.g.,

> "What implications has it for the being of Jesus in time that He was in time in this way too, as the Resurrected? ... The answer is that the particular content of the particular recollection of this particular time of the apostolic community consisted in the fact that in this time the man Jesus was manifested among them in the mode of God." (pp. 447 f.)

(19) Ib., p. 99. ("...dass wir es in der Existenz dieses Menschen mit der Identität seines Tuns als eines wahren Menschen mit dem Tun des wahren Gottes zu schaffen haben. Es ist also die dem menschlichen Wesen widerfahrende Gnade das Ereignis dieses Tuns." - S. 110.)

(20) Ib., p. 89.

(21) The grace of this event also brings about our discernment of its truth (ib., p. 100). On the circle between the Holy Spirit and the story see below Chapter 9.

(22) Ib., pp. 104 ff.

(23) But cf. §49.2 "The Divine Accompanying" in III.3 where he uses the particularity of revelation to correct philosophical notions, e.g. on Aquinas p. 133.

(24) IV.2, p. 116, S. 129.

(25) Ib., p. 116.

(26) Ib., p. 70.

(27) _Evangelische Theologie_, Heft 10, Okt. 1962, S. 535-57.

(28) Ib., S. 541, cf. S. 544.

(29) Ib., S. 538.

(30) E.g. IV.2, p. 40.

(31) Ib., p. 85.

(32) Op. cit., Vol. II, Pt. I, p. 122.

(33) Cf. on Judas, Chapter 5 above and especially the Appendix to that chapter. On nothingness in IV.2 see p. 367, where wrong choices are said to "derive from the kingdom of the dead which (Jesus Christ) closed, from the nothingness which he reduced to nothingness in His life".

(34) Ib., p. 184.

134

(35) Ib.

(36) Ib., pp. 66 ff.

(37) Cf. Appendix to Chapter 5.

(38) Op. cit., e.g. p. 475.

(39) E.g. III.2, p. 522.

(40) E.g. II.1, §31.3.

(41) Cf. III.2, pp. 447 f., quoted above, note 18.

(42) E.g. III.2, p. 449.

CHAPTER 8. GOD AND TIME

"The difference between those who think like Robbe-
Grillet and those who think like Norman Mailer is re-
markably like the difference diagnosed three hundred
years ago, by Pascal - 'the first modern man' - between
the mode of thinking of the philosophers and that of the
poets or storytellers. Pascal's famous opposition between the God of the Philosophers and the God of Abraham,
Isaac and Jacob is in the first place an opposition
between styles of language. But Pascal knew well enough,
as we do also, that the choice of style is also the
choice of a whole world view. When the poets and storytellers talked of God in the language of Mailer's
'savages', by way of metaphor, they were also choosing
its accompanying metaphysic. Whereas, when the philosophers, remote ancestors of Robbe-Grillet's liberated
man, spoke of Him they did so (if at all) in the soph-
isticated abstract language of geometrically-defined
objects and value-free physical laws. Now the baneful
intellectual dissociation which Pascal diagnosed as
afflicting Christianity in his own time is far from
cured today: indeed, its ravages are as evident as
ever." (1)

Barth's doctrine of God is perhaps the most thorough attempt in history
to present the God of the storytellers. In Chapter 2 I described his development towards a theology whose negative verdict on natural theology was balanced by a concentration on biblical stories. In Chapter 5 I examined in
detail one part of his doctrine of God and showed the extnet to which it is
dependent upon those stories; and all the other chapters have also had something to say on this subject. In this chapter I will further illustrate it
from C.D.I.1 and II.1 and will then discuss Barth's doctrine on a topic about
which philosophers too have had much to say, God's eternity.

(i)

The clearest and most accurate account of the relation of Barth's hermeneutics to his doctrine of God is in E. Jüngel's Gottes Sein ist im Werden
(2). He suggests that the whole C.D. is an exegesis of "Gott entspricht sich"
which is the "Ereignis der Selbstidentifikation Gottes" (3). He sees that
Barth's doctrine of God poses the hermeneutical problem

"in seiner Äussersten Konzentration. Das Sein Gottes
ist das hermeneutische Problem der Theologie. Genauer:
dass das Sein Gottes geht, ist das hermeneutische Problem
schlechthin." (4)

Jüngel's book can be taken as a tribute to the centrality of the interpretation of narratives in the C.D., and the commentator who has followed up the implications of this most comprehensively is Robert Jenson (5) who says bluntly that the plot of Jesus' story is for Barth the plot of God's being (6).

I will now make some remarks about Barth's doctrine of the Trinity adding detailed support in Appendix A to this chapter.

Claude Welch, in his comparison of Barth's doctrine of the Trinity with others in modern theology, makes a good case for the originality and strength of Barth's doctrine lying not in its conclusions or structure, but in the way it is grounded in revelation (7). He sees it avoiding both scriptural literalism (the "proof text" method) and rationalistic or quasi-rationalistic deduction of the doctrine (8). It is with this distinctiveness that I am concerned, and its result can be stated in many ways: that Barth "actualizes" the doctrine of God; that he achieves a radical integration of Deus in se and Deus revelatus; that his theology is christocentric; that the ontological and hermeneutical circles are one; that there is a primal history corresponding to Jesus' history; that there is nothing to be known of God "above", "behind" or "beyond" revelation; that the immanent and economic Trinity coincide; or that the concept of "repetition" is central in understanding the threefoldness of the Trinity.

Barth's scriptural basis itself is examined in Appendix A, the main points being that Barth describes the Trinity as an order in God expressed in the interrelation of crucifixion, resurrection and Pentecost; that his doctrine of appropriation is biassed towards christocentricity; and that the hermeneutical function of his concept of God's freedom is to enable him to assert God's transcendence in spite of his method's "scandal of particularity". I will now add to this last point by remarking on the one passage in Barth's doctrine of the Trinity which elaborates on the hermeneutical problem (9). It comes under the heading of the interpretation of the revelation to man, which is an appropriation of the Holy Spirit. Earlier Barth was concerned to deny the distinction between form and content in revelation(10) while yet asserting God's freedom in relation to the form of Jesus' humanity which he assumes (11). The hermeneutical support for this is on pp. 373 ff., where the form of narrative is seen as inseparable from revelation, and God's freedom is related to the "special historicity" of the biblical narratives. What this amounts to is an assertion that whatever the error in the "general historicity" of the narratives God is still free to speak through the details given in the text (12). It is conceivable that the Holy Spirit could instruct through the results of historical criticism, but Barth will not allow it. It is also conceivable that the Holy Spirit could speak through myth, but Barth will not allow that either. The result is that the Holy Spirit is "tied down" to the biblical narrative of the Son, just as the Father is (13), and, moreover, to a particular classification of that narrative which I have called "realistic".

This last point is seen in the distinction between myth and saga (14): saga intends history and is irreducible to general truths; but myth only pretends to be history while really conveying some truth which can be expressed otherwise than through the narrated events, and so is a "non-spatial, timeless truth, in other words, a human creation" (15). This contrast avoids the case of narratives such as realistic novels which intend fictional history, and so, while not mythical by Barth's definition, are human creations. The logic of Barth's position is to accept the biblical stories as novels in which the attempt to draw the line between fact and fiction is impossible, but also superfluous because God chooses to speak through them. Thus God's freedom is the crucial argument for establishing the authority of the biblical narratives in Barth's doctrine of revelation, and it is therefore also the main element in his doctrine of the inspiration of Scripture(16).

(ii)

I now move to Barth's doctrine of God in C.D.II.1. The first chapter of the volume, The Knowledge of God, deals with the epistemological problems in Barth's distinctive way which owes much to his use of biblical narratives. The distinction between primary and secondary objectivity, the arguments against natural theology, the concept of the hiddenness of God and the understanding of analogy are all tied into my theme. In Appendix B to this chapter I show in detail how this is so. Of particular importance in it is the correlation of primary and secondary objectivity with eternity and time, and a statement which is the nearest Barth comes to an "Anknüpfungspunkt", in seeing the forty days of post-resurrection appearances as God's "unambiguous" secondary objectivity. The identification of the dialectic of analogy with the ordered relation of crucifixion to resurrection is also of great significance for Barth's whole scheme, as is the understanding of God's free personal presence as the preemption of every analogia entis.

The latter part of II.1 gives Barth's doctrine of the attributes or perfections of God as "the One who loves in freedom". His procedure is to begin from the question: Who is God? It is answered by reference to his acts. In this way the concept of identity, or personality, is kept as formal as possible (17): the understanding of what a person is is gained by finding out what sort of subject those acts indicate. "The real person is not man but God" (18). This person is made known in the one human person we can be sure is a real person, Jesus Christ (19). So the incarnation is the starting-point for knowledge of God's attributes. In line with this there are frequent assertions that the correct way of arriving at God's attributes is to go from the "particular" to the "general" (20); and even when Barth agrees with the conclusions of earlier doctrines of God he insists that his method is necessary for the doctrine to be sound:

> "The fundamental error of the whole earlier doctrine of
> God is reflected in this arrangement: first God's being
> in general, then his triune nature.... But...God's
> revelation is first and last a Gospel." (21)

Since both God's love (22) and his freedom (23) are identified with his revelation in Jesus Christ and since a basic principle guiding Barth's doctrine is that

> "every individual perfection in God is nothing but God
> Himself and therefore nothing but every other divine
> perfection" (24),

it is worthwhile examining each perfection as an interpretation of the story of Jesus Christ.

Each pair in which Barth treats the prefections combines consideration
of God's love and freedom, with the emphasis in the pairs of §30 on love and
in those of §31 on freedom. Barth had in §29 surveyed previous ways of or-
ganising the attributes of God (psychological, religio-genetic, historico-
intuitive) and had favoured that which understands "two moments" in God, of
freedom and of love (25). As he treats the prefections it becomes clear that
the relationship of the two moments is to be understood through the crucifixion and resurrection. It is the resurrection which demonstrates the freedom of God in the loving act of the crucifixion; and the irreversible order
of the two events in their rendering of one identity shows how such attributes as God's judgement (expressing his holiness) and grace are held together.

> "It is puzzling how the heart of the New Testament
> message, viz., the passion narrative and the indissoluble
> connection between Christ's death and resurrection as
> directly and indirectly attested in so many apostolic
> texts, can be so disregarded that even momentarily we
> can lose sight of the necessity of seeing the grace of
> God in His judgement and therefore His judgement in His
> grace." (26)

It is essential to Barth's method in this doctrine that, in all his rich
reflection and his use of the O.T. and of traditional dogmatic material, the
perfections as he defines them must be "cashed" in terms of these two events
which for him sum up the incarnation. This is the hallmark of his method's
distinctiveness, and not the way in which he selects and groups the perfections - of that, as he says, it is the case that "methodus est arbitraria"(27)
and it would be wrong to see that scheme as anything other than one among
several possible ways in which Barth answers the question: "Who and what
is God?" (28)

How Barth's method is worked out in various perfections is told in
Appendix C to this chapter. There it is clear that the perfections of the
divine loving lend themselves fairly straightforwardly to being given their
content by the story of Jesus Christ. It is under the heading of God's
freedom, as understood by Barth, that traditional "general" ideas about God
such as transcendence, independence and infinity arise, and Barth's interpretation of them is perhaps the most severe test of his story-centred method.
His solution is what might be called a descriptive metaphysics in support of
the overarching story. Appendix C shows how, under the headings of unity,
constancy, omnipotence and glory, he describes a transcendent person with
characteristics dictated by the story of Jesus Christ. The two perfections
I have omitted there are omnipresence and eternity. If Barth's theology had
made more use of the concept of causality then omnipotence could not have
been relegated to the appendix, and the same could be said for unity and
constancy if substance were an important category for him. Since, however,
he has no interest in the theoretical relation of omnipotence to occurrence
in general (except to assert that it is one of free determination by God,
ordered towards the event of Jesus Christ), and since his nearest equivalent
tp Aquinas' "substance" is "act" or "event", one needs to go elsewhere for
his fundamental categories. "Act" and "event" give the clue: they need a
place and time in order to exist, and so omnipresence and eternity are crucial

to his metaphysics of the overarching story.

God's presence is not for Barth a general, uniform presence everywhere, but a particular, differentiated presence both to himself within the Trinity and also to us, with as many varieties as there are places and people (29). His position involves taking literally biblical statements which apply spatial concepts to God:

> "We must not think, then, that it is meant or at
> least has to be understood only symbolically, pictorially
> and indirectly when in the Old and New Testaments God is
> constantly characterised and described as the possessor
> of a place or location.... Had the Lord not been at this
> particular Beth-El, then the dreams of this particular
> man would have been idle fancies. And then the whole
> covenant between God and man as a definite covenant
> with definite men would have been invalid both at that
> time and for all time." (30)

From this it is plain what a heavy investment in the realism of the biblical stories Barth's theology makes. But there is also an ordering of the stories. The special presence they tell of and the general presence (or at least "no non-presence" (31)) they imply are all understood as pointing to the special presence in Jesus Christ (32). Barth's statements about this make it both unique (33) and inclusive:

> "It is the one unique and simple presence, the
> proper presence of God as the one and simple God in
> His creation, in which both His special presence in
> all its diversity and also his general presence with
> its dynamic identity possess their beginning and end." (34)

> "God's most proper space ('der eigenste Raum Gottes')
> is itself the space which this man occupies in the cradle
> and on the cross, and which He therefore cannot leave or
> lose again, for, as His resurrection and ascension re-
> veal, it is now his permanent place ('sein bleibender
> Raum')...the reality of the divine space, by which all
> other spaces are created, preserved and surrounded." (35)

This is where the logic of Barth's method leads, not only to realistic stories being the highest form of religious language, but to the choice of one such story as the revelation of the sphere of reality in which all men live, with all other reality (and God's presence in it) as "secondary" (36) or "symbolic" (37) or "sacramental" (38). The same logic is applied to the eucharistic conflict between Lutheran and Reformed theology, enabling Barth to combine the Reformed stress on the distinctiveness of Jesus Christ's space and the need for a hierarchy with the Lutheran stress on his human corporeal omni-presence. As in the similar dispute over Christ's divinity and humanity (39) the bias of Barth's method is Lutheran and he makes up for this by all the stronger assertions of the hierarchy.

My quotation above from p. 486 on "God's proper space" leads to two comments.

Firstly there is the question of God's own space, which Barth earlier presented as his first differentiation of omnipresence (40). There he supports his statements with various scriptural quotations taken literally (41) but what he says later about Jesus Christ is the decisive ground for his statements about the space of the Trinity. In ascribing space to the Trinity Barth is again carrying to the limit his anthropomorphic story language, and affirming, by the analogia fidei, of Deus in se what he discovers in Deus revelatus. His method does not allow him to say that God is non-spatial, and the concept of repetition of the same identity as applied to the Trinity also forbids it since without some sort of space there would be simply undifferentiated identity (42). This is one of many areas in which Barth differs sharply from a psychological conception of the Trinity. It is possible to conceive of a mind which is non-spatial (43) and so to have a coherent theory of inner-trinitarian relations without the concept of divine space. But for Barth such a theory is ruled out by his choice of revelation history as the only analogy of the Trinity. Given this, there must be some analogue of created space in God.

Secondly, there is the question of the relation of time to space contained in the phrase "His permanent place". This points to how Barth makes universal and transcendent the space of the story. He does it by importing his conception of eternity. Without the temporal dimension omnipresence would be the sort of "static" concept which Barth abhors, and this is why he focuses on God's special presence in a history. Space is a necessary component in his doctrine of God, but time is the more fundamental category (44). The particularity of both the space and the time of God's presence in Jesus Christ is necessary, but the permanence of that presence and its capacity to be relevant to all ages is a temporal problem; and the identity of Jesus Christ (and through him, of God) is for Barth rendered by a certain sequence of events in time, in which space is presupposed, but whose crucial feature, that of irreversible direction, is a property peculiar to time (45).

(iii)

The way is now prepared for treating Barth's doctrine of time, and I will first give a survey of its role in his theology, beginning with this chapter's concern, the doctrine of God.

Richard Roberts describes Barth's exposition of eternity in C.D.II.1 as

> "the temporal explanation of the consistently developed
> doctrine of the divine perfections" (46),

and justifies his claim at length. For my purpose it is important to note that Barth's definition of eternity is tailor-made for making Jesus Christ's history eternal:

> "Eternity is the simultaneity of beginning, middle and
> end, and to that extent it is pure duration." (47)

There is a double thrust here, towards both an overarching simultaneity and also an irreversible ordering (48) within it which allows eternity to be the prototype (49) of time. In terms of the history of Christian thought, Barth has fused the Boethian totum simul with an Augustinian structure reminiscent of archetypes (50), and his originality is in making this serve the world of the overarching story as the ultimate guarantee that it is the real world in its rendering of God's identity. It is a metaphysics which centres on the temporal transcendence and freedom of God, which affirms the ultimacy of temporal categories in the priority of eternity over being (51), and which pervades every doctrine in the C.D. Perhaps the clearest statement of its significance for my theme is the following:

"We have good reason to give clear emphasis...to the concepts of the pre-temporality, supra-temporality and post-temporality of the eternal God. For a great deal depends on this truth and on the legitimacy of these concepts. It is only if they are true and legitimate that the whole content of the Christian message - creation as the basis of man's existence, established by God, reconciliation as the renewal of his existence accomplished by God, redemption as the revelation of his existence to be consummated by God... - can be understood as God's word of truth and not as the myth of a pious or impious self-consciousness, the comfortless content of some human monologue which has no real claim upon us, the substance of a well-meant pastoral fiction, mere wishful thinking or a terrifying dream. The Christian message cannot be distinguished from a myth or a dream of this kind unless God's eternity has temporality in the sense described, and God is really pre-temporal, supra-temporal and post-temporal." (52)

Yet even to arrive at this transcendent guarantee that the story is not a novel Barth starts from the story, as he forcefully states, for it is from that that we know that "eternity became time". How he bases this doctrine on the resurrection will be shown later in the chapter, but now I complete my brief survey of the role of time in the C.D.

Roberts shows its pervasiveness with a thoroughness that needs no repetition. He shows its place in the areas I listed at the end of Chapter 7 above, notably the realtion between election and incarnation (54), the doctrine of analogy (55), and the two natures of Christ (56). He also discusses its role in the doctrine of creation (57) which Chapter 6 above has already indicated, and in the integration of christology and soteriology (58) which I have described as the resurrection demonstrating the inclusive overarching character of the Gospel story. What Barth is attempting in each case, as Roberts makes clear, is to solve the traditional Christian problem of how to distinguish God's sovereign and eternal being from his temporal creation while at the same time affirming the humanity and divinity of Christ.

Roberts discerns a systematic ambiguity in Barth's thought on time, with Barth always relating time and eternity in a theological circle and

never defining them by their disparate attributes. He says that Barth over-
stretches a few key concepts, and concludes:

> "Whenever Barth seeks to temporalize God by utilizing
> the method of analogia fidei this becomes a species of
> ontological and semantic parasitism. Certain concepts
> have to draw semantic vitality from what they deny."(59)

In other words there is a flaw in the "temporal ontology" (60) of the C.D.
which inevitably results in the fuzziness found in the doctrine of the two
natures in Chapter 7 above. So my analysis there to some extent confirms
Roberts' judgement, and criticisms which I have made in other chapters add
further support.

Yet I am not satisfied with resting there, for Roberts' conceptual
analysis does not seem to me to take sufficient account of the nature of
the story from which Barth's concepts draw their vitality. In particular,
Roberts' complaint about the paucity and overstretching of Barth's temporal
concepts does not recognise his unique use of one part of the gospel story:
the forty days of post-resurrection appearances (61). It is for Barth a
temporal concept, and one which resists Roberts' method of analysis, for
the main judgement which one must make about it is as to whether Barth's
use of it interprets the story correctly. The rest of this chapter will
attempt to arrive at such a judgement.

(iv)

That the resurrection, which has been shown in previous chapters to
be the main determinant of Barth's theological perspective, is also the
key to his doctrine of time and eternity is recognised by Roberts:

> "The resurrection is the completion and realization of
> the doctrine of time in the C.D....."(62).

> "The pattern of temporality in eternity (and thus in
> 'primal history'), the succession of past, present and
> future without division or limitation which informs the
> act of God in election, is fulfilled in the resurrection."(63)

As has already been shown in this chapter Barth correlates the primary and
secondary objectivity of God with eternity and time respectively and sees
the Forty Days as the time of God's unambiguous secondary objectivity.
Other volumes support this unique status of the Forty Days (64), and I will
now draw on a literary critic to elucidate their function in Barth's interpretation of them.

Frank Kermode, in The Sense of an Ending. Studies in the theory of
fiction (65) discusses apocalyptic and fiction in the light of our need for
patterns, especially that of "beginning, middle and end", in order to make
sense of history and our place in it. The Bible he takes as a familiar
model of history:

> "Ideally, it is a wholly concordant structure, the end is
> in harmony with the beginning, the middle with the beginning
> and end." (66)

He discusses kairos and chronos and the "time-redeeming" function of concords (67), typology (68), books as "fictive models of the temporal world"
or "bibliocosms" (69), myth (70), and the role of the imagination in making
concords (71), and he sees the loss of the "six-days world" - the belief that
the world was created in six days according to Genesis - as far more disturb-
ing in its cultural effects than the Copernican revolution (72). The novel
is the area of modern culture which he examines in order to show characteristic ways of coping with the loss of the concordant biblical world, and he
is well aware of the similarities between the attempts of novelists to offer
worlds of meaning and the work of theologians. For him both are engaged in
comprehending present reality through modifying the paradigms of the past(73).

From all this it is clear that Kermode's book suggests more ways in
which Barth's theology is related to literary criticism, for Barth too works
with a "bibliocosm", lays great store by its patterns and concords, and
modifies the traditional paradigm with the aim of replacing the "six-days
world" by the "A.D.1 - 30 world" (74). For Barth the ultimate concord is of
course that of God and man in Jesus Christ, and the temporal revelation of
this is in the concord of eternity with time in the Forty Days:

> "During these forty days the presence of God in the
> presence of the man Jesus was no longer a paradox." (75)

It is here that a concept employed by Kermode is especially illuminating.
He takes the term aevum from Aquinas, who meant by it the time of angels,
a third duration between time and eternity, and shows how equivalent concepts have been used to describe the time of books:

> "for in the kind of time known by books a moment has
> endless perspectives of reality. We feel, in Thomas
> Mann's words, that 'in their beginning exists their
> middle and their end, their past invades the present
> and is invaded by concern for the future.' The con-
> cept of aevum provides a way of talking about this un-
> usual variety of duration - neither temporal nor
> eternal, but, as Aquinas said, participating in both
> the temporal and the eternal. It does not abolish time
> or spatialize it; it co-exists with time, and is a
> mode in which things can be perpetual without being
> eternal." (76)

Kermode sees the aevum in its various modes as a "concord-fiction" which
tries to resolve the dissonance between time and eternity, and which today
is found largely in novels or poems, though once it was more common in
tragedies and the theology of angels (77).

The Forty Days opens and closes with angels, and one of Barth's discussions of the literary nature of the accounts comes in The Limits of
Angelology (78). There he says that angels are particularly "figures of
biblical saga and legend", the content of which can "be grasped only by

divinatory imagination", and elsewhere too (79) he remarks on the imaginative, fictional characteristics of the accounts. The parallels of the resurrection stories in Barth with the aevum in Kermode are striking: they are imaginatively composed and grasped stories whose time is neither ordinary time nor eternity (for the Forty Days have an end) and whose function is to reveal the concordance between eternity and time.

Barth would, of course, reject the suggestion that there is a tertium quid between time and eternity, for that would be to threaten the true humanity and divinity of Christ after his resurrection and defeat the purpose of the definition of saga. A key difference between Aquinas' aevum and Barth's Forty Days is that Aquinas allows a distinct medium inter aeternitatem et tempus, utroque participans (80), whereas Barth only allows a different literary genre and mode of apprehension, while remaining "Chalcedonian" on the distinction and unity of time and eternity. In his angelology too he is at pains to qualify the mediation of angels so that it only supports Jesus Christ's sole mediation (81). He therefore means the Forty Days as a tertium quid quoad nos (82), and expresses it in literary and epistemological terms. His critique of Aquinas' angelology further serves to bring out the literary bias of his method (83).

This invocation of the literary imagination (and Barth even polemically suggests the importance of another aspect of the imagination, a sense of humour, in dealing with angels (84) and the resurrection (85)!) in an epistemological role at this crucial point in Barth's theology is, as this dissertation tries to show, consistent with the C.D. as a whole; and when Roberts decides that too few temoral concepts carry too much weight he does not notice the use of the Forty Days as equivalent to the concept of aevum (as understood by Kermode), nor the accompanying claim to an imaginative resolution as in poetry or novels. This sort of claim is, however, notoriously difficult to judge. Barth's final appeal is always to faith, i.e. to whether the story "works" in this way for the reader. Yet his interpretation is not the only one even within the Church, and one must at least ask whether it does justice to the stories of the Forty Days.

(v)

My verdict on this is that there is a similar mixture of insight and distortion to that found, for example, in his interpretation of Judas in Chapter 5 above. The insight is similar to Kermode's into the function of the aevum of Aquinas and in literature, and I have already illustrated that (86). The distortion is that the content of the Gospel accounts of the resurrection appearances does not bear out Barth's claim that they represent a unique fulfilment and completeness, a manifestation of eternity in time. They have much more the character of "sendings" into the future, and there is at least as much promise as fulfilment. Jenson notes this (87), and much of the work of theologians such as Moltmann and Pannenberg can be seen as an effort to do better justice to the tension between promise and fulfilment than did Barth. His absolutising of the Forty Days goes well beyond the perception of their literary function. It is related to his modification of the traditional paradigm, for in that paradigm the resurrection and Parousia were not at all one event for Jesus, and there was little temptation to transfer "the sense of an ending" to the resurrection. The resurrection and the appearances are immensely important in the story even when they are recognised as in one sense interim events. Barth's virtual "closure" at this point overburdens them, as Roberts affirms of other temporal concepts, and violates their "realistic" element as one link in a chain of events.

A more general criticism concerns the way Barth uses his doctrine of eternity based on the resurrection to make the story "inclusive". Even if one grants the concept of an overarching story (and it is not my task to argue about that), Barth may be presumptuous in claiming that it conforms so closely to the story of Jesus' life. His whole way of thinking is so much in the pattern of "correspondences" that he concentrates his considerable capacity for amazement on the resurrection and so loses the tang of novelty and surprise in his account of events since then and to come. Perhaps his problem was that for all the significance of his invocation of the imagination it still has the sound of being a last resort, and not a recognition of its many possibilities in theology.

In connection with this second criticism I will conclude by drawing on the author of my opening quotation to make a suggestion about the structure of Barth's theology. Wicker adapts the linguistic analysis of Saussure and Roman Jakobson to the study of novels. He lays out a binary structure based on two operations, selection and combination, which are present in all language use and rest on complementary principles:

> "For the act of selection always implies the possible
> substitution of a different but similar item, in place
> of the item chosen, without disturbance of the functional
> arrangement, or 'context' as a whole. Whereas the act
> of combination always sets up a functional arrangement
> or structure such that this arrangement could take a
> number of different forms without affecting the actual
> choice of the items included in it." (88)

In Barth's theology, where God is the primary speaker, the stress is on the first of these. Election decides the whole plot of salvation, and we enter into it by substitution. The second principle is anathema to Barth at the level of the overarching story. It suggests a refusal to correspond to God's plan and a desire to change the providential structure of life. Above all he fears the distortion of Jesus Christ that results from entering him into other stories. This is bound to affect his spirituality in its attempt to relate Jesus' story to ours, and the next chapter will deal with this.

(1) Brian Wicker, op. cit., pp. 4 ff.

(2) Op. cit.

(3) Ib., S. 36.

(4) Ib., S. 10.

(5) Especially in God after God. The God of the Past and the God of the Future seen in the Work of Karl Barth (New York 1969).

(6) Ib., p. 106.

(7) The Trinity in Contemporary Theology (London 1953), e.g. pp. 203 ff.

(8) E.g. p. 197.

(9) C.D.I.1, pp. 373 ff.

(10) E.g. ib., p. 351. Cf. I.2, pp. 492 ff.

(11) E.g. I.1, pp. 363, 367-72.

(12) See especially ib., pp. 374-6.

(13) Ib., p. 448. See Appendix A.

(14) Ib., pp. 375 ff.

(15) Ib., p. 378.

(16) See C.D.I.2, pp. 508-37 - inspiration is not a property of the text or an experience of the author but is the promise of the Holy Spirit's free presence when Scripture is read in the Church. N.B. pp. 509, 514, 519, 525, 526, 530, 532.

(17) For a discussion of the formality or otherwise of concepts of identity see Hans Frei, The Identity of Jesus Christ, op. cit., Chapter 9. Frei's understanding there is what I have in mind when I use the concept of identity in this dissertation.

(18) C.D.II.1, p. 272.

(19) Ib., p. 286.

(20) E.g. pp. 297 ff., 310-4, 329, 337 ff., 346 ff., 352 f.

(21) Ib., pp. 348 f.

(22) E.g. ib., p. 274.

(23) E.g. ib., p. 315.

(24) Ib., p. 333.

(25) Ib., pp. 337 ff.

(26) Ib., p. 364.

(27) Ib., p. 352.

(28) Ib., p. 353.

(29) E.g. ib., pp. 468, 476.

(30) Ib., pp. 478 f.

(32) Ib., pp. 483 f.

(33) E.g. on the gratia unionis ib., pp. 485 f.

(34) Ib., p. 484.

(35) Ib., p. 486; S. 547.

(36) Ib., p. 485.

(37) Ib., p. 486. This does not appear as a contradiction of his previous insistence on literalism if "symbolic" is taken in a typological sense - the genre is realistic but a higher reality is also indicated.

(38) Ib., p. 486.

(39) See Chapter 7 above, p. 131 f.

(40) Ib., pp. 470 ff.

(41) E.g. pp. 474 ff.

(42) Op. cit., p. 468.

(43) Most traditional Christian theology and philosophy supposed so; for a lucid modern defence of the project see J.R. Lucas, A Treatise on Space and Time (London 1973), Ch. 27.

(44) Cf. Lucas, op. cit., p. 3: "Time is more fundamental than space. Indeed, time is the most pervasive of all the categories."

(45) Cf. Lucas, op. cit., p. 56: "We shall see space as time-like, but with the direction taken out."

(46) Op. cit., p. 134.

(47) C.D.II.1, p. 608.

(48) In eternity, he says, "there is order and succession" - ib., p. 615. For a philosophical parallel to Barth's concern for succession in eternity see the suggestion of A.C. Ewing with which he concludes his Value and Reality. The Philosophical Case for Theism (London 1973), pp. 280 ff.

(49) E.g. C.D.II.1, p. 612.

(50) See Roberts, op. cit., Ch. IV.

(51) E.g. C.D.II.1, pp. 609 f.

(52) Ib., p. 620.

(53) Ib., p. 616.

(54) See Roberts, op. cit., Chapters 6 and 7.

(55) Ib., Ch. III.

(56) Ib., Ch. VII.

(57) Ib., Ch. VIII.

(58) Ib., Chapters VII, Ix.

(59) Ib., p. 474.

(60) Ib., p. 474.

(61) Though Roberts does note their importance - ib., pp. 200, 349.

(62) Ib., p. 201.

(63) Ib., p. 202.

(64) E.g. III.2, p. 449, IV.1, p. 301.

(65) Op. cit.

(66) Ib., p. 6.

(67) Ib., pp. 46 ff.

(68) Ib., pp. 48, 58 f.

(69) Ib., p. 54.

(70) Ib., pp. 39 ff., 104, 172, 176.

(71) Ib., p. 89, Ch. IV, p. 144.

(72) Ib., pp. 166 ff.

(73) E.g. ib., p. 128:

   "In speaking of a continual attempt on the part of the clerisy to
   relate, by frequent alteration, an inherited paradigm to a changed
   sense of reality, we may strain the attention of hearers so long as
   we speak of physics or law or theology, but as soon as the subject
   is the novel the argument drops into perfectly familiar context."

(74) E.g. C.D.I.2, p. 58 on fulfilled time. Cf. III.2, where Barth gives
   his fullest treatment of time. Not only does he say: "Time in its
   beginning was enclosed by His (Jesus') time, and to that extent was
   itself His time" (III.2, p. 484), but also concludes that although
   "the arch of His time" is yet to be completed, "Nothing which will
   be has not already taken place in Easter Day" (ib., p. 489), and for
   Jesus the resurrection and parousia are a single event (ib., p. 490).
   In C.D.I.2, where Barth gives his first comprehensive account of time
   under the heading The Time of Revelation, he orders all time on either
   side of the resurrection, the story of which is "the subject whose
   predicate is all the other narratives" (p. 114). He expounds the con[
   cordances between the time of expectation and time of recollection,
   but assigns "absolute uniqueness" to the resurrection, of which he
   says: "Recollection of eternal time, which is what recollection of
   the risen One is, is necessarily recollection of a time which over-
   arches our time, and which therefore cannot be confined to the datable
   time with which it is in the first instance related." (Ib., p. 116:
   "Erinnerung ewiger Zeit, wie es die Erinnerung an den Auferstandenen
   ist, das ist ja notwendig Erinnerung einer Zeit, die unsere Zeit über-
   greift, die also nicht auf jene datierbare Zeit, auf die sie sich zu-
   nächst bezieht, beschränkt sein kann" - S. 128.) It is of course
   essential for Barth that the resurrection is the key not only to the
   concord within the Bible but between the Bible and our individual
   stories too.

(75) C.D.III.2, p. 449.

(76) Op. cit., pp. 71 f.

(77) Ib., p. 89.

(78) C.D.III.3, pp. 374 ff.

(79) E.g. III.2, p. 452, where he accepts that forty is a common O.T. significant number and is "not to be taken literally but typically", and
   admits the vagueness of the topography of the accounts with their
   "imaginative, poetic style of historical saga" and a "corresponding
   obscurity" ("in der phantasierenden und dichtenden Gestaltungsart und
   in der Dunkelheit der geschichtlichen Sage" - S. 542). I am prescinding
   at present from the fact that what gives the accounts their importance
   for Barth is that they also point to a real event.

(80) C.f. F.N. Brabant, Time and Eternity in Christian Thought (London
   1937), pp. 74 ff.

(81) C.D.III.3, pp. 411 ff.

(82) Cf. his assertion that resurrection and Parousia are one event for Jesus (C.D.III.2, p. 490), and his discussion of heaven (III.3, pp. 418 ff.).

(83) Ib., pp. 390-401. As Barth and Kermode both observe, the drive behind Aquinas' elaboration of his angelology is that of comprehensive intellectual understanding, which demands an account of this realm of creatures. Barth condemns him for giving an "abstract" angelology (p. 391) and for "merely making philosophical and not theological decisions" and therefore not arriving at "angels in the biblical sense of the term" (p. 393), and he concludes by seeing the whole edifice as a projection of man's intellect, a gigantic alter ego (pp. 400 ff.). Barth's alternative is to understand angels purely from their role in the biblical stories, and this leads him, not to the limits of understanding in the realm of theory, but to realising that the limits of communication by historical description necessitate assigning angels (and the Forty Days, which openand close with angels) to another genre more suited to the imagination's aesthetic understanding. Wicker (op. cit., p. 6) remarks upon Aquinas' "undervaluing the cognitive value of poetry and narrative in theology". The divergence between Barth and Aquinas on angels is a symptom of the split noted by Wicker in the opening quotation of this chapter (cf. the debate provoked by Bernard Lonergan's Method in Theology, in particular the attack on Lonergan's Thomist approach by Fergus Kerr on the grounds that Lonergan fails to appreciate the imaginative uses of language ("Bernard Lonergan's Method. A Response to William Matthews", New Blackfriars, Vol. 57, No. 669, Feb. 1976, pp. 59-71)). Kermode's transcription of Aquinas' aevum to the sphere of literature is therefore paralleled by Barth's rejection of Aquinas' intellectualist account of angels in favour of a literary account, but in both Aquinas and Barth angels help to signify the harmony between time and eternity.

(84) III.3, p. 369.

(85) III.2, p. 447.

(86) The insight overlaps with that into what Stern calls "the realism of assessment", and it is significant that Stern can say:

> "All assessments and judgements are inescapably connected with a sequence of events in time. The various ways of presenting time in literature may thus turn out to be best approached via the various kinds of assessment - realistic or other - at work in a given fictional whole." (On Realism, op. cit., p. 130)

(87) God after God, op. cit., pp. 157 ff.

(88) Op. cit., p. 14.

Appendix A to Chapter 8

<u>Barth's Doctrine of the Trinity in C.D.I.1</u>

Throughout this doctrine Barth stresses that its purpose is, solely by interpreting the Scriptures, to answer the question: Who is God? (1) Scripture gives the answer "in the form of narrating a story or series of stories" (2). Barth has already made his fundamental move (variously described above p. 137), e.g.:

> "Revelation is, of course, the predicate of God, but in
> such a way that the predicate coincides exactly with God
> Himself." (3)

So the stage is set for defining the Trinity in terms of relations discovered in the biblical narratives. This he does, the decisive events being the threefold climax of the N.T. story. At key points in his exposition Barth looks to the relation between Good Friday, Easter and Pentecost as the expression of the relations within the Trinity.

Firstly, in <u>The Root of the Doctrine of the Trinity</u>, he sums up the N.T. evidence as follows:

> "As by unveiling we ultimately mean nothing but
> Easter, and then, with an inevitable glance back at
> the course of revelation, by veiling nothing but
> Good Friday, so now, with a glance forward, with a
> glance at man in whom and for whom revelation be-
> comes an event, with a glance at the threshold over
> which revelation enters history, we mean nothing
> but Pentecost, the outpouring of the Holy Spirit." (4)

Secondly, when he discusses the doctrine of appropriations in <u>Three-in-Oneness</u> he adds to the two traditional rules prohibiting arbitrariness and exclusiveness a third rule of <u>sola scriptura</u>, explaining it as follows:

> "As surely as Scripture is meant to be read in
> its context as the witness to God's revelation;
> as surely as e.g. Good Friday, Easter and Pentecost
> merely unite in asserting what they should assert,
> so surely we must declare that all God's operation,
> as we are bound to conceive it on the basis of His
> revelation, is a single act, occurring simultaneously
> and unitedly in all His three modes of existence." (5)

Finally, in <u>The Meaning of the Doctrine of the Trinity</u> Barth says that "the Church doctrine of the Trinity is a self-enclosed circle" (6), and that the trinitarian God's

> "characteristic proofs in the N.T. are indicated by
> Good Friday, Easter and Pentecost, and accordingly
> His name indicated as that of the Father, the Son

and the Holy Spirit" (7).

Barth thus establishes the world of the Gospel story (including by typology,
as explained above in Chapters 5 and 6, the O.T. story) as the only source
for knowledge of the Trinity, and he devotes a section, Vestigium Trinitatis
(8), to denying all claims to insight into the trinitarian nature of God
other than those appealing to

> "the form which God Himself in His revelation has
> assumed in our language, world and humanity" (9).

I have already suggested with the help of Colin Gunton's dissertation
how such an approach is a modification of Anselm's method in the direction
of a narrative-based christocentricity (10), and I will now illustrate this
further from the way Barth treats the "appropriations" of the members of
the Trinity.

Barth wants to have both perichoresis (the interchangeable inter-
penetration of the three members) and particular appropriations. His way
of upholding the possibility of this is not to claim that the concepts are
logically compatible but that the biblical story compels us to hold both (11).
There is thus an argument parallel to that for the divinity and humanity of
Jesus discussed in Chapter 7 above: it is a consistently "double-aspect"
interpretation of stories concluding both that opera trinitatis ad extra
sunt indivisa and that this identity-in-act is threefold (12). In the way
the appropriations are distributed the christocentric bias of the theology
is clear.

Creation is the main appropriation of the Father (13). Chapter 6
above has already shown how Barth makes this doctrine christocentric. In
I.1 he does the same: his argument for the Father being the creator even
ignores Genesis and uses only the cross and resurrection of Jesus (14).
This is supported by stating that the Bible

> "formally...shows the content of the revelation of the
> Father to be completely limited and tied down by its
> impartation in the Person of the revealer, Jesus of
> Nazareth" (15).

The distinctive attribute of the Father throughout the doctrine of the Trinity
is freedom. The whole doctrine depends upon

> "God's freedom to distinguish Himself from Himself, to
> become other than Himself, and yet to remain as He was" (16).

The difficulty of this notion is soon eased by the qualification:

> "That He reveals himself as the Son is what is primarily
> meant by saying that He reveals Himself as the Lord" (17);

and it is eased further in the following pages by taking the freedom of God
to mean his freedom to reveal or not to reveal himself to particular people
through the form of the humanity of Jesus as described in the Bible.

153

What Barth does is to focus on the Son as the form of revelation, assert the inseparability of form and content, and define the appropriation of the Father and of the Holy Spirit through the concept of freedom within this world of meaning. The Father has expressed his freedom in choosing to act in the particular way related by the story. The Holy Spirit is the expression of God's freedom in bringing about the appropriation of the story by men (18). God's freedom is therefore the concept with which Barth both ensures the transcendence of God and enables his identity to be defined by the tight particularity of the story. Jüngel puts this point another way when he says that Barth's doctrine of the Trinity fulfils the same function as Bultmann's demythologising by preventing God being treated as an "object" (19). The danger of God being "objectified" is acute in Barth's concentration on the story, for God's being is defined through his action and the story tells the action. Hence the need for the great emphasis in the C.D. on God's freedom, grace, initiative. This structures the whole theology through the irreversible analogia fidei between God and man, but ita hermeneutical function is simple: it enables the story to be the all-embracing world of meaning. This is clearest in the doctrine of election, where God freely decides that a certain stretch of history will enclose all other history by containing his own temporal self-repetition.

NOTES to Appendix A to Chapter 8

(1) E.g. I.1, pp. 345, 351, 354, 361, 380, 399, 427, 436 ff.

(2) Ib., p. 362.

(3) Ib., p. 343.

(4) Ib., p. 380, cf. p. 382.

(5) Ib., p. 430.

(6) Ib., p. 436.

(7) Ib., p. 437.

(8) Ib., pp. 383 ff.

(9) Ib., p. 399.

(10) See Chapter 2 above, pp. 23 f.

(11) E.g. ib., pp. 454 ff.

(12) Cf. p. 416 on the baptism of Jesus.

(13) Ib., p. 441 ff.

(14) Ib., pp. 444-7.

(15) Ib., p. 448. ("...das biblische Zeugnis...den der Offenbarung des Vaters formal schlechterdings bedingt und gebunden sein lässt durch seine Mitteilung in der Person des Offenbarers Jesus von Nazareth" - S. 411.)

(16) Ib., p. 367.

(17) Ib., p. 368.

(18) The Son's freedom is expressed in his obedience as told by the story - cf. IV.1.

(19) Op. cit., S. 33 f.

Appendix B to Chapter 8

Barth on the Knowledge of God in C.D.II.1

§25 <u>The Fulfilment of the Knowledge of God</u> begins, as one would expect, from an <u>a posteriori</u> position on knowledge of God: he is knowable because he is already known in his revelation. Barth's main concept in this section is his distinction between the primary and secondary objectivity of God. The latter is the way God mediates his reality to man. It is found in the history between God and man which is recounted in the O.T. and N.T. (1), and culminates in the "unambiguous" secondary objectivity of God in the forty days of post resurrection appearances, in which the apostles "know the primary objectivity and hence God Himself" (2).

As a piece of theory the distinction simply formalises Barth's method of arriving at his understanding of who God is. It also allows one to see the method as a middle way between a doctrine of God as pure Subject who cannot be talked about <u>in se</u> at all, and a doctrine of God which has a natural theology (i.e., argues from other forms of secondary objectivity than the biblical history). Another way of stating this middle way is that Barth wishes to affirm the freedom of God in relation to history (his primary objectivity), and also to claim that God has chosen one way of expressing himself and no other (his secondary objectivity). Of special importance to the latter part of Chapter 8 is the fact that Barth also interprets eternity as God's primary objectivity and time as his secondary objectivity (3).

The fundamental methodological clue to the whole chapter is the statement that

> "God is the One whose being can be investigated only in
> the form of a continuous question as to His action" (4).

§§25-27 can be seen as Barth's support for that quotation. The "only" is championed against natural theology, and the gathering of positive doctrine from the biblical history is defended by Barth's doctrine of analogy.

Natural theology never has a chance in Barth's theology because God is defined as the "Subject of this (i.e. biblical) history" (5). It would of course be possible to see the same God at work in, for example, other religions, but Barth's conception of the freedom of God is that it has chosen to restrict itself to one definitive revelation. This is most clearly stated in the discussion of analogy:

> "All kinds of things might be analogous of God, if God
> had not and did not make a very definite delimited use
> of His omnipotence in His revelation." (6)

The main questions which remain as to natural theology are about its possible presence in the Bible and the way in which man may be open to the God of the Bible. On the first, Barth poses the question as to whether, besides the main strand of God speaking and acting in history, there are two "independent" strands in the Bible, one which refers to direct confirmation by the

Holy Spirit and another which is the confirmation man can gather from the cosmos (7). (This is a loaded question, for it ignores the fact that few natural theologies in the Christian tradition uphold any such "independence" but rather wish to affirm various sorts of interrelation.) Barth concludes that the Holy Spirit works by illuminating the history, and that none of biblical man's experience of God can be understood apart from the history. The final reason for this is that man's true situation is "objectively" the result of that history (8).

As regards the second question, man's openness to God, Barth devotes a separate section, §26.2 The Readiness of Man, to it and arrives at a similar conclusion amounting to an assertion of the overarching biblical story as the world in which we live. Natural theology is accused of telling the wrong story about man's openness to God (9). The only true story about this is that of Jesus (10) and other men may participate through the Holy Spirit in "the person and work of Jesus Christ" (11).

Before Barth treats analogy he has a section on The Hiddenness of God. This guards in advance the freedom of God, for even when he has revealed himself in history and the Bible he still has the initiative over whether this may "become truth" (12), for the individual by grace. This is the same point as that on the freedom of the Holy Spirit in the Trinity, discussed above in Chapter 8 and Appendix A.

In discussing analogy in §27.2 The Veracity of Man's Knowledge of God there is the same concern to guard God's freedom. The emphasis is on God enabling man to participate in God's knowledge of Himself, leading to thanks, praise, awe and παρρησία . The latter typifies what Barth means by analogical language in theology: speaking freely on the basis of revelation in the confidence that God gives power and confirmation to what is said (13). This points to the root of Barth's objection to the analogia entis. For him the analogia entis is always preempted by the free personal presence of God who is always there to be invoked and to give knowledge of himself through particular correspondences (knowledge for which the analogia entis searches in the nature of the correspondences themselves). In hermeneutics the analogia fidei has the same effect as the concept of God's freedom, allowing Barth to concentrate on the biblical narrative in the way he does. In §27.2 before the discussion of analogy Barth champions the use of anthropomorphisms in the Bible and theology by asserting the freedom of God to be described in this way (14). When he comes to analogy he insists that his use of the term is

"not...a systematic but an exegetical decision" (15).

He then develops his position up to a final explanation of why there can be no calculation of the degrees of similarity and dissimilarity in our concept of God (16). The reason is that God both veils and unveils himself in his revelation, and in neither case is it a matter of quantity. When one remembers that God's veiling is expressed in the crucifixion and his unveiling in the resurrection (17) the following important quotation suggests how Barth's doctrine of analogy is determined by his interpretation of the story in a modification of the theology of his Epistle to the Romans:

"If we want to describe the relationship between

157

the two concepts (i.e. veiling and unveiling), and
therefore the explanation of the concept of analogy,
as dialectical, we must always note that what is involved is an ordered dialectic, and indeed one which
is teleologically ordered." (18)

The unity of the two is their common subject, God: it is "His unveiling"
and "His veiling" (19). Thus we see the concept of analogy being "cashed"
in terms of the relationship between events in a story which renders God's
identity in Jesus Christ.

This is made explicit in the final pages of §27.2 which also conclude
the whole chapter on The Knowledge of God (20). There Barth admits that he
has offered a circular argument and asks how it can be shown to be a circulus
veritatis. He denies appeals to any presupposition invoked to give systematic certainty, whether faith, the Holy Spirit, the Church, Christian experience, the Trinity or Jesus Christ and says that we are never immune to
temptation and testing. Then, however, in a characteristic move, he says
that there is a sphere in which the testing has already been undergone for
us, and the comfort of faith hascome to us (21). This is of course the
history of Jesus Christ, with the crucifixion as the "original and proper"
meaning of testing and the resurrection the meaning of comfort.

"And faith consists absolutely in the fact that
we want to know only about the temptation and comfort
that have come upon Jesus Christ, only about His cross
and resurrection as the question, really directed to
us but in this way really answered for us, of our
action: of the correctness of our line of thought;
of the limits and the veracity of our knowledge of
God." (23)

My conclusion is that Barth's doctrine of analogy only claims to be
relevant to one story, and so of course repudiates more general theories (24).
The analogia fidei tries to explain how this story tells us of God. The
simple answer is: by faith in the story's main character. The further
question is: How does it tell us about Him? The answer to that is: by
telling about his crucifixion (which for Barth sums up all Jesus' earthly
life as well as the history of Israel) and resurrection. How Barth develops
a doctrine of God's attributes using this method is the subject of the rest
of C.D.II.1.

NOTES to Appendix B to Chapter 8

(1) II.1, p. 19.

(2) Ib., p. 20.

(3) Ib., p. 61.

(4) Ib., p. 61. Cf. II.1, Ch. VI, <u>The Reality of God in Act</u>, e.g.
     e.g. p. 261, cf. Appendix C.

(5) Ib., p. 80.

(6) Ib., p. 232.

(7) Ib., p. 99 f.

(8) Ib., p. 111.

(9) E.g. pp. 146 ff.

(10) Ib., p. 148.

(11) Ib., p. 157.

(12) Ib., p. 194.

(13) E.g. p. 231.

(14) Ib., pp. 221 ff.

(15) Ib., p. 227.

(16) Ib., pp. 234 ff.

(17) Cf. above, Appendix A on the Trinity.

(18) Ib., p. 236.

(19) Ib.

(20) Ib., pp. 243 ff.

(21) Ib., p. 252.

(22) Ib., p. 254.

(23) Ib., p. 254.

(24) Cf. in §27.2 the excursus criticising Quenstedt for the role of "our
      own being or creaturely being in general" (ib., p. 241) in his treat-
      ment of analogy.

Barth on the Perfections of God in C.D.II.1

The first perfections of the divine loving which Barth treats are his grace and holiness (1). I have already quoted in Chapter 8 the key passage from p. 364. The description of the incarnation as the archetypal form of grace (2) is the basis of all that is said in this section §30.1, for holiness is understood as another name for that focal point of grace (3), with the O.T. seen as having various strands which come together in Jesus' cross and resurrection (4).

In §30.2 <u>The Mercy and Righteousness of God</u>, Barth says that this, like every other pair of perfections, is simply a deepening of insight into God's grace and holiness (5). God's mercy, defined as his "readiness to share in sympathy the distress of another" (6), is summed up by the crucifixion seen as substitutionary atonement (7), and the discussion of God's righteousness ranges through O.T. and N.T., to arrive at "the meaning and intention of scripture" (8), Jesus Christ, whose crucifixion shows the wrath and the just judgement of God as well as his mercy (for "He endured it from both sides" (9)), and whose resurrection is the confirmation and revelation of God's righteousness and mercy (10). These events are throughout interpreted inclusively:

> "We do not believe if we do not live in the neighbour-
> hood of Golgotha." (11)

§30.3 <u>The Patience and Wisdom of God</u> defines patience as giving space and time in expectation of a free response (12). Barth again gives O.T. examples, but concludes that these give an ambiguous verdict on whether God is patient (13). The unambiguous statement is, of course, Jesus Christ, and his lifetime alone is "strictly speaking" (14) the time which God gives, in which we may participate. Christ's substitutionary suffering and death is emphasised as the content of this patience. This is also true of God's wisdom, whose "eternally concrete expression" is the cross of Christ (15). The eternal election and providence ordering everything towards crucifixion and resurrection is the main content of Barth's concept of God's wisdom.

In §31 Barth begins with the unity and omnipresence of God. The latter, with the attribute of eternity, is dealt with in the body of Chapter 8. In the unity of God Barth sees two aspects, uniqueness and simplicity, but as the latter was dealt with in his doctrine of the Trinity he concentrates on the uniqueness. He finds those concepts of unity given by mathematics, logic and metaphysics to be colourless and general,and goes to the Bible for colour and particularity (16). The unity and uniqueness that he discovers there are in God's acts (17) and above all in Jesus Christ:

> "In the events which not only are caused by God or proceed
> from Him, but which are identical with His being and
> action, He reveals Himself and is known in His being as
> the One who is unique." (18)

Further:

> "The unique New Testament proof of the uniqueness of God"

is Jesus' substitutionary death (19).

The next pair is God's constancy and omnipotence. Constancy (20) is a concept which expands on God's unity and so develops the interpretation of the Bible as rendering one Subject. Barth distinguishes it from the idea of immutability, which, he thinks, does not allow real life to God. He says that it is

> "a proof and a manifestation of God's constant vitality
> that God has a real history in and with the world created
> by Him",

in which he is the same as he is in eternity (21).

The existence of evil raises the most serious doubt about God's constancy. Barth answers this in two moves. Firstly, he contends that if evil were not possible creation would not be distinct from God (22). This allows him to deny that evil reflects on God's integrity, and to portray God's constancy in his election, answering evil in advance in a way that even makes it seem a felix culpa. Secondly, election is founded on Jesus Christ and the crisis as regards constancy comes, in this view, at the crucifixion. Does this represent a contradiction in God? At stake here are Barth's doctrines of the Trinity and of the incarnation as well as the perfections of constancy. His answer is an exposition of Phil. 2.5 ff. (23) in which he maintains that the self-emptying involved no surrender of deity, only a hiding of it. The key statement is

> "He is not a God who is what He is in a majesty behind
> this condescension, behind the cross on Golgotha. On
> the contrary, the cross on Golgotha is itself the divine
> majesty...." (24)

The definition of deity which emerges is therefore circular within the Gospel story: God is the being who is expressed in the crucifixion (25). Barth ends the exposition on constancy with an attack on Protestant orthodoxy for its "abstract" understanding of God's real will and its general doctrine of providence which abstracts from the "supremely particular event" (26).

Parallel to the attack on immutability is the attack on general notions of omnipotence in the discussion of that perfection (27). The predicate, omnipotence, is defined by the Subject, God (28), who is defined by the biblical history (29). The latter point is made in various ways: that

> "we must recognise His capacity, His potentia absoluta,
> only in the capacity chosen by Him, in His potentia
> ordinata. We no longer need reckon with the possibility
> that He could have acted differently" (30);

that "the deus absconditus is none other than the Deus revelatus" and so "we count on a greater omnipotence but not a different one" (31);

that God's will is not infinite because it "fixes a sphere which it does not overstep.... There is no outside this sphere" (32);
that Protestant orthodoxy, for all the usefulness of its distinctions in God's will, did not grasp clearly either that God's eternal decision is "to be described genuinely and compulsorily in these temporal forms", or that "to say that God moves in certain directions is not a mere figure of speech.... It is an eternal reality in Himself" (33);
and that Jesus Christ is the concrete time and place from which God exercises his omnipotence (34).

So much for the "particular" in the move from the particular to the general (35), but one must also ask about the "general" and this introduces the other strand in this section, the freedom of God.

Barth asserts God's freedom by distinguishing between God's omnicausality and his omnipotence (36), or between what he does do and what he can do (37). Yet the whole thrust of his method is to prove such possibility from the fact of God's action (e.g., above, the <u>potentia absoluta</u> from the <u>potentia ordinata</u>), and so what God can do is never given any content other than the assertion that what he does do shows him to be a free agent and so capable of acting further in the same character (e.g., above, a "greater" but "not a different" omnipotence). In line with this the long treatment of God's knowledge and will (38) aims to show "the freedom of His personality" and does so by drawing on the Bible to describe

"the sovereignty, the superiority, the penetrating and comprehensive capacity of His knowledge, decision and resolve"(39).

Since much of the substance of this section reappears in the doctrine of election to which I have already devoted a chapter, I will confine myself to one final comment. This is that the story-based concept which is essential to the presentation of the superiority and freedom of God's knowledge and will is that of time: God's knowledge includes foreknowledge, and his will is an eternal decision. So the perfection of omnipotence is also illuminated by the theme of the latter part of Chapter 8.

In expounding the final perfection, God's glory, Barth overflows with lyrical language. The basic theme is familiar: all God's glory is brought together in Jesus Christ (40), whose beauty is the beauty of God and is the way to the beauty of the Trinity and of the perfections (41), whose crucifixion changes our idea of what beauty is (42), and whose glorification by us is summed up as the giving of thanks for the atonement (43). Once again Barth has defined a perfection by the events of the story, though the stress here is on God's control over whether the story speaks to us of what Barth finds there (44). The excursus on pp. 665 f. illustrates in miniature what Barth means in practice by the <u>analogia fidei</u> and is a suitable conclusion for this appendix. The analogy is the face of Christ:

"No other speaks at the same time of the human suffering of the true God and the divine glory of the true man. This is the function of the face of Christ alone." (45)

The knowledge of this is faith, and is inseparable from knowing Christ's crucifixion and resurrection (in that order), understood as the fulfilment of the Old Testament (46).

162

NOTES to Appendix C to Chapter 8

(1) II.1, pp. 351 ff.

(2) Ib., p. 354.

(3) Ib., p. 359.

(4) Ib., pp. 363 ff.

(5) Ib., p. 368.

(6) Ib., p. 369.

(7) E.g. ib., p. 375. Cf. pp. 399 ff.

(8) Ib., p. 394.

(9) Ib., p. 397.

(10) Ib., pp. 394, 404.

(11) Ib., p. 406. Cf. pp. 403 ff.

(12) Ib., p. 408.

(13) Ib., p. 416.

(14) Ib., p. 417.

(15) Ib., p. 438.

(16) Ib., p. 447. Cf. p. 457 on sola scriptura.

(17) Ib., pp. 450 ff.

(18) Ib., p. 445.

(19) Ib., p. 457. ("der einzige neutestamentliche Beweis für die Einzigkeit
     Gottes" - S. 514.)

(20) Ib., pp. 490 ff.

(21) Ib., p. 502.

(22) Ib., p. 503.

(23) Ib., pp. 516 ff.

(24) Ib., p. 517.

(25) But there is no discussion of the issue Moltmann, op. cit., is facing: does God die? Barth's answer is of course "No", for God raises Jesus from the dead, and remains constant in this way. Barth discusses the alternative of a split in God in IV.1, pp. 184 ff. and rejects it, suggesting in the process many ideas which help in elucidating II.1.

(26) II.1, p. 521. Cf. above Chapter 5 on the decretum absolutum.

(27) Ib., pp. 522 ff.

(28) Ib., p. 524.

(29) E.g. ib., pp. 599-607.

(30) Ib., p. 541.

(31) Ib., p. 542. ("Wohl mit einer grösseren, aber nicht mit einer anderen Allmacht haben wir zu rechnen." - S. 610.)

(32) Ib., pp. 555 f.

(33) Ib., p. 593.

(34) Ib., p. 605.

(35) Ib., p. 602.

(36) Ib., p. 528.

(37) E.g. ib., p. 531.

(38) Ib., pp. 543 ff.

(39) Ib., p. 543.

(40) Ib., p. 643.

(41) Ib., p. 662.

(42) Ib., p. 665.

(43) Ib., p. 668.

(44) Ib., p. 665.

(45) Ib., p. 666.

(46) Ib., p. 665.

CHAPTER 9. THE SPIRITUALITY OF THE CHURCH DOGMATICS

>"We say amisse,
>   This or that is:
>Thy word is all, if we could spell." (1)

>"Much troubled, till I heard a friend expresse,
>That all things were more ours by being his." (2)

(i)

By the spirituality of the C.D. I mean what Barth says there about the
appropriation of the Gospel and about the way of life to which this leads.
Reading (or hearing) the Bible plays a role in both of these, and this is
the aspect I will examine, suggesting that to consider the C.D. as an ascesis
of Bible reading is helpful in understanding its method.

The previous chapters have accumulated much evidence to support this
approach. When Barth in Safenwil was searching for a new foundation for his
theology he found it in the "strange new world of the Bible", and the hermeneutical circle which can be discerned in his Römerbrief is that between
crucifixion and resurrection. Barth's turn to dogmatic theology in the
traditional sense was accompanied by an emphasis on the "Nachdenken" of biblical narratives. In the C.D. his equivalent of Anselm's "name" for God as
the one quo nihil maius cogitari potest was "the one who reveals Himself as
the Lord", thus making his doctrine of revelation fundamental, and together
with it the Bible as the written record of God's self-revelation (3). Throughout the C.D. the self that God reveals is decisively articulated by biblical
stories; but to receive this there must be an accompanying imaginative and
intellectual ascesis which sustains and defends the sense believed given to
the world by this divine self-disclosure. This leads to polemics against
natural theology in all its forms and against various styles of philosophy
which flourished during and after the Enlightenment. Barth's comprehensive
alternative world of meaning is an overarching story which is not the traditional one from creation to parousia but is the lifetime of Jesus Christ.
A doctrine of time based on an interpretation of the resurrection supports
the inclusiveness of that stretch of time, and the Old Testament history and
all world history are "figured" into it.

The spirituality of the C.D. is therefore mainly an exposition of ways
in which Christian life should correspond to Jesus Christ's history, with
conversion as the believer's participation in it:

>"It is in His (Jesus Christ's) conversion that we are
>engaged. It is in His birth, from above, the mystery
>and miracle of Christmas, that we are born again. It
>is in His baptism in Jordan that we are baptised with
>the Holy Spirit and with fire. It is in His death on
>the cross that we are dead as old men, and in His re-

surrection in the garden of Joseph of Arimathaea that
we are risen as new men. Who of us then, in relation
to our own conversion or that of others, can seriously
know any other terminus for this event than the day of
Golgotha, in which He accomplished in our place and for
us all the turning and transforming of the human situation,
and as He did so was crowned as the royal man He was, our
Lord?" (4)

This is part of a discussion of sanctification as a participatio
Christi which involves a lifetime of such "conversion", and its radical
doctrine of substitution, in which men are drawn into the history of their
substitute, Jesus Christ, is at the heart of the subjective side of Barth's
doctrine of reconciliation. Barth's description of it in C.D.IV.1 is:

"His history is as such our history. It is our true
history (incomparably more direct and intimate than
anything we think we know as our history)." (5)

The effect of justification by faith alone is to have one's own self "de-
mythologized" (6), one's identity exchanged for Jesus Christ's (which includes one's "real" identity), the stories in terms of which one conceives
oneself replaced by this story. Earlier in the C.D. Barth's most comprehensive
statement of this spirituality was in III.2, where the christocentric anthropology culminates in the section on "Man in his time", and the time of Jesus
is seen as embracing all men (7), with the resurrection as the key to understanding this (8). This is in turn grounded in Barth's christocentric doctrine of God, which involves a theocentric perspective on all human experience,
again with a temporal ontology (9).

One might sum up this central theme in the spirituality of the C.D. by
saying that, where Catholic theology might speak of participation in the
sacraments, Barth (with increasing emphasis as the C.D. proceeds) takes the
incarnation as "the one and only sacrament" (10). Where an ontology of substance might speak of "transubstantiation" Barth's theology supports what
might be called "transtemporalization". This focuses spirituality on our
presence with Jesus Christ in his history. The "staggering simplicity" of
the Holy Spirit is that "He is no other than the presence and action of Jesus
Christ Himself" (11), the working of God in men to awaken them to their real
situation in the overarching story (12). This is the basic "rule" for Bible
reading given in the C.D.: to acknowledge the world of the overarching biblical story as the real world par excellence, of which one's own story is a
part, and to which it must correspond.

(ii)

Three traditional headings in spirituality are beauty, goodness and
truth. Barth believed theology to be the most beautiful of the sciences,
and his doctrine of God's perfections culminate with a discussion of God's
and theology's beauty (13). The influence of Mozart's music pervades his
theology - without it, he said, "I could not think of what moves me person-
ally in theology, in politics" (14) - and the C.D. lends itself to discussion

in aesthetic terms. I have attempted this in my use of literary parallels, and have shown how deeply Barth's concern to preserve the integrity of biblical narratives conditions his theological reflection. He takes account of the realistic form of many biblical narratives, especially the Gospels, and makes it a constant criterion in his own judgements and in his polemics against others. His three main examples of the beauty of God are God's perfections, triunity and incarnation (15), and in each case I have shown how his distinctive interpretation of biblical narratives shapes his doctrine. I have also suggested how his distortions, especially his tendency to press stories too far in the service of christocentricity, greatly affect his theology; but such questions are best left to my third heading, truth. Indeed it often seems artificial to treat independently the aesthetic strand in the C.D., yet in discussing its spirituality the implied ascesis of beauty must be noted (16).

Goodness is another theme treated christocentrically by Barth. The goodness of the Christian is no less hidden in Christ than is his justification (17). Barth insists that ethics is part of dogmatics (18), but its place is a subordinate one (19). This is an implication of the priority of Gospel over law, God's command being understood as the permission and freedom to respond appropriately to the good news of what he has done (20). The precise way in which Barth argues from the Bible to his particular ethical conclusions in C.D.III.4 (the only volume in the C.D.devoted to special ethics) is not my concern in this work, partly because it would require a dissertation in itself (21). Besides, the subordinate role Barth accords to ethics points to his understanding of the earlier parts of the doctrine of God, creation and reconciliation as the main guides to his method.   It is sufficient here to point to the common form of the discussions about God's perfections and about human ethics. In each the radical particularity of the Gospel and the christocentricity of Barth's theology are made compatible with universality and inclusiveness by an appeal to freedom (22).

For Barth, it is the freedom of Jesus Christ which is the paradigm and power of Christian action, and so the main place to look for his ascesis of goodness is in his doctrine of reconciliation, where the later sections of each volume deal with the appropriate free response (faith, love, hope) to the truth of the earlier sections. In each part of C.D.IV the transition to the response is a discussion of the resurrection - "The Verdict of the Father" in IV.1, "The Direction of the Son" in IV.2 and "The Promise of the Spirit" in IV.3.1:

> "The particular event of His resurrection is thus the
> primal and basic form of His glory, of the outgoing and
> shining of His light, of His expression, of His Word as
> His self-expression, and therefore of His outgoing and
> penetration and entry into the world around and ourselves,
> of His prophetic work. It is to this event that the New
> Testament witness refers, and on this that it builds, when
> it speaks of the universality of the particular existence
> of Jesus Christ, of the inclusiveness of His specific
> being and action, of the continuity in which He has His
> own special place but reaches out from it to embrace ours
> too, to comprehend us men, to address and claim and treat
> and illumine us as His own people which we are in virtue

167

of His being and action, and thus to find a form among
us and in us." (23)

Therefore the free presence of Jesus Christ is what is to be responded
to, with gratitude for that grace being the first action of Christian living,
and sin defined as failure to respond appropriately. I will discuss Barth's
culminating account of Christian life in C.D.IV.3 later in this chapter and
in an appendix, but conclude now with this related point: that the spirituality of the C.D. is dominated by the person of the resurrected Jesus, and
that therefore it is primarily a spirituality of knowledge, a knowledge which
has endless personal and practical implications but which is first of all
knowledge of a person distinct from ourselves who is portrayed in the Bible.
This doctrine of a particular person who is still present (with his history
of A.D. 1-30) is Barth's bastion against mysticism, existentialism, Roman
Catholic ecclesiology, Mariology and analogia entis, liberal Protestantism,
the hermeneutical gap and much else, and is the key to the simplicity of the
spirituality he found in Abel Burckhardt's hymns (24). It also points, as
did my remarks on beauty, to the third heading, truth, as the main one under
which to show the distinctiveness of Barth's spirituality.

The whole C.D. is an ascesis of truth, and the question of appropriation
is met by a doctrine of the freedom of the Holy Spirit (25), and by the claim
that the best apologetics is good dogmatics. Each volume of the C.D. insists
on the knowledge of God and man to be found in Jesus Christ, and in previous
chapters I have tried to show something of the way in which Barth elicits it
from biblical narratives. There Barth's opposition to world-views found in
post-Enlightenment thinkers, especially those which pivot on the human subject of experience, was clear, and his diagnosis of the faults characteristic
of Neoprotestantism (especially Schleiermacher) and Christian existentialism
(especially Bultmann) was that they had succumbed to this man-centred approach. His answer was to put the self of Christ at the centre, but in order
to support his case he needed his own account of human self-understanding.
So he described man's true identity as correspondence with Jesus Christ.
Christianity therefore involves not only seeing all the lines in the Bible
converging on Jesus Christ but also appropriating his identity as our own.
The clarity and simplicity of this basis for theological anthropology is
preserved by rejecting historical criticism and other challenges to the
story as told in the Bible. Once this is done Barth has a stronghold against
post-Kantian theories of the self, for the true self is now described in a
series of events told in a realistic story. Schleiermacher and Bultmann are
bound to be rejected because, while each is christocentric in his own way,
in their hermeneutics they do not accept the realistic story of Jesus Christ
as their datum for reflection, and they acknowledge other bases for understanding the self. The simplicity of Barth's solution is enhanced by being
so self-contained. The story has a beginning, a middle and an end; its
realism means that it renders its own world of meaning by the interaction
of character and event, and by means of figuration it can embrace all history. There need therefore be no concern about some things in which modern
theology has invested an enormous amount of energy. For example, the relevance of the Gospel to human nature is not a problem, since the Gospel defines human nature; the possibility of God becoming man, or of man rising
from the dead, or of miracles, is proved, not by argument, but by the fact
of their occurrence in the real world of the story; and all the attempts
to discover or generate links between us and the Gospels across the

hermeneutical gap are superfluous because the story embraces our time.

All of this amounts to a distinctive spirituality of knowledge. It is more Hegelian than Kantian: the involvement of men in the historical unfolding of the ratio of the immanent Trinity (26). The spirituality is most comprehensively described theocentrically, as participation in God's own ascesis in time and eternity. Barth's understanding of the resurrection, however, differentiates him from Hegel. For Barth the incarnation can never be the symbol of a larger dialectic moving to a fuller consummation. Rather the light of the resurrection reveals that the "Urgeschichte" in God has been played out in history, and that the meaning of history is not a dialectic but a person who embodies the "dialectic" of crucifixion and resurrection and is present to all history as its Lord. Thus there is the twofold distinctiveness of prior completion and personal presence.

(iii)

The themes of completion and presence reach their greatest intensity in C.D.IV.3, and in the Appendix to this chapter I show how they are there tightly woven into a spirituality of knowledge which is supported by appeal to biblical narratives. The resurrection again appears as the conditio sine qua non of Barth's spirituality, and I will now comment critically on Barth's understanding of that event and the related issue of natural theology.

I have attempted in Chapters 3 and 4 above to discern the literary logic of Barth's interpretation of the resurrection by analysing his presentation of it in C.D.IV.1, by applying to it such concepts as the "realism of assessment" and the "middle distance", and by suggesting how he avoids pitfalls in post-Enlightenment hermeneutics of narrative in the areas of ostensive reference, abstracted meaning and subjectivity. In Chapter 8 I proposed Kermode's literary application of Aquinas' aevum as a model for Barth's view of the resurrection. In all these ways Barth appeared as a sensitive interpreter of the Gospels, but there were criticisms too, in particular of his "closure" of the overarching story with the forty days of post-resurrection appearances (27). This has been confirmed in the Appendix to this chapter, where it is noted how Barth's affirmation of the completion of the primary story depends on understanding the resurrection, Pentecost and the parousia as three forms of the same event. The obvious difficulty for spirituality in this is that it is hard to see the significance of history now in progress: everything significant has already happened. This is a problem that many of Barth's successors have tackled, notably J. Moltmann and W. Pannenberg, whose common thrust (for all their differences) is towards a theological understanding of the incompleteness of history, and who draw on Hegel in their attempts.

The closure of the Ascension is closely related to Barth's tendency to see Jesus' story as a "Bildungsroman", in which his identity is complete at the crucifixion and becomes the universal "Bildungsroman" through the resurrection. This, as I have shown, devalues the realism of the Gospels, for example by forcing men's experience of suffering into a "secondary" relation to Jesus' experience (28). That, however, is only the tip of the iceberg, for the whole of Barth's anthropology is affected by the significance he gives to the story of Jesus. The Gospels are written using methods of

character portrayal common to their time (29), which are thin in comparison
with those used by, for example, the great realistic novelists.   Barth
recognises this, yet still uses them as the main source of his anthropology,
a procedure which shows its greatest signs of strain in C.D.III.2.   There,
for example, Barth defines the "basic form of humanity" (30) in a way which
claims to be based on the man Jesus.   Yet while all the characteristics which
he lists might be found in Jesus (though one might doubt the centrality of
"gladness") the principle of selection is not given, and the similarity to
twentieth century personalist philosophies (e.g. Martin Buber's) is so
striking that the story of Jesus appears to be a peg on which to hang gen-
eralisations about man inspired by other sources.

     The problem is most acute when Barth takes "Jesus, Whole Man" as the
basis for his account of man's constitution as body, soul and spirit (31).
Here the poverty of the Gospel accounts is most apparent, and Barth's own
actualist approach to human identity least applicable.   Since he rules out
other ways of understanding man's distinctiveness he is forced here too to
see it solely in terms of participation in the biblical history:

> "Spirit is the <u>conditio sine qua non</u> of the being of
> man as soul of his body.   There is value in reminding
> ourselves, of course, that the same is also to be said
> of the beast.   It is only by the Spirit of God the
> Creator that they also live and are soul of their body.
> What distinguishes man from beast is the special move-
> ment and purpose with which God through the Spirit gives
> him life, and, connected with this, the special spirit-
> uatlity of his life, which is determined by the fact that
> God has not only made him in his constitution as soul of
> his body, but destined him in this constitution for that
> position of a partner of the grace of His covenant." (32)

Here, as G.S. Hendry points out in a work which includes much criticism of
Barth's spirituality that supports my argument, the determination of the
natural man by the Spirit is deprived completely of "the element of subject-
ivization" (33), a point which will recur later in this chapter.   So Barth's
reaction against theological appeals to human consciousness and his ban on
extra-biblical anthropological sources, together with his way of relying
on biblical narratives, lead either to impoverishment (as in his account
of man's constitution) or to smuggling in richer substance (as in his conception of the basic form of humanity).

     There is a further problem with the "special spirituality" of the "new
man".   The Christian is certainly conscious of Jesus Christ through the Holy
Spirit, but Barth consistently denies that reflection on the varieties of
such consciousness has a valid place in dogmatics.   His "Bildungsroman"
Jesus, whose story embraces ours, is made as objective as possible, always
distinct from our consciousness of him through his identification with the
events of his earthly history.   The resurrection guarantees this "eternal-
ising" of the story and, in Wicker's terms (34), leads to a spirituality
dominated by "substitution", our true identity being found by participating
in Jesus' history.   The alternative, rejected mode, which Wicker called
"combination", by contrast refuses to allow the events of A.D. 1-30 such
general significance, and is open to Jesus being involved in very different

170

stories and structures stressing his role as servant.

One criticism of Barth from this viewpoint is that even the New Testament gives different versions of Jesus's story, and that to understand them involves the whole complex business of historical and redaction criticism, with the subjective stances of the various N.T. authors inextricably bound up with their witness to Jesus Christ. This is especially true of the resurrection accounts, and the criticisms of Barth by Van Harvey (35), Christopher Evans (36) and Peter Selby (37) all make this point convincingly, yet without endorsing Bultmann. Barth, however, could plausibly reply that there is still enough of a basic pattern to support his "substitutionary" spirituality. The force of the "combination" alternative is greater in its appeal to world and church history as a source of new combinations and developments which deny the closure at Ascension. This allows theology to risk being shaped by its exchanges with many disciplines and by such reflections as Hans Urs von Balthasar's on the lives of individual saints (38).

This leads into the problem of natural theology. In Appendix B to Chapter 8 above I noted how Barth's question to the Bible about natural theology was loaded in favour of his own answer, and that he did not take seriously the force of "both...and..." positions. I will not here offer a full alternative to Barth's view of natural theology, but will suggest how this dissertation helps to show its weakness. I will use first a Protestant, then a Catholic illustration.

Søren Kierkegaard wrote:

> "If one does not maintain strictly the relation between
> philosophy (the purely human view of the world, the human
> standpoint) and Christianity but begins straightway, with-
> out special penetrating investigations of this relation,
> to speculate about dogma, one can easily achieve appar-
> ently rich and satisfying results. But things can also
> turn out as with marl at one time, when, without having
> investigated it and the soil, people used it on any sort
> of land - and got excellent yields for a few years but
> afterwards found that the soil was exhausted." (39)

I have used realistic novels as a purely human standpoint, and I suggest that Barth's ignoring of such sources for anthropology is an impoverishment, as he makes demands on the Bible which cannot be met by it, and does not adequately explore the possibility that the Bible itself contains an exigence towards natural theology (40). The problem of generalising the one story is greatest in relation to the resurrection. There Barth has the right "middle distance" perspective on the story, but in attempting to generalise through his own story-based doctrine of time he is tied too closely to one set of events and appears to usurp God's freedom to make new combinations in the same perspective. The resurrection, with the accompanying doctrine of time, is also applied retrospectively to the earlier parts of the biblical story in a way which upsets the human ecology by making the Bible seem like a "Bildungs-roman".

Barth and Kierkegaard both agree on a radical "scandal of particular-ity" at the heart of Christianity, but they differ on the "how" of spirit-

uality, the necessity or not of the sort of "anthropological contemplat-
ion" (41) which was Kierkegaard's version of natural theology. In exploring
subjectivity Kierkegaard's existentialism is at one with the tradition of
Schleiermacher. In one of his last writings Barth offered an interpretation
of both traditions in meliorem partem as theologies of the Holy Spirit, and
granted (on certain conditions) that pneumatology is a valid standpoint from
which to give an account of all theology (42). Yet, given his strictly
christocentric, substitutionary conception of human identity, it is hard to
imagine the C.D. accommodating Kierkegaard's wrestling with the problems of
the post-Kantian shift to subjectivity. Indeed, as Hendry shows, the exclusion of such problems is an important motive in Barth's minimising of
the role of the human spirit in Christianity (43). I would further suggest
that another motive was Barth's own political role. A natural theology
which would deal adequately with modern reality would have much to learn
from Barth's own practice in relation to the political events of his time
(44). These were the constant background of and a considerable influence
upon his theology, which in turn had some effect upon them. His spirituality, with its emphasis on the Church's mission ad extra (45) and its use of
the Gospels with slogan-like etraightforwardness and force, is well suited
to communal solidarity andstruggle, an arena in which the introspective
intensity of a Kierkegaard is not usually encouraged.

My second source of comparison is the thought of Pierre Teilhard de
Chardin. He suggests another way in which Barth's theology uses biblical
narratives to make a self-sufficient totality which buys its completeness
and invulnerability at too high a price. In Chapter 6 above I showed how
Barth recognises the Genesis stories of creation as imaginative, poetic
sagas which include elements of ancient "science", but that he saw their
main reference being to God and to the history of the covenant. An alternative interpretation is that they also intend to say something about creation
per se and that any doctrine of creation which does not try, as the Genesis
writers did, to incorporate contemporary scientific knowledge is shirking
its duty. Teilhard's writings are an example of an attempt to do this, and
at the very least they give to scientific facts the force of imagination by
integrating them into a spirituality (46). By contrast there is in Barth's
theology an alienation from the natural sciences, which are at least as
important an element of modernity as are subjectivity and politics (47).

(iv)

Many of the above criticisms of Barth have been for his way of drawing
sharp lines by appealing to narratives which it is possible to interpret in
less exclusive ways. Yet the other side of Barth's exclusiveness is his all-
pervading invocation of freedom. The reconciliation of particularity and
freedom is the formal problem of his spirituality, as of his doctrine of
God and his ethics. The combination is possible because its source and model
is the freedom of God in a particular person, Jesus Christ. A neutral human
free will is excluded (48): one is either acting freely in correspondence
with God's will or one is a slave to sin. As Hans Urs von Balthasar says,
freedom is "the ultimate foundation of Barth's anthropology" and is "a
mysterious realm where self-determination and obedience, independence and
imitation, act upon and clarify each other" (49). This realm of "free"

action is, as I have shown, defined mainly by certain biblical narratives.
Much of Barth's exegesis is about continuities and differentiations within
this narrative realm, expressed in the discovery of analogies, patterns,
"lines", distortions and other features. Yet Barth preserves "the freedom
of the Word" by not claiming demonstrative status for his exegesis. For
him it is always incomplete and useless unless completed by the free presence of Jesus Christ, and is only valid in the circulus virtuosus of a story
telling about a person who is present to confirm it. Hence he concludes a
section on the freedom of the Word as follows:

> "Because it is the decisive activity prayer must take
> precedence even of exegesis" (50),

for prayer freely recognises the presence of Jesus Christ and the ordering
between God and man. The theme of the impossibility of theology without
prayer runs right through the C.D. (51) but there is no interest in the
wisdom of the traditional spirituality on the subject. Instead, typically,
the concentration is on the identity of theGod to whom prayer is addressed,
and it is in Barth's claims to knowledge of that that the distinctiveness
and vulnerability of his spirituality lies.

Hans Urs von Balthasar has written that "saints who have spent years,
even their whole lives, occupied in contemplating one single mystery in the
life of our Lord are theologically in the right" (52). The heart of Barth's
theology is the sequence of crucifixion and resurrection, and, even though
those saints were generally less exclusive in their claims, it is in their
tradition that Barth's concentrated reflection stands (53). The spirituality
that results embraces beauty, goodness and truth, and it also has a characteristic "tone". This is a blend of astonishment and thanks:

> "The statement 'God reveals Himself' must be a statement
> of utter thankfulness, a statement of pure amazement, in
> which is repeated the amazement of the disciples at
> meeting the risen One." (54)

This fires the repeated exploration of the Gospel events in the C.D., it is
the attitude and action in which beauty, goodness and truth come together
there, and it is also the ground from which Barth might launch a counter-
attack on his critics. For is not thanks the continuation of a completed
event? And might not an event be so astonishingly rich that the significance of all subsequent history might consist in becoming more and more
thankful for it, in thought, speech and action?

(1) George Herbert, "The Flower".

(2) Ib., "The Holdfast".

(3) See above Chapter 2.

(4) C.D.IV.2, p. 583.

(5) p. 548.

(6) Ib., pp. 547, 618.

(7) E.g. p. 440.

(8) E.g. p. 442 ff.

(9) See above Chapters 5 and 8.

(10) C.D.IV.2, p. 55. Cf. ib., p. 107; IV.4, p. 102: "the sacrament of the history of Jesus Christ."

(11) Ib., IV.2, pp. 322 f.

(12) Ib., pp. 553-584.

(13) Ib., II.1, pp. 650 ff.

(14) Busch, op. cit., p. 410.

(15) C.D.II.1, pp. 657 ff.

(16) E.g. The primacy of storytelling in Barth's method can be linked with his objections to organ solos in liturgy and to works of art in churches (C.D.IV.3.2, pp. 866 ff.). But there are more pervasive topics that have their place here, such as the structuring of the C.D., with its original order of presentation, and the style of the C.D., not just its use of language but the spiralling method of presentation, and the sheer verbosity, which can be seen as the product of a type of medit- ation and discipline at the opposite end of the spectrum to the gnomic precision of Patanjali, Pascal or Simone Weil.

(17) E.g. C.D.I.2, p. 782.

(18) Ib., pp. 782-796; II.2, pp. 509-551.

(19) Ib., I.2, p. 795.

(20) Ib., II.2, Chapter VIII passim.

(21) Cf. R.E. Willis, The Ethics of Karl Barth (Leiden 1971).

(22) See above Chapter 8 and the freedom motif throughout C.D.III.4; also below in this chapter.

(23) C.D.IV.3.1, p. 281; Cf. Chapter 3 above.

(24) See above Chapter 2.

(25) E.g. "Even the New Testament, although time and again it places the Holy Spirit in between the event of Christ on the one hand and the Christian community on the other, does not really tell us anything about the How, the mode of His working." (C.D.IV.1, p. 649)

(26) At a formal, conceptual level Barth's method is often uncannily Hegelian in its motion. He sets typological interpretation in the pattern of a dualistic, dialectical interplay which then becomes a complex, comprehensive unity, as is shown e.g. in Chapter 5 above.

(27) See above Chapter 8.

(28) See above Chapter 7.

(29) See Graham Stanton, op. cit., above Chapter 4.

(30) pp. 222-85.

(31) Ib., pp. 325 ff.

(32) Ib., p. 359.

(33) The Holy Spirit in Christian Theology (London 1957), pp. 51 f.

(34) See above Chapter 8, p. 146.

(35) Op. cit. above, Chapter 4, Appendix.

(36) Op. cit. above, Chapter 4, Appendix.

(37) Look for the Living. The Corporate Nature of Resurrection Faith (London 1976), Chapter 3.

(38) For Barth's rejection of von Balthasar's position on this see C.D.IV.1, p. 768.

(39) Journals and Papers, Vol. III (London 1970), 3253.

(40) E.g. a realistic story in itself raises questions about the nature of surrounding reality (especially people), whose investigation is not an optional extra in theology.

(41) The phrase is from Kierkegaard's journals, and is employed frequently by Gregor Malantschuk to describe this basic element in Kierkegaard's method (in his masterly work, Kierkegaard's Thought, Princeton 1971).

(42) Schleiermacher-Auswahl, op. cit., S. 311 f. This standpoint on Barth's own theology is taken by Philip Rosato in his massive Tübingen dissertation Karl Barth's Theology of the Holy Spirit. God's noetic realization of the ontological relationship between Jesus Christ and all men (1975).

(43) Op. cit., pp. 51 f., 96-117.

(44) See Busch, op. cit., passim; Marquardt, op. cit., passim.

(45) Op. cit., pp. 52 f., 96-117.

(46) Cf. Emile Rideau, Teilhard de Chardin. A Guide to his Thought (London 1967); Henri de Lubac, The Faith of Teilhard de Chardin (London 1965).

(47) There is a "stimulating question" that Barth poses in C.D.IV.3.2, p. 756, but which he did not live to answer, "concerning the Holy Spirit as the principle of life which rules not merely in the history of the saved community but also in the whole created cosmos as such". T.F. Torrance is the theologian who has most ably tried to fill the scientific gap in Barth's position, but, whatever the nature of the continuity between the work of the two the gap in Barth's position remains.

(48) On human freedom see e.g. C.D.I.2, pp. 203-42;   II.1, pp. 128-78, 567-97; II.2, pp. 305-506, 583-630; III.2, pp. 265-85; III.3, pp. 58-288; III.4, passim; IV.1, pp. 740-79; IV.2, pp. 499-613, 824-40; IV.3.2, pp. 647-80.

(49) Op. cit., p. 110.

(50) C.D.I.2, p. 695.

(51) E.g. "Prayer is the attitude apart from which dogmatic work is impossible" (ib., I.1, p. 25); "Theological work is surely inconceivable and impossible at any time without prayer. All the gulfs and contradictions which occur in it have their final cause in the fact that it is not everywhere carried through in the fellowship of prayer." (Ib., IV.3.2, p. 882)

(52) A Theology of History (New York 1963), p. 67.

(53) For a recent attempt to present Christian doctrine and spirituality from within one event, the transfiguration, see H.E.W. Slade, Exploration into Contemplative Prayer (London 1975). Slade explicitly (p. 173) adopts Barth's view of time in support of his own spirituality, which differs greatly from Barth's in its understanding of natural theology and other religions.

(54) C.D.I.2, p. 65.

The Spirituality of C.D.IV.3

The aim of C.D.IV.3 is to expound reconciliation as an event which

> "reveals itself, not as a truth but as <u>the</u> truth, in
> which all truths, the truth of God particularly and the
> truth of man, are enclosed, not as truths in themselves,
> but as rays or facets of its truth." (1)

This reconciliation is identical with the history of Jesus Christ (2) and
with the history of God himself (3), and it "determines all history and embraces all other histories" (4). It is only to be accepted in the form the
Bible presents it (5). Our knowledge of it occurs when Jesus Christ draws
us into his history and makes it our experience (6), and Barth defines what
the Bible means by knowledge as follows:

> "What it really means is the process or history in
> which man, certainly observing and thinking, using his
> senses, intelligence and imagination, but also his will,
> action and 'heart', therefore as a whole man, becomes
> aware of another history which in the first instance
> encounters him from without, and becomes aware of it in
> such a compelling way that he cannot be neutral towards
> it, but finds himself summoned to disclose and give him-
> self to it in return, to direct himself, according to
> the law which he encounters in it, to be taken up into
> its movement, in short, to demonstrate the acquaintance
> which he has been given with this other history in a
> corresponding alteration of his own being, action and
> conduct." (7)

Knowledge thus defined is the basic concept of Barth's spirituality because
it enables union with Christ while at the same time preserving distinction.
Barth can say that reconciliation really takes place in Christian knowledge(8)
and can attack the "constant and widespread devaluation of the concept of
knowledge" (9) in metaphysics, moralism, sacramentalism and existentialism
because for him the content of reconciliation is Jesus Christ, who lives and
speaks now, not just

> "spiritually but physically, in the very spatio-temporal
> form of His than history.... As the history which over-
> laps all others, that of Jesus Christ takes place prim-
> arily, but in the particular history of Christian knowl-
> edge it also takes place again and again secondarily." (10)

The completeness of this history is upheld in two complementary ways.
First there is its grounding in God's election (11) which, Barth maintains,
does not at all weaken its character as real history but rather enlightens
it as that (12). Secondly there is the resurrection which reveals this

divine origin, and which completes the history so decisively that world history is already totally determined by it (13) and the giving of the Holy Spirit and the return of Christ as judge are only new forms of the same event (14). It is this twofold completion which guarantees the centrality of knowledge in Barth's spirituality, for to receive the good news is first of all to recognise that the true state of the world, however preposterous this may appear now, is that it has already been reconciled in Christ (15). This is the "realism" that shows other forms of realism to be illusions (16), and allows Barth to answer as he does his leading question on spirituality:

> "In what conceivable form of self-understanding can man think of himself as one who is really the old man no longer but this new man with the child in the cradle of Bethlehem?" (17)

The completeness is also a justification for Barth's rejection of natural theology (18), which in this volume is considerably less polemical than earlier, but yet quite firm, as his rules on pp. 110 ff. make clear. All "true words" must be appropriated to Jesus Christ, credited to the freedom of God and the universality of the resurrection's effect (19).

The completeness, finally, is obviously put in doubt by the existence of suffering, evil and sin. Much is said about these in IV.3, but no further significant arguments are added to those in the earlier volumes which I have already discussed (20). The completeness is supported by a temporal ontology in which evil andsin can be affirmed as really past, and by Jesus' history embracing all history, including its evil, sin and suffering. Yet what is said in IV.3 does develop Barth's spirituality of knowledge, as the form of sin discussed there is that of falsehood. This, he says, is "sin in its most highly developedform" (21). It is the distortion or denial of the knowledge of Jesus Christ, and he sees it operating especially within the Church and theology. It is significant for my theme that his strongest attack is on attempts to systematise the encounter with Jesus Christ, thus impinging on God's freedom. He takes his chief biblical example of systematising from the story (mixed saga and realism) in the Book of Job. The advice given to Job by his friends is not false in itself but is "strikingly unhistorical" in its offering of "timeless truths" (22) in abstraction from the ongoing history of Yahweh with Job, in which there is "new knowledge, the truth itself breaking through in all its virgin freshness" (23).

When Barth in C.D.IV.3.2 discusses the implications of the theology of IV.3.1 for individual and corporate Christian life his main term is "vocation". This is the "total alteration" of a man due to the address of Jesus Christ (24), an awakening which is analogous to the resurrection (25). It leads into sharing Jesus Christ's history (26), to which the Christian's history is an imperfect analogy (27). This sharing is inseparable from the task that is given, that of witnessing to Jesus Christ on the basis of the knowledge given by him (28). Only this knowledge and witness are allowed by Barth as a decisive distinction of the Christian in contrast to other men, for he holds that Christ lives objectively in all men as the Mediator (29). This leads him into extensive criticism of other Christian concepts of salvation. His main polemic is against "holy egoism", whether individual or collective, which does not see that vocation is primarily to universal mission,with personal liberation or suffering a subsidiary matter (30). Thus once again spirituality is centred on knowledge of Christ and participation

178

in his history. This is what lets him say that "in the standing of the Christian we have a model of supreme objectivity" (31), the Christian's special grace being to "live out the great history of liberation in his own little history" (32), which is done primarily by proclaiming the truth of the great history, addressing all men as Christiani in spe.

NOTES to Appendix to Chapter 9

(1) p. 8.

(2) Ib., p. 4. Cf. pp. 165 ff.

(3) Ib., p. 40.

(4) Ib., p. 42.

(5) Ib., p. 44.

(6) E.g. ib., p. 182.

(7) Ib., pp. 183 f.

(8) Ib., pp. 216 ff.

(9) Ib., p. 218.

(10) Ib., p. 224 ("nicht nur geistig sondern auch leiblich, genau in der raumzeitlichen Gestalt seiner damaligen Geschichte..." - S. 256).

(11) E.g. ib., pp. 227 ff.

(12) Ib., p. 233.

(13) E.g. ib., p. 301.

(14) Ib., p. 293.

(15) E.g. ib., p. 241.

(16) Ib., p. 249.

(17) Ib., p. 249.

(18) E.g. ib., p. 117.

(19) Ib., pp. 116 f.

(20) See above Chapter 5 and Appendix.

(21) C.D.IV.3.1, p. 374.

(22) Ib., pp. 459.

(23) Ib., p. 459.

(24) p. 508.

(25) Ib., p. 511.

(26)   E.g. ib., p. 535.

(27)   Ib., p. 663.

(28)   E.g. ib., pp. 573 ff. Note the certainty ascribed to the knowledge
       of faith, and its link with the resurrection, e.g.

           "Precisely as the statement of faith it is a statement of
           certain knowledge established with a force which cannot
           be excelled or even equalled.... As surely as God lives....
           As surely as Jesus Christ lives...so surely does the com-
           munity of Jesus Christ really exist for the world." - Ib., p. 785 f.

(29)   Ib., pp. 604 f.

(30)   Ib., pp. 561-680.

(31)   Ib., p. 653.

(32)   Ib., p. 654.

CHAPTER 10.   CONCLUSION

> "When it finally becomes known who the greatest theo-
> logian of this century really was, perhaps it will
> turn out to be some little man or woman quietly en-
> gaged in Bible study on whom the light will shine." (1)

In this quotation, as in the one with which my first chapter opened,
Barth suggests the standard by which he asks to be judged: fidelity to the
Bible. I have followed his attempt to be faithful to certain biblical narratives, and in the process I have, I hope, explained why in his case exegesis and theological statement are so tightly locked together. I have discussed his doctrines of election, creation and Christ, and in the most recent
two chapters have drawn the threads together under the headings of time and
spirituality. I will not now recapitulate details of my conclusions there,
but will set out in the most general terms two of the weightiest issues in
Barth's theology as I have described it.

The first is the way Barth affirms that God exists and is of a very
particular character. This "scandal of particularity" is also the scandal
of Barth's theology, for it is supported not only by a confident claim to
knowledge of God but also by radical attack on post-Enlightenment world-
views. His chief way of expressing this is through the dominance of one
story over all others, with the guarantee of the story being the presence
of Christ. The story is like a finger which, for all its shaking and its
warts, points to Christ; and it is the only witness we have, so that it
must be the authority on God and on the new state of the world since the
resurrection, and the criterion against which world-views are measured.
There are many points at which one may diverge from Barth, and some have
emerged in previous chapters, but now I will just underline what from
within the perspective of this thesis seems to be his chief danger: that
of claiming to find more knowledge in the one story than is there. "Reading in" to the story outside elements is a staple of his traditionally typological method, and, given his pre-suppositions (especially his doctrines
of providence and of time) it is possible to support it, though it is not
currently fashionable. Yet Barth goes beyond the tradition in his use of
it, notably in his new concentrated version of the overarching story. This
story has in the C.D. to bear a colossal weight under which it shows signs
of twisting, and to prop it up Barth needs either to claim a "consciousness
in excess of the story" (2), or else to deny theological weight to factors,
such as historical criticism, subject-centred anthropology and the natural
sciences, which many theologians consider important. Further, in traditional terms what is most lacking is anagogical exegesis, and it is this gap
that Moltmann, Pannenberg, Jenson and others have tried to fill in a modern
mode. Barth's alternative in the C.D. (though he never wrote his doctrine
of redemption) is his doctrine of Jesus Christ as prophet in IV.3, and I
suspect that it is in wrestling with the problems of presence and completion as laid out in Chapter 9 and its Appendix that one faces the deepest
dogmatic issues raised by Barth.

Secondly, the other side of Barth's way of describing God's particular-

ity and universality is his understanding of man as "secondary". This is
the revolution in anthropology corresponding to his christocentric revolt
against post-Enlightenment world-views. He continually emphasises man's
derivative nature with "terms like image...copy, correspondence, analogy...
likeness, similarity" (3), and attacks the concept of human autonomy. In
this he is in a long tradition of Christian thought about creation, atonement, justification, grace, obedience, humility and much else, that has often
scandalised those who see humanity otherwise; but it is not my task to comment on that debate. Yet even within a Christian perspective that goes a
long way with Barth there are problems here, again stemming from his form of
christocentricity. The main one is his tendency to offer a "Bildungsroman"
Christ whose relations with other men are distorted. The dogmatic expression of this is the rejection of the λόγος ἄσαρκος , making Christ's humanity coeternal with his divinity, and solving the problem of the unity of
divinity and humanity in Christ at the expense of a gap between his humanity
and ours (4). Here again is knowledge in excess of the story.

Yet I have also in this study tried to show the magnitude and plausib-
ility of Barth's achievement. He grasped better than most exegetes in recent
centuries the significance of realistic narrative form in the Bible. He then
concentrated his reflection on this feature, shared by novels and historical
writing, and this raises a range of complex issues which his critics must not
bypass, such as the relation of fact to fiction, the role of imagination in
knowing, the status of realistic narrative as religious language, the way in
which works of literature cross the hermeneutical gap, and the doctrine of
the Holy Spirit. With great economy (in method if not words) he presented
his doctrines by appealing mainly to biblical narratives, and was above all
concerned to assert that the chief difficulty with them is in the astonishing
content of the message, which necessitates, if true, a revolution in knowledge
and existence. Above all, by having the resurrection as his main methodological principle he shows an insight into the logic of the Gospel which leaves
apologetic concerns behind and draws attention, at length, to the dicisive-
ness for the identity of Christianity of the question of the presence of the
risen Christ.

"Barth told Scholz that academic theology was based
on the resurrection of Jesus Christ from the dead. 'He
looked at me earnestly and said: 'That goes against all
the laws of physics, mathematics and chemistry, but now
I understand what you mean.''"(5)

183

NOTES to Chapter 10

(1)   Barth's speech at his eightieth birthday celebrations, 9 May 1966,
        in Fragments Grave and Gay, Ed. M. Rumscheidt (London 1971), p. 112.

(2)   Cf. above Chapter 5 on Judas;   also Chapter 8 on time, Chapter 9 on
        anthropology.

(3)   C.D.III.2, p. 319.

(4)   For perceptive criticism of Barth on this point see R. Jenson, Alpha
        and Omega. A Study in the Theology of Karl Barth (New York 1963),
        pp. 162 ff.

(5)   Busch, op. cit., p. 207.

BIBLIOGRAPHY
_____

   This gives the works (in the language and edition which I have used,
with the place of publication of each work given in the language of its
title) which are of particular importance for this study. Works of Barth
in I and II are, except for the K.D., listed in the order of their publication in German, the date of original publication being given in square
brackets when it differs from the edition cited.

I.   Works of Karl Barth cited:

      Die Kirchliche Dogmatic I.1 - IV.4 and Registerband (Zürich 1938-1970).
      I.1 first published 1932. E.T. Church Dogmatics I.1 - IV.4 (Edinburgh
      1936-1969).

      Der Römerbrief (Bern 1919).

      Der Römerbrief, Zweite (völlig veränderte) Auflage (München 1922).
      E.T. (of sixth edition) The Epistle to the Romans (Oxgord 1933).

      The Word of God and the Word of Man (New York 1957) [1924].

      Die Auferstehung der Toten (München 1924).

      Die christliche Dogmatik im Entwurf: I. Die Lehre vom Worte Gottes.
      Prolegomena zur christlichen Dogmatik (München 1927).

      Erklärung des Philipperbriefes (München 1927. E.T. London 1962).

      Theology and Church (New York 1962) [1928].

      "Der heilige Geist und das christliche Leben", in Zur Lehre vom hei-
      ligen Geist (München 1930).

      Anselm: Fides Quaerens Intellectum. Anselm's proof of the existence
      of God in the context of his theological scheme (London 1960) [1931].

      "Das erste Gebot als theologisches Axiom" in Zwischen den Zeiten
      (München 1933).

      "Nein! Antwort an Emil Brunner", in Theologische Existenz Heute, Heft
      16 (München 1934).

      Die protestantische Theologie im 19. Jahrhundert (Zürich 1947. E.T.
      London 1972).

      "Rudolph Bultmann - An attempt to understand him", in Kerygma and Myth,
      Vol. II, ed. H.-W. Bartsch (London 1962) [1952].

      Revolutionary Theology in the Making. Barth-Thurneysen Correspondence,
      1914-1925 (London 1964) [1956, 1958].

      Preface to La Prédestination by Pierre Maury (Genève 1957).

      "Introduction to Theology. Questions to and discussion with Dr. Karl
      Barth", in Criterion (a publication of the Divinity School of the Uni-
      versity of Chicago), Vol. 2, No. 1 (Winter 1963).

      "Denken heisst: Nachdenken", in Zürcher Woche, 15 Jg., Nr. 24 (14.6.
      1963).

"Nachwort" in Schleiermacher-Auswahl, ed. H. Bolli (München 1968).

Karl Barth - Rudolf Bultmann. Briefwechsel 1922-1966 herausg. B. Jaspert (Zürich 1971).

Fragments Grave and Gay, ed. M. Rumscheidt (London 1971).

II. Other works of Barth consulted:

Credo (London 1964) [1935].

"Evangelium und Bildung", in Theologische Studien, Heft 2 (Zürich 1938).

The Knowledge of God and the Service of God according to the teaching of the Reformation (London 1938).

Dogmatics in Outline (London 1966) [1947].

"Humanismus", in Theologische Studien, Heft 28 (Zürich 1949).

The Humanity of God (London 1967) [1953-1957].

Das Grösste Drama aller Zeiten by Dorothy L. Sayers: translated, with an introduction, by Karl Barth, from the English The Greatest Drama ever staged (Zürich 1959).

"Philosophie und christliche Existenz" in Philosophie und Theologie. Festschrift für Heinrich Barth. Zum 70. Geburtstag (Basel 1960).

"A Theological Dialogue", in Theology Today, Vol. XIX, No. 2 (Princeton July 1962).

Evangelical Theology: An Introduction (London 1963) [1962].

Ad Limina Apostolorum. An Appraisal of Vatican II (Richmond, Virginia 1968).

How I Changed my Mind (Edinburgh 1969).

Das christliche Leben. Die Kirchliche Dogmatik IV.4. Fragmente aus dem Nachlass. Vorlesungen 1959-1961, herausg. Hans-Anton Drewes und Eberhard Jüngel (Zürich 1976).

III. Other works cited:

Allott, Miriam
    Novelists on the Novel (London 1959).

Auerbach, E.
    Mimesis. The Representation of Reality in Western Literature (Princeton 1969).

    Scenes from the Drama of European Literature (New York 1959).

    Literary Language and its Public in Late Latin Antiquity and in the Middle Ages (London 1965).

Balthasar, Hans Urs von
   Karl Barth. Darstellung und Deutung seiner Theologie (Köln 1962.
   E.T. New York 1972).

   A Theology of History (New York 1963).

Bambrough, R.
   Reason, Truth and God (London 1969).

   (ed.) Wisdom. Twelve Essays (Oxford 1974).

Barr, J.
   The Bible and the Modern World (London 1973).

Berkouwer, G.C.
   The Triumph of Grace in the Theology of Karl Barth (London 1956).

Bouillard, H.
   Karl Barth. Vol. I Genese et Evolution de la Theologie Dialectique.
   Vol. II Parts 1 and 2 Parole de Dieu et Existence Humaine (Aubier
   1957).

Brabant, F.N.
   Time and Eternity in Christian Thought (London 1937).

Braithwaite, R.
   An Empiricist's View of the Nature of Religious Belief (Cambridge 1955).

Buess, E.
   "Zur Prädestinationslehre Karl Barths", in Theologische Studien, Heft
   43 (Zürich 1955).

Bultmann, R.
   Theology of the New Testament Vol. I (New York 1951).

Burg, D. and Feifer, G.
   Solzhenitsyn (London 1972).

Busch, E., Fangmeier, J., Geiger, M. (Herausg.)
   Parrhesia. Karl Barth zum 80. Geburtstag (Zürich 1966).

Clayton, J.P. (ed.)
   Ernst Troeltsch and the Future of Theology (Cambridge 1976).

Come, A.
   An Introduction to Barth's Dogmatics for Preachers (London 1963).

Crites, S.
   "The Narrative Quality of Experience", in Journal of the American
   Academy of Religion (Sept. 1971).

Danto, A.C.
   Analytical Philosophy of History (Cambridge 1965).

Dunlop, J.R., Haugh, R. and Klimoff, A.
   Aleksandr Solzhenitsyn. Critical Essays and Documentary Materials
   (London 1975).

Elton, G.R.
   Political History: Principles and Practice (London 1970).

Evans, C.F.
   Resurrection and the New Testament (London 1970).

Ewing, A.C.
   Value and Reality. The Philosophical Case for Theism (London 1973).

Forster, E.M.
   Aspects of the Novel (London 1962).

Frei, H.W.
   The Eclipse of Biblical Narrative. A Study in eighteenth and nineteenth century hermeneutics (New Haven and London 1974).

   The Identity of Jesus Christ. The Hermeneutical Bases of Dogmatic
   Theology (Philadelphia 1975).

Fritzsche, H.-G.
   Das Christentum und die Weltanschauungen. Zugleich eine Einführung in
   Kirchliche Dogmatik Karl Barths unter vorwiegend "apologetischem" Ge-
   sichtspunkt (Hamburg-Bergstedt 1962).

Gardner, Helen
   The Business of Criticism (Oxford 1959).

Grant, D.
   Realism (London 1970).

Gunton, C.
   The Doctrine of God in Barth and Hartshorne (Manuscript supplied by
   the author, based on his Ph.D. thesis, King's College, London University 1975).

Halperin, J. (ed.)
   The Theory of the Novel (London 1974).

Hardy, Barbara
   Tellers and Listeners. The Narrative Imagination (London 1975).

Harvey, Van A.
   The Historian and the Believer (London 1967).

Hendry, G.S.
   The Holy Spirit in Christian Theology (London 1957).

Herbert, George
   Collected Poems (Oxford 1961).

Hick, J.
   Evil and the God of Love (London 1968).

Hickling, C. and Hooker, Morna (eds.)
   What about the New Testament? Essays in Honour of Christopher Evans
   (London 1975).

Jenson, R.W.
   Alpha and Omega. A study in the theology of Karl Barth (New York 1964).

   God after God. The God of the Past and the God of the Future, seen in
   the work of Karl Barth (New York 1969).

Johnson, R.C.
   "The Legacy of Karl Barth", in Reflection, Vol. 66, No. 4 (New Haven,
   Conn. May 1969).

Jones, H.
   Biblical Theology and the Concept of Story. Unpublished paper (Mainz

University 1975).

Josipovici, G.
The World and the Book (London 1971).

Jüngel, E.
Gottes Sein ist im Werden (Tübingen 1966).

"Die Möglichkeit theologischer Anthropologie auf dem Grunde der Analogie. Eine Untersuchung zum Analogieverständnis Karl Barths", in Evangelische Theologie, Heft 10 (Oct. 1962).

Kähler, M.
Der sogenannte historische Jesus und der geschichtliche, biblische Christus (München 1969).

Kelsey, D.
The Uses of Scripture in Recent Theology (Philadelphia 1975).

Kermode, F.
The Sense of an Ending. Studies in the Theory of Fiction (London 1966).

Kerr, F.
"Bernard Londergan's Method. A Response to William Matthews", in New Blackfriars, Vol. 57, No. 669 (Feb. 1976).

Kierkegaard, S.
Journals and Papers, Vol. III (London 1970).

Konrad, J.-F.
Abbild und Ziel der Schöpfung. Untersuchungen zur Exegese von Gen.1 und 2 in Barths Kirchlicher Dogmatik III.1 (Tübingen 1962).

Kort, W.A.
Narrative Elements and Religious Meaning (Philadelphia 1975).

Koselleck, R. and Stempel, W.-D. (Herausg.)
Geschichten und Geschichte (München 1972).

Koselleck, R.
"Historia Magistra Vitae" in Natur und Geschichte. Karl Löwith zum 70. Geburtstag (Stuttgart 1967).

Krötke, W.
Sünde und Nichtiges bei Karl Barth (Berlin 1970).

Lindemann, W.
Karl Barth und die kritische Schriftauslegung (Hamburg-Bergstedt 1973).

Lonergan, B.
Method in Theology (London 1972).

Lubac, H. de
The Faith of Teilhard de Chardin (London 1965).

Lucas, J.R.
A Treatise on Space and Time (London 1973).

Lukačs, G.
The Theory of the Novel: A Historico-philosophical Essay on the Forms of Great Epic Literature (Cambridge, Mass. 1971).

Lüthi, K.
  Gott und das Böse. Eine biblisch-theologische und systematische These
  zur Lehre vom Bösen, entworfen in Auseinadersetzung mit Schelling und
  Karl Barth (Zürich 1961).

McIntyre, J.
  The Shape of Christology (London 1966).

Malantschuk, G.
  Kierkegaard's Thought (Princeton 1971).

Marquardt, F.-W.
  Theologie und Sozialismus. Das Beispiel Karl Barths (München 1972).

Millar, A.
  Realism and Understanding: Some Problems in the Philosophy of Religion.
  Unpublished Ph.D. thesis (Cambridge University 1973).

Miller, J.E. (ed.)
  Theory of Fiction: Henry James (Lincoln, Nebraska 1972).

Moltmann, J.
  The Crucified God (London 1974).

Nelson, W.
  Fact or Fiction. The Dilemma of the Renaissance Storyteller (Cambridge,
  Mass. 1973).

Nineham, D.E.
  New Testament Interpretation in an Historical Age (London 1976).

  The Use and Abuse of the Bible (London 1976).

O'Grady, C.
  The Church in the Theology of Karl Barth, Vol. I (London 1968).

  The Church in Catholic Theology: Dialogue with Karl Barth Vol. II
  (London 1969).

Parker, T.H.L. (ed.)
  Essays in Christology for Karl Barth (London 1956).

Patrides, C.A.
  The Grand Design of God. The Literary Form of the Christian View of
  History (London 1972).

Plumb, J.H.
  The Death of the Past (London 1969).

Rideau, E.
  Teilhard de Chardin: A Guide to his Thought (London 1967).

Ritschl, D.
  Notes on the Concept of Story in Relation to the Quest for Human
  Identity. Unpublished paper (Ecumenical Institute, Bossey 1975).

Roberts, R.
  Eternity and Time in the Theology of Karl Barth. An essay in dogmatic
  and philosophical theology. Unpublished Ph.D. thesis (Edinburgh University 1975).

Rosato, P.J.
  Karl Barth's Theology of the Holy Spirit. God's noetic realization

of the ontological relationship between Jesus Christ and all men.
Unpublished doctoral dissertation (Tübingen University 1975).

Roth, R.P.
Story and Reality. An essay on truth (Grand Rapids, Michigan 1973).

Rumscheidt, M.
Revelation and Theology. An Analysis of the Barth - Harnack Correspondence of 1923 (Cambridge 1972).

Scammell, M.
Review of Lenin in Zürich in The Times Literary Supplement No. 3867
(April 23, 1976).

Schlichting, W.
Biblische Denkform in der Dogmatik. Die Vorbildlichkeit des Biblischen
Denkens für die Methode der Kirchlichen Dogmatik Karl Barths (Zürich
1971).

Scholes, R. and Kellogg, R.
The Nature of Narrative (New York 1966).

Selby, P.
Look for the Living. The Corporate Nature of the Resurrection Faith
(London 1976).

Simon, U.
Story and Faith in the Biblical Narrative (London 1975).

Slade, H.E.W.
Exploration into Contemplative Prayer (London 1975).

Solzhenitsyn, A.
A Day in the Life of Ivan Denisovitch (London 1971).

The First Circle (London 1968).

Cancer Ward (London 1974).

The Gulag Archipelago (London 1974, 1975).

August 1914 (London 1972).

Lenin in Zürich (London 1976).

Stanton, G.N.
Jesus of Nazareth in New Testament Preaching (Cambridge 1974).

Stern, J.P.
On Realism (London 1973).

History and Allegory in Thomas Mann's "Doktor Faustus" (London 1975).

"Mann in his Time", in The Times Literary Supplement No. 3822 (6 June
1975).

Te Selle, Sallie
Literature and Christian Life (New Haven 1966).

Tolkien, J.R.R.
Tree and Leaf (London 1964).

Torrance, T.F.
Karl Barth: An Introduction to his Early Theology 1910-1931 (London
1962).

Trilling, L.
    Sincerity and Authenticity (London 1974).

Watt, I.
    The Rise of the Novel (London 1957).

Weber, O.
    Karl Barth's Church Dogmatics. An Introduction Report on Vols. I.1
    to III.4 (London 1953).

Weinrich, H.
    "Narrative Theology" in Concilium, Vol. 5, No. 9 (May 1973).

Welch, C.
    The Trinity in Contemporary Theology (London 1953).

Wellek, R. and Warren, A.
    Theory of Literature (London 1949).

Wharton, J.A.
    "The occasion of the Word of God. An unguarded essay on the character
    of the Old Testament as the meaning of God's story with Israel", in
    Austin Seminary Bulletin, Vol. LXXXIV, No. 1 (Sept. 1968).

Wicker, B.
    The Story-Shaped World. Fiction and Metaphysics: Some variations
    on a theme (London 1975).

Willis, R.E.
    The Ethics of Karl Barth (Leiden 1971).

Zwanger, H.
    Sage und Mythos in Karl Barths Kirchlicher Dogmatik. Ein Beitrag
    zum Verständnis Barthscher Hermeneutik. Unpublished doctoral disser-
    tation (Tübingen University 1974).

IV.   Works concerning Barth consulted but not cited:

Allen, E.L.
    The Sovereignty of God and the Word of God. A guide to the thought of
    Karl Barth (London 1950).

Bettis, J.D.
    "Is Karl Barth a Universalist?" in Scottish Journal of Theology, Vol.
    20, No. 4 (Edinburgh 1967).

Blanshard, B.
    Reason and Belief (London 1974).

Bowden, J.
    Karl Barth (London 1971).

Brown, James
    Kierkegaard, Heidegger, Buber and Barth. A study of subjectivity and
    objectivity in existentialist thought (New York 1962).

Camfield, F.W. (ed.)
    Reformation Old and New. A Tribute to Karl Barth (London 1947).

Clark, G.H.
 Karl Barth's Theological Method (Philadelphia 1963).

Ehrenburg, H.
 "The inherent problem in Barth's theology" in The Churchman (Jan-Mar
 1941).

Fairweather, A.M.
 The Word as Truth (London 1944).

Frei, H.W.
 "Karl Barth, Theologian", in Reflection, Vol. 66, No. 4 (New Haven,
 Conn. May 1969).

Fuchs, E.
 "Der Theologe Karl Barth. Zu seinem 80. Geburtstag" in Zeitschrift
 für Theologie und Kirche, 63 J. Heft 2 (Tübingen Jun. 1966).

Geyer, H.-G.
 Freispruch und Freiheit. Theologische Aufsätze für Walter Kreck zum
 64. Geburtstag (München 1974).

Glasse, J.
 "Barth on Feuerbach", in Harvard Theological Review, Vol. 57, No. 2
 (Cambridge, Mass. April 1964).

Godsey, J.
 "The Architecture of Karl Barth's Church Dogmatics" in Scottish
 Journal of Theology, Vol. 9 (Edinburgh 1956).

Guinnessey, B.
 "Karl Barth: The Primacy of Scripture", in Unitas, Vol. 8 (New York
 1966).

Hartwell, H.
 The Theology of Karl Barth. An Introduction (Philadelphia 1964).

Hamer, J.
 Karl Barth (London 1962).

Kemmer, A.
 "Die Mystik in Karl Barths Kirchlicher Dogmatik", in Freiburger Zeitschrift für Philosophie und Theologie, 7 Bd. (1960).

Klappert, B.
 Die Auferstehung des Gekreuzigten (Neukirchen 1971).

Lanzenauer, R.H. von
 "Die Grundlagen der religiösen Erfahrung bei Karl Barth", in Abhand-
 lungen zur Philosophie und Psychologie der Religion, Heft 11 (Würzburg
 1927).

McKinney, R.W.A.
 The Role of the Historical Jesus in the Theology of Karl Barth. Unpublished D.Phil dissertation (Oxford University 1969).

Meckels, E.
 Analogie bei Erich Przywara und Karl Barth. Das Verhältnis von Offen-
 barungstheologie und Metaphysik (Neukirchen 1974).

Miskotte, K.H.
    "Über Karl Barths Kirchliche Dogmatik. Kleine Präludien und Phantasien", in Theologische Existenz Heute, Neue Folge Nr. 89 (München 1961).

Moltmann, J. (Herausg.)
    Die Anfänge der dialektischen Theologie (München 1962).

Moltmann, J.
    Theology of Hope (London 1967).

Pannenberg, W.
    Theology and the Philosophy of Science (London 1976).

Pauck, W.
    Karl Barth: Prospect of a new Christianity? (London 1931).

Pöhlmann, H.G.
    Analogia entis oder analogia fidei? Die Frage der Analogie bei Karl Barth (Göttingen 1965).

Runia, K.
    Karl Barth's Doctrine of Holy Scripture (Grand Rapids, Michigan 1962).

Schmid, F.
    Hermeneutik und Ontologie in einer Theologie des Wortes Gottes (Tübingen 1963).

Smart, J.D.
    The Divided Mind of Modern Theology (Philadelphia 1967).

Smith, Noel
    "Karl Barth on the doctrine of the inspiration of the Scripture in the history of the Church", in Scottish Journal of Theology, Vol. 2, No.2 (Edinburgh 1949).

Storch, M.
    Exegesen und Meditationen zu Karl Barths Kirchlicher Dogmatik (München 1964).

Vogel, M.H.
    "The Barth-Feuerbach Confrontation", in The Harvard Theological Review, Vol. 59, No. 1 (Cambridge, Mass. Jan. 1966).

Willems, B.
    Karl Barth. An Ecumenical Approach to his Theology (New York 1965).

Wingren, G.
    Theology in Conflict (Edinburgh 1958).

Zahrnt, H.
    The Question of God. Protestant Theology in the Twentieth Century (London 1969).

194